Pro JavaScript™ Techniques

John Resig

Apress®

Lead Editor: Chris Mills
Technical Reviewer: Dan Webb
Editorial Board: Steve Anglin, Ewan Buckingham, Gary Cornell, Jason Gilmore, Jonathan Gennick, Jonathan Hassell, James Huddleston, Chris Mills, Matthew Moodie, Dominic Shakeshaft, Jim Sumser, Keir Thomas, Matt Wade
Project Manager: Tracy Brown Collins
Copy Edit Manager: Nicole Flores
Copy Editor: Jennifer Whipple
Assistant Production Director: Kari Brooks-Copony
Production Editor: Laura Esterman
Compositor: Linda Weidemann, Wolf Creek Press
Proofreader: April Eddy
Indexer: Broccoli Information Management
Artist: April Milne
Cover Designer: Kurt Krames
Manufacturing Director: Tom Debolski

Distributed to the book trade worldwide by Springer-Verlag New York, Inc., 233 Spring Street, 6th Floor, New York, NY 10013. Phone 1-800-SPRINGER, fax 201-348-4505, e-mail orders-ny@springer-sbm.com, or visit http://www.springeronline.com.

For information on translations, please contact Apress directly at 2560 Ninth Street, Suite 219, Berkeley, CA 94710. Phone 510-549-5930, fax 510-549-5939, e-mail info@apress.com, or visit http://www.apress.com.

The source code for this book is available to readers at http://www.apress.com in the Source Code/ Download section and on the book's web site at http://jspro.org.

Contents at a Glance

PART 1 ■ ■ ■ Introducing Modern JavaScript

PART 2 ■ ■ ■ Professional JavaScript Development

PART 3 ■ ■ ■ Unobtrusive JavaScript

PART 4 ■ ■ ■ Ajax

PART 5 ■ ■ ■ The Future of JavaScript

PART 6 ■ ■ ■ Appendixes

Contents

PART 1 ▪▪▪ Introducing Modern JavaScript

PART 2 ▪▪▪ Professional JavaScript Development

PART 3 ■ ■ ■ Unobtrusive JavaScript

▪CHAPTER 9   Building an Image Gallery 191

PART 4 ▪▪▪ Ajax

▪CHAPTER 10   Introduction to Ajax. 215

PART 5 ▪▪▪ The Future of JavaScript

PART 6 ▪▪▪ Appendixes

About the Author

JOHN RESIG is a programmer and entrepreneur who has a passion for the JavaScript programming language. He's the creator and lead developer of the jQuery JavaScript library and the lead developer on many web-based projects. When he's not programming, he enjoys watching movies, writing in his web log (`http://ejohn.org/`), and spending time with his girlfriend, Julia.

About the Technical Reviewer

■DAN WEBB is a freelance web application developer who has most recently been working with Vivabit, where he is developing Event Wax, a web-based event management system. He also recently coauthored the Unobtrusive JavaScript Plugin for Rails and the Low Pro extension to Prototype.

Dan is a JavaScript expert who has spoken at @media 2006, RailsConf, and The Ajax Experience. He has written for A List Apart, HTML Dog, and SitePoint, and he is a member of the UK web design group the Brit Pack. He blogs regularly about Ruby, Rails, and JavaScript at his site, `http://www.danwebb.net/`. He recently became a member of the newly formed Prototype Core Team.

Acknowledgments

I'd like to take this opportunity to thank everyone who made this book possible. It was a tremendous amount of work, and I appreciate all the help and guidance that I received along the way.

I'd like to thank my editor, Chris Mills, for finding me and encouraging me to write this book. He conceptualized much of its structure, flow, and groundwork; without him, this project would not have happened.

I'd also like to thank my technical editor, Dan Webb, for thoroughly checking my code and reminding me of the finer points of the JavaScript language. Due to his effort, the code in this book should work as expected and be presented in a way that is correct and understandable.

I'd like to thank my copy editor, Jennifer Whipple, and my production editor, Laura Esterman, for helping to keep the book readable and comprehensible, and for dealing with my many follies and inconsistencies.

I also want to thank Tracy Brown Collins, my project manager, for keeping me in line, organized, and (generally) on top of my deadlines.

I'd also like to thank Julia West and Josh King for sticking with me through the long days and weeks of writing, while I was shirking my other responsibilities. Julia was by my side every day, making sure that I always met my deadlines, keeping me strong, and encouraging me to work hard.

Finally, I would like to thank my family and friends for supporting me and encouraging me throughout the years.

PART 1

■ ■ ■

Introducing Modern JavaScript

## CHAPTER 1

Modern JavaScript Programming

The evolution of JavaScript has been gradual but persistent. Over the course of the past decade, the perception of JavaScript has evolved from a simple toy language into a respected programming language used by corporations and developers across the globe to make incredible applications. The modern JavaScript programming language—as it has always been—is solid, robust, and incredibly powerful. Much of what I'll be discussing in this book will show what makes modern JavaScript applications so different from what they used to be. Many of the ideas presented in this chapter aren't new by any stretch, but their acceptance by thousands of intelligent programmers has helped to refine their use and to make them what they are today. So, without further ado, let's look at modern JavaScript programming.

Object-Oriented JavaScript

From a language perspective, there is absolutely nothing modern about object-oriented programming or object-oriented JavaScript; JavaScript was designed to be a completely object-oriented language from the start. However, as JavaScript has "evolved" in its use and acceptance, programmers of other languages (such as Ruby, Python, and Perl) have taken note and begun to bring their programmatic idioms over to JavaScript.

Object-oriented JavaScript code looks and behaves differently from other object-capable languages. I'll go into depth, discussing the various aspects of what makes it so unique, in Chapter 2, but for now, let's look at some of the basics to get a feel for how modern JavaScript code is written. An example of two object constructors can be found in Listing 1-1, demonstrating a simple object pairing that can be used for lectures in a school.

Listing 1-1. *Object-Oriented JavaScript Representing a Lecture and a Schedule of Lectures*

```
// The constructor for our 'Lecture'
// Takes two strings, name and teacher
function Lecture( name, teacher ) {
    // Save them as local properties of the object
    this.name = name;
    this.teacher = teacher;
}
```

```javascript
// A method of the Lecture class, used to generate
// a string that can be used to display Lecture information
Lecture.prototype.display = function(){
    return this.teacher + " is teaching " + this.name;
};

// A Schedule constructor that takes in an
// array of lectures
function Schedule( lectures ) {
    this.lectures = lectures;
}

// A method for constructing a string representing
// a Schedule of Lectures
Schedule.prototype.display = function(){
    var str = "";

    // Go through each of the lectures, building up
    // a string of information
    for ( var i = 0; i < this.lectures.length; i++ )
        str += this.lectures[i].display() + " ";

    return str;
};
```

As you can probably see from the code in Listing 1-1, most of the object-oriented fundamentals are there but are structured differently from other more common object-oriented languages. You can create object constructors and methods, and access and retrieve object properties. An example of using the two classes in an application is shown in Listing 1-2.

Listing 1-2. *Providing a User with List of Classes*

```javascript
// Create a new Schedule object and save it in
// the variable 'mySchedule'
var mySchedule = new Schedule([
    // Create an array of the Lecture objects, which
    // are passed in as the only argument to the Lecture object
    new Lecture( "Gym", "Mr. Smith" ),
    new Lecture( "Math", "Mrs. Jones" ),
    new Lecture( "English", "TBD" )
]);

// Display the Schedule information as a pop-up alert
alert( mySchedule.display() );
```

With the acceptance of JavaScript among programmers, the use of well-designed object-oriented code has also become more popular. Throughout the book I'll attempt to show different pieces of object-oriented JavaScript code that I think best exemplifies code design and implementation.

Testing Your Code

After establishing a good object-oriented code base, the second aspect of developing profes-
sional-quality JavaScript code is to make sure that you have a robust code-testing environment. The need for proper testing is especially apparent when you develop code that will be
actively used or maintained by other developers. Providing a solid basis for other developers
to test against is essential for maintaining code development practices.

In Chapter 4, you'll look at a number of different tools that can be used to develop a good
testing/use case regime along with simple debugging of complex applications. One such tool
is the Firebug plug-in for Firefox. Firebug provides a number of useful tools, such as an error
console, HTTP request logging, debugging, and element inspection. Figure 1-1 shows a live
screenshot of the Firebug plug-in in action, debugging a piece of code.

Figure 1-1. *A screenshot of the Firefox Firebug plug-in in action*

The importance of developing clean, testable code cannot be overstated. Once you begin
developing some clean object-oriented code and pairing it together with a proper testing
suite, I'm sure you'll be inclined to agree.

Packaging for Distribution

The final aspect of developing modern, professional JavaScript code is the process of packaging code for distribution or real-world use. As developers have started to use more and more
JavaScript code in their pages, the possibility for conflicts increases. If two JavaScript libraries
both have a variable named *data* or both decide to add events differently from one another,
disastrous conflicts and confusing bugs can occur.

The holy grail of developing a successful JavaScript library is the ability for the developer
to simply drop a <script> pointer to it and have it work with no changes. A number of techniques and solutions exist that developers use to keep their code clean and universally
compatible.

The most popular technique for keeping your code from influencing or interfering with
other JavaScript code is the use of namespaces. The ultimate (but not necessarily the best or

most useful) example of this in action is a public user interface library developed by Yahoo, which is available for anyone to use. An example of using the library is shown in Listing 1-3.

Listing 1-3. *Adding an Event to an Element Using the Heavily Namespaced Yahoo UI Library*

```
// Add a mouseover event listener to the element that has an
// ID of 'body'
YAHOO.util.Event.addListener('body','mouseover',function(){

    // and change the background color of the element to red
    this.style.backgroundColor = 'red';

});
```

One problem that exists with this method of namespacing, however, is that there is no inherent consistency from one library to another on how it should be used or structured. It is on this point that central code repositories such as JSAN (JavaScript Archive Network) become immensely useful. JSAN provides a consistent set of rules for libraries to be structured against, along with a way to quickly and easily import other libraries that your code relies upon. A screenshot of the main distribution center of JSAN is shown in Figure 1-2.

I will discuss the intricacies of developing clean, packageable code in Chapter 3. Additionally, the importance of other common stumbling points, such as event-handling collision, will be discussed in Chapter 6.

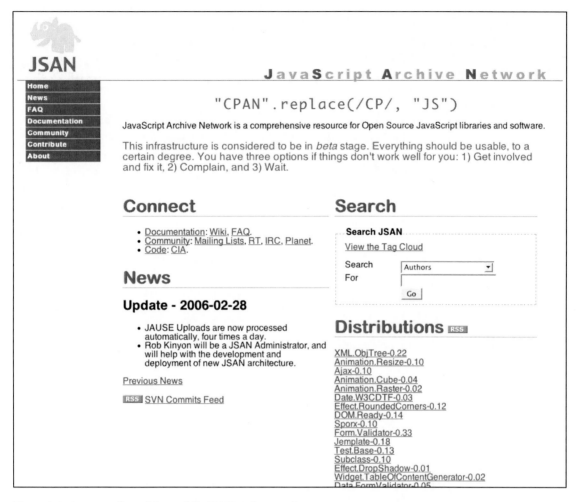

Figure 1-2. *A screenshot of the public JSAN code repository*

Unobtrusive DOM Scripting

Built upon a core of good, testable code and compliant distributions is the concept of unobtrusive DOM scripting. Writing unobtrusive code implies a complete separation of your HTML content: the data coming from the server, and the JavaScript code used to make it all dynamic. The most important side effect of achieving this complete separation is that you now have code that is perfectly downgradeable (or upgradeable) from browser to browser. You can use this to offer advanced content to browsers that support it, while still downgrading gracefully for browsers that don't.

   Writing modern, unobtrusive code consists of two aspects: the Document Object Model (DOM), and JavaScript events. In this book I explain both of these aspects in depth.

The Document Object Model

The DOM is a popular way of representing XML documents. It is not necessarily the fastest, lightest, or easiest to use, but it is the most ubiquitous, with an implementation existing in most web development programming languages (such as Java, Perl, PHP, Ruby, Python, and JavaScript). The DOM was constructed to provide an intuitive way for developers to navigate an XML hierarchy.

Since valid HTML is simply a subset of XML, having an efficient way to parse and browse DOM documents is absolutely essential for making JavaScript development easier. Ultimately, the majority of interaction that occurs in JavaScript is between JavaScript and the different HTML elements contained within a web page; and the DOM is an excellent tool for making this process simpler. Some examples of using the DOM to navigate and find different elements within a page and then manipulate them can be found in Listing 1-4.

Listing 1-4. *Using the Document Object Model to Locate and Manipulate Different DOM Elements*

```
<html>
<head>
    <title>Introduction to the DOM</title>
    <script>
    // We can't manipulate the DOM until the document
    // is fully loaded
    window.onload = function(){

        // Find all the <li> elements in the document
        var li = document.getElementsByTagName("li");

        // and add a ared border around all of them
        for ( var j = 0; j < li.length; j++ ) {
            li[j].style.border = "1px solid #000";
        }

        // Locate the element with an ID of 'everywhere'
        var every = document.getElementById( "everywhere" );

        // and remove it from the document
        every.parentNode.removeChild( every );

    };
    </script>
</head>
<body>
    <h1>Introduction to the DOM</h1>
    <p class="test">There are a number of reasons why the
        DOM is awesome, here are some:</p>
```

```
<ul>
    <li id="everywhere">It can be found everywhere.</li>
    <li class="test">It's easy to use.</li>
    <li class="test">It can help you to find what you want, really quickly.</li>
</ul>
</body>
</html>
```

The DOM is the first step to developing unobtrusive JavaScript code. By being able to quickly and simply navigate an HTML document, all resulting JavaScript/HTML interactions become that much simpler.

Events

Events are the glue that holds together all user interaction within an application. In a nicely designed JavaScript application, you're going to have your data source and its visual representation (inside of the HTML DOM). In order to synchronize these two aspects, you're going to have to look for user interactions and attempt to update the user interface accordingly. The combination of using the DOM and JavaScript events is the fundamental union that makes all modern web applications what they are.

All modern browsers provide a number of events that are fired whenever certain interactions occur, such as the user moving the mouse, striking the keyboard, or exiting the page. Using these events, you can register code that will be executed whenever the event occurs. An example of this interaction is shown in Listing 1-5, where the background color of the <li>s change whenever the user moves his mouse over them.

Listing 1-5. *Using the DOM and Events to Provide Some Visual Effects*

```
<html>
<head>
    <title>Introduction to the DOM</title>
    <script>
    // We can't manipulate the DOM until the document
    // is fully loaded
    window.onload = function(){

        // Find all the <li> elements, to attach the event handlers to them
        var li = document.getElementsByTagName("li");
        for ( var i = 0; i < li.length; i++ ) {

            // Attach a mouseover event handler to the <li> element,
            // which changes the <li>s background to blue.
            li[i].onmouseover = function() {
                this.style.backgroundColor = 'blue';
            };
```

```
            // Attach a mouseout event handler to the <li> element
            // which changes the <li>s background back to its default white
            li[i].onmouseout = function() {
                this.style.backgroundColor = 'white';
            };

        }

    };
    </script>
</head>
<body>
    <h1>Introduction to the DOM</h1>
    <p class="test">There are a number of reasons why the
        DOM is awesome, here are some:</p>
    <ul>
        <li id="everywhere">It can be found everywhere.</li>
        <li class="test">It's easy to use.</li>
        <li class="test">It can help you to find what you want, really quickly.</li>
    </ul>
</body>
</html>
```

JavaScript events are complex and diverse. Much of the code and applications in this book utilize events in one way or another. Chapter 6 and Appendix B are completely dedicated to events and their interactions.

JavaScript and CSS

Building upon your base of DOM and event interactions comes dynamic HTML. At its core, dynamic HTML represents the interactions that occur between JavaScript and the CSS information attached to DOM elements.

Cascading style sheets (CSS) serve as the standard for laying out simple, unobtrusive web pages that still afford you (the developer) the greatest amount of power while providing your users with the least amount of compatibility issues. Ultimately, dynamic HTML is about exploring what can be achieved when JavaScript and CSS interact with each other and how you can best use that combination to create impressive results.

For some examples of advanced interactions, such as drag-and-drop elements and animations, take a look at Chapter 7, where they are discussed in depth.

Ajax

Ajax, or Asynchronous JavaScript and XML, is a term coined in the article "Ajax: A New Approach to Web Applications" (http://www.adaptivepath.com/publications/essays/archives/000385.php) by Jesse James Garrett, cofounder and president of Adaptive Path, an information architecture firm. It describes the advanced interactions that occur between the client and the server, when requesting and submitting additional information.

The term *Ajax* encompasses hundreds of permutations for data communication, but all center around a central premise: that additional requests are made from the client to the server even after the page has completely loaded. This allows application developers to create additional interactions that can involve the user beyond the slow, traditional flow of an application. Figure 1-3 is a diagram from Garrett's Ajax article that shows how the flow of interaction within an application changes due to the additional requests that are made in the background (and most likely without the user's knowledge).

classic web application model (synchronous)

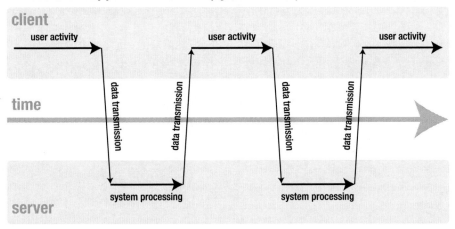

Ajax web application model (asynchronous)

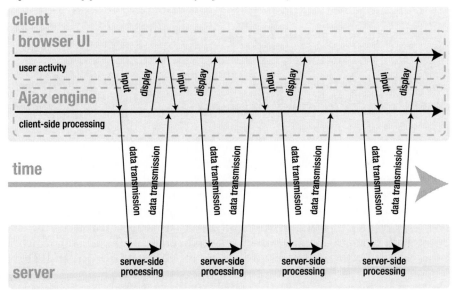

Figure 1-3. *A diagram from the article "Ajax: A New Approach to Web Applications," showing the advanced, asynchronous interaction that occurs between the client and a server*

Since the original release of the Garrett article, the interest of users, developers, designers, and managers has been piqued, allowing for an explosion of new applications that make use of this advanced level of interaction. Ironically, while there has been this resurgence in interest, the technology behind Ajax is rather old (having been used commercially since around the year 2000). The primary difference, however, is that the older applications utilized browser-specific means of communicating with the server (such as Internet Explorer–only features). Since all modern browsers support XMLHttpRequest (the primary method for sending or receiving XML data from a server), the playing field has been leveled, allowing for everyone to enjoy its benefits.

If one company has been at the forefront of making cool applications using Ajax technology, it's Google. One highly interactive demo that it released just before the original Ajax article came out is Google Suggest. The demo allows you to type your query and have it be autocompleted in real time; this is a feature that could never be achieved using old page reloads. A screenshot of Google Suggest in action is shown in Figure 1-4.

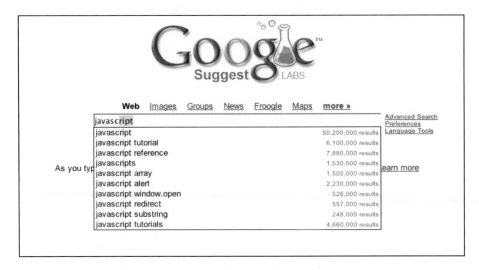

Figure 1-4. *A screenshot of Google Suggest, an application available at the time of Garrett's Ajax article that utilized the asynchronous XML techniques*

Additionally, another revolutionary application of Google is Google Maps, which allows the user to move around a map and see relevant, local results displayed in real time. The level of speed and usability that this application provides by using Ajax techniques is unlike any other mapping application available and has completely revolutionized the online mapping market as a result. A screenshot of Google Maps is shown in Figure 1-5.

Even though very little has physically changed within the JavaScript language, during the past couple years, the acceptance of JavaScript as a full-blown programming environment by such companies as Google and Yahoo shows just how much has changed in regard to its perception and popularity.

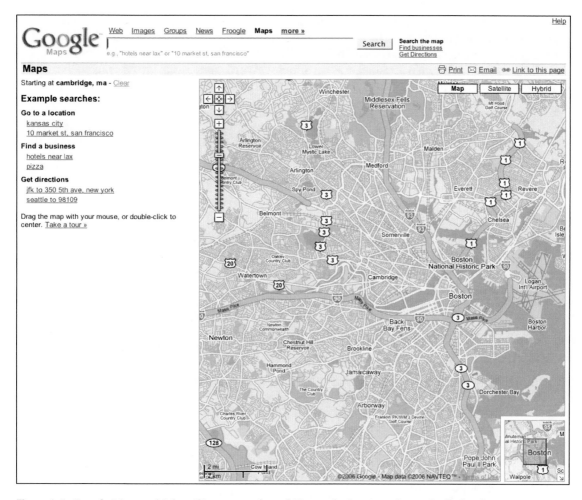

Figure 1-5. *Google Maps, which utilizes a number of Ajax techniques to dynamically load location information*

Browser Support

The sad truth of JavaScript development is that since it is so tied to the browsers that implement and support it, it is also at the mercy of whichever browsers are currently the most popular. Since users don't necessarily use the browsers with the best JavaScript support, we're forced to pick and choose which features are most important.

What many developers have begun to do is cut off support for browsers that simply cause too much trouble when developing for them. It's a delicate balance between supporting browsers due to the size of their user base and supporting them because they have a feature that you like.

Recently Yahoo released a JavaScript library that can be used to extend your web applications. Along with the library, it also released some design pattern guidelines for web developers to follow. The most important document to come out of it (in my opinion) is Yahoo's official list of browsers that it does and doesn't support. While anyone, and any corporation, can do something similar, having a document provided by one of the most trafficked web sites on the Internet is entirely invaluable.

Yahoo developed a graded browser support strategy that assigns a certain grade to a browser and provides different content to it based upon its capabilities. Yahoo gives browsers three grades: A, X, and C:

- A-grade browsers are fully supported and tested, and all Yahoo applications are guaranteed to work in them.

- An X-grade browser is an A-grade browser that Yahoo knows exists but simply does not have the capacity to test thoroughly, or is a brand-new browser that it's never encountered before. X-grade browsers are served with the same content as A-grade browsers, in hopes that they'll be able to handle the advanced content.

- C-grade browsers are known as "bad" browsers that do not support the features necessary to run Yahoo applications. These browsers are served the functional application contents without JavaScript, as Yahoo applications are fully unobtrusive (in that they will continue to work without the presence of JavaScript).

Incidentally, Yahoo's browser grade choices just so happen to coincide with my own, which makes it particularly appealing. Within this book, I use the term *modern browser* a lot; when I use that phrase, I mean any browser that has grade-A support deemed by the Yahoo browser chart. By giving you a consistent set of features with which to work, the learning and development experience will become much more interesting and much less painful (all by avoiding browser incompatibilities).

I highly recommend that you read through graded browser support documents (which can be found at `http://developer.yahoo.com/yui/articles/gbs/gbs.html`), including the browser support chart shown in Figure 1-6, to get a feel for what Yahoo is attempting to accomplish. By making this information available to the general web-developing public, Yahoo is providing an invaluable "gold standard" for all others to reach, which is a great thing to have.

For more information about all the browsers that are supported, see Appendix C of this book where the shortcomings and advantages of each browser are discussed in depth. More often than not, you'll find all of the A-grade browsers to be on the cutting edge of development, providing more than enough features for you to develop with.

When choosing what browsers you wish to support, the end result ultimately boils down to a set of features that your application is able to support. If you wish to support Netscape Navigator 4 or Internet Explorer 5 (for example), it would severely limit the number of features that you could use in your application, due to their lack of support for modern programming techniques.

	Win 98	Win 2000	Win XP	Mac 10.0	Mac 10.2	Mac 10.3	Mac 10.3.x	Mac 10.4
IE 7.0	n/a	n/a	A-grade	n/a	n/a	n/a	n/a	n/a
IE 6.0	A-grade	A-grade	A-grade	n/a	n/a	n/a	n/a	n/a
IE 5.5	A-grade	A-grade	n/a	n/a	n/a	n/a	n/a	n/a
IE 5.0	C-grade	C-grade	n/a	C-grade	C-grade	C-grade	C-grade	C-grade
Netscape 8.0	X-grade	X-grade	A-grade	n/a	n/a	n/a	n/a	n/a
Firefox 1.5	A-grade	A-grade	A-grade	A-grade	A-grade	A-grade	A-grade	A-grade
Firefox 1.0.7	A-grade	A-grade	A-grade	A-grade	A-grade	A-grade	A-grade	A-grade
Mozilla 1.7.12	X-grade	X-grade	A-grade	X-grade	X-grade	X-grade	X-grade	X-grade
Opera 8.5	X-grade	X-grade	A-grade	C-grade	C-grade	C-grade	X-grade	X-grade
Safari 1.0	n/a	n/a	n/a	X-grade	n/a	n/a	n/a	n/a
Safari 1.1	n/a	n/a	n/a	X-grade	X-grade	n/a	n/a	n/a
Safari 1.2	n/a	n/a	n/a	X-grade	X-grade	X-grade	n/a	n/a
Safari 1.3	n/a	n/a	n/a	n/a	n/a	X-grade	A-grade	n/a
Safari 2.0	n/a	n/a	n/a	n/a	n/a	n/a	n/a	A-grade

Figure 1-6. *The graded browser support chart provided by Yahoo*

However, knowing which browsers are modern allows you to utilize the powerful features that are available in them, giving you a consistent base from which you can do further development. This consistent development base can be defined by the following set of features:

Core JavaScript 1.5: The most current, accepted version of JavaScript. It has all the features necessary to support fully functional object-oriented JavaScript. Internet Explorer 5.0 doesn't support full 1.5, which is the primary reason developers don't like to support it.

XML Document Object Model (DOM) 2: The standard for traversing HTML and XML documents. This is absolutely essential for writing fast applications.

XMLHttpRequest: The backbone of Ajax—a simple layer for initiating remote HTTP requests. All browsers support this object by default, except for Internet Explorer 5.5–6.0; however, they each support initiating a comparable object using ActiveX.

CSS: An essential requirement for designing web pages. This may seem like an odd requirement, but having CSS is essential for web application developers. Since every modern browser supports CSS, it generally boils down to discrepancies in presentation that cause the most problems. This is the primary reason Internet Explorer for Mac is less frequently supported.

The combination of all these browser features is what makes up the backbone of developing JavaScript web applications. Since all modern browsers support the previously listed features (in one way or another), it gives you a solid platform to build off of for the rest of this book. Everything discussed in this book will be based on the assumption that the browser you're using supports these features, at the very least.

Summary

This book is an attempt to completely encompass all modern, professional JavaScript programming techniques as they are used by everyone from individual developers to large corporations, making their code more usable, understandable, and interactive.

In this chapter we looked at a brief overview of everything that we're going to discuss in this book. This includes the foundations of professional JavaScript programming: writing object-oriented code, testing your code, and packaging it for distribution. Next you saw the fundamental aspects of unobtrusive DOM scripting, including a brief overview of the Document Object Model, events, and the interaction between JavaScript and CSS. Finally you looked at the premise behind Ajax and the support of JavaScript in modern browsers. All together, these topics are more than enough to take you to the level of a professional JavaScript programmer.

PART 2

■ ■ ■

Professional JavaScript Development

CHAPTER 2

■ ■ ■

Object-Oriented JavaScript

Objects are the fundamental units of JavaScript. Virtually everything in JavaScript is an object and takes advantage of that fact. However, to build up a solid object-oriented language, JavaScript includes a vast arsenal of features that make it an incredibly unique language, both in possibilities and in style.

In this chapter I'm going to begin by covering some of the most important aspects of the JavaScript language, such as references, scope, closures, and context, that you will find sorely lacking in other JavaScript books. After the important groundwork has been laid, we'll begin to explore the important aspects of object-oriented JavaScript, including exactly how objects behave and how to create new ones and set up methods with specific permissions. This is quite possibly the most important chapter in this book if taken to heart, as it will completely change the way you look at JavaScript as a language.

Language Features

JavaScript has a number of language features that are fundamental to making the language what it is. There are very few other languages like it. Personally, I find the combination of features to fit just right, contributing to a deceptively powerful language.

References

A fundamental aspect of JavaScript is the concept of references. A *reference* is a pointer to an actual location of an object. This is an incredibly powerful feature The premise is that a physical object is never a reference. A string is always a string; an array is always an array. However, multiple variables can refer to that same object. It is this system of references that JavaScript is based around. By maintaining sets of references to other objects, the language affords you much more flexibility.

Additionally, an object can contain a set of properties, all of which are simply references to other objects (such as strings, numbers, arrays, etc.). When multiple variables point to the same object, modifying the underlying type of that object will be reflected in all variables. An example of this is shown in Listing 2-1, where two variables point to the same object, but the modification of the object's contents is reflected globally.

Listing 2-1. *Example of Multiple Variables Referring to a Single Object*

```
// Set obj to an empty object
var obj = new Object();

// objRef now refers to the other object
var objRef = obj;

// Modify a property in the original object
obj.oneProperty = true;

// We now see that that change is represented in both variables
// (Since they both refer to the same object)
alert( obj.oneProperty === objRef.oneProperty );
```

I mentioned before that self-modifying objects are very rare in JavaScript. Let's look at one popular instance where this occurs. The array object is able to add additional items to itself using the push() method. Since, at the core of an Array object, the values are stored as object properties, the result is a situation similar to that shown in Listing 2-1, where an object becomes globally modified (resulting in multiple variables' contents being simultaneously changed). An example of this situation can be found in Listing 2-2.

Listing 2-2. *Example of a Self-Modifying Object*

```
// Create an array of items
var items = new Array( "one", "two", "three" );

// Create a reference to the array of items
var itemsRef = items;

// Add an item to the original array
items.push( "four" );

// The length of each array should be the same,
// since they both point to the same array object
alert( items.length == itemsRef.length );
```

It's important to remember that references only point to the final referred object, not a reference itself. In Perl, for example, it's possible to have a reference point to another variable, which also is a reference. In JavaScript, however, it traverses down the reference chain and only points to the core object. An example of this situation can be seen in Listing 2-3, where the physical object is changed but the reference continues to point back at the old object.

Listing 2-3. *Changing the Reference of an Object While Maintaining Integrity*

```
// Set items to an array (object) of strings
var items = new Array( "one", "two", "three" );
```

```
// Set itemsRef to a reference to items
var itemsRef = items;

// Set items to equal a new object
items = new Array( "new", "array" );

// items and itemsRef now point to different objects.
// items points to new Array( "new", "array" )
// itemsRef points to new Array( "one", "two", "three" )
alert( items !== itemsRef );
```

Finally, let's look at a strange instance that appears to be one of object self-modification, but results in a new nonreferential object. When performing string concatenation the result is always a new string object rather than a modified version of the original string. This can be seen in Listing 2-4.

Listing 2-4. *Example of Object Modification Resulting in a New Object, Not a Self-Modified Object*

```
// Set item equal to a new string object
var item = "test";

// itemRef now refers to the same string object
var itemRef = item;

// Concatenate some new text onto the string object
// NOTE: This creates a new object, and does not modify
// the original object.
item += "ing";

// The values of item and itemRef are NOT equal, as a whole
// new string object has been created
alert( item != itemRef );
```

References can be a tricky subject to wrap your mind around, if you're new to them. Although, understanding how references work is paramount to writing good, clean JavaScript code. In the next couple sections we're going to look at a couple features that aren't necessarily new or exciting but are important to writing good, clean code.

Function Overloading and Type-Checking

A common feature in other object-oriented languages, such as Java, is the ability to "overload" functions to perform different behaviors when different numbers or types of arguments are passed to them. While this ability isn't immediately available in JavaScript, a number of tools are provided that make this quest entirely possible.

Function overloading requires two things: the ability to determine how many arguments are provided, and the ability to determine the type of the arguments that are provided. Let's start by looking at the number of arguments provided.

Inside of every function in JavaScript there exists a contextual variable named *arguments* that acts as a pseudo-array containing all the arguments passed into the function. Arguments isn't a true array (meaning that you can't modify it, or call .push() to add new items), but you can access items in the array, and it does have a .length property. There are two examples of this in Listing 2-5.

Listing 2-5. *Two Examples of Function Overloading in JavaScript*

```
// A simple function for sending a message
function sendMessage( msg, obj ) {
    // If both a message and an object are provided
    if ( arguments.length == 2 )
        // Send the message to the object
        obj.handleMsg( msg );

    // Otherwise, assume that only a message was provided
    else
        // So just display the default error message
        alert( msg );
}

// Call the function with one argument - displaying the message using an alert
sendMessage( "Hello, World!" );

// Otherwise, we can pass in our own object that handles
// a different way of displaying   information
sendMessage( "How are you?", {
    handleMsg: function( msg ) {
        alert( "This is a custom message: " + msg );
    }
});

// A function that takes any number of arguments and makes
// an array out of them
function makeArray() {
    // The temporary array
    var arr = [];

    // Go through each of the submitted arguments
    for ( var i = 0; i < arguments.length; i++ ) {
        arr.push( arguments[i] );
    }

    // Return the resulting array
    return arr;
}
```

Additionally, there exists another method for determining the number of arguments passed to a function. This particular method uses a little more trickiness to get the job done, however. We take advantage of the fact that any argument that isn't provided has a value of *undefined*. Listing 2-6 shows a simple function for displaying an error message and providing a default message if one is not provided.

Listing 2-6. *Displaying an Error Message and a Default Message*

```
function displayError( msg ) {
    // Check and make sure that msg is not undefined
    if ( typeof msg == 'undefined' ) {
        // If it is, set a default message
        msg = "An error occurred.";
    }

    // Display the message
    alert( msg );
}
```

The use of the typeof statement helps to lead us into the topic of type-checking. Since JavaScript is (currently) a dynamically typed language, this proves to be a very useful and important topic. There are a number of different ways to check the type of a variable; we're going to look at two that are particularly useful.

The first way of checking the type of an object is by using the obvious-sounding typeof operator. This utility gives us a string name representing the type of the contents of a variable. This would be the perfect solution except that for variables of type object or array, or a custom object such as user, it only returns object, making it hard to differentiate between all objects. An example of this method can be seen in Listing 2-7.

Listing 2-7. *Example of Using Typeof to Determine the Type of an Object*

```
// Check to see if our number is actually a string
if ( typeof num  == "string" )
    // If it is, then parse a number out of it
    num = parseInt( num );

// Check to see if our array is actually a string
if ( typeof arr == "string" )
    // If that's the case, make an array, splitting on commas
    arr = arr.split(",");
```

The second way of checking the type of an object is by referencing a property of all JavaScript objects called constructor. This property is a reference to the function used to originally construct this object. An example of this method can be seen in Listing 2-8.

Listing 2-8. *Example of Using the Constructor Property to Determine the Type of an Object*

```
// Check to see if our number is actually a string
if ( num.constructor == String )
    // If it is, then parse a number out of it
    num = parseInt( num );

// Check to see if our string is actually an array
if ( str.constructor == Array )
    // If that's the case, make a string by joining the array using commas
    str = str.join(',');
```

Table 2-1 shows the results of type-checking different object types using the two different methods that I've described. The first column in the table shows the object that we're trying to find the type of. The second column is the result of running typeof Variable (where *Variable* is the value contained in the first column). The result of everything in this column is a string. Finally, the third column shows the result of running Variable.constructor against the objects contained in the first column. The result of everything in this column is an object.

Table 2-1. *Type-Checking Variables*

Variable	typeof Variable	Variable.constructor
{ an: "object" }	object	Object
["an", "array"]	object	Array
function(){}	function	Function
"a string"	string	String
55	number	Number
true	boolean	Boolean
new User()	object	User

Using the information in Table 2-1 you can now build a generic function for doing type-checking within a function. As may be apparent by now, using a variable's constructor as an object-type reference is probably the most foolproof way of valid type-checking. Strict type-checking can help in instances where you want to make sure that exactly the right number of arguments of exactly the right type are being passed into your functions. We can see an example of this in action in Listing 2-9.

Listing 2-9. *A Function That Can Be Used to Strictly Maintain All the Arguments Passed into a Function*

```
// Strictly check a list of variable types against a list of arguments
function strict( types, args ) {

    // Make sure that the number of types and args matches
    if (  types.length != args.length ) {
```

```
        // If they do not, throw a useful exception
        throw "Invalid number of arguments. Expected " + types.length +
            ", received " + args.length + " instead.";
    }

    // Go through each of the arguments and check their types
    for ( var i = 0; i < args.length; i++ ) {
        //
        if ( args[i].constructor != types[i] ) {
            throw "Invalid argument type. Expected " + types[i].name +
                ", received " + args[i].constructor.name + " instead.";
        }
    }
}

// A simple function for printing out a list of users
function userList( prefix, num, users ) {
    // Make sure that the prefix is a string, num is a number,
    // and users is an array
    strict( [ String, Number, Array ], arguments );

    // Iterate up to 'num' users
    for ( var i = 0; i < num; i++ ) {
        // Displaying a message about each user
        print( prefix + ": " + users[i] );
    }
}
```

Type-checking variables and verifying the length of argument arrays are simple concepts at heart but can be used to provide complex methods that can adapt and provide a better experience to the developer and users of your code. Next, we're going to look at scope within JavaScript and how to better control it.

Scope

Scope is a tricky feature of JavaScript. All object-oriented programming languages have some form of scope; it just depends on what context a scope is kept within. In JavaScript, scope is kept within functions, but not within blocks (such as while, if, and for statements). The end result could be some code whose results are seemingly strange (if you're coming from a block-scoped language). Listing 2-10 shows an example of the implications of function-scoped code.

Listing 2-10. *Example of How the Variable Scope in JavaScript Works*

```
// Set a global variable, foo, equal to test
var foo = "test";
```

```
// Within an if block
if ( true ) {
    // Set foo equal to 'new test'
    // NOTE: This is still within the global scope!
    var foo = "new test";
}

// As we can see here, as foo is now equal to 'new test'
alert( foo == "new test" );

// Create a function that will modify the variable foo
function test() {
    var foo = "old test";
}

// However, when called, 'foo' remains within the scope
// of the function
test();

// Which is confirmed, as foo is still equal to 'new test'
alert( foo == "new test" );
```

You'll notice that in Listing 2-10, the variables are within the global scope. An interesting aspect of browser-based JavaScript is that all globally scoped variables are actually just properties of the window object. Though some old versions of Opera and Safari don't, it's generally a good rule of thumb to assume a browser behaves this way. Listing 2-11 shows an example of this global scoping occurring.

Listing 2-11. *Example of Global Scope in JavaScript and the Window Object*

```
// A globally-scoped variable, containing the string 'test'
var test = "test";

// You'll notice that our 'global' variable and the test
// property of the the window object are identical
alert( window.test == test );
```

Finally, let's see what happens when a variable declaration is misdefined. In Listing 2-12 a value is assigned to a variable (foo) within the scope of the test() function. However, nowhere in Listing 2-12 is the scope of the variable actually declared (using var foo). When the foo variable isn't explicitly defined, it will become defined globally, even though it is only used within the context of the function scope.

Listing 2-12. *Example of Implicit Globally Scoped Variable Declaration*

```
// A function in which the value of foo is set
function test() {
    foo = "test";
}

// Call the function to set the value of foo
test();

// We see that foo is now globally scoped
alert( window.foo == "test" );
```

As should be apparent by now, even though the scoping in JavaScript is not as strict as a block-scoped language, it is still quite powerful and featureful. Especially when combined with the concept of closures, discussed in the next section, JavaScript reveals itself as a powerful scripting language.

Closures

Closures are means through which inner functions can refer to the variables present in their outer enclosing function after their parent functions have already terminated. This particular topic can be very powerful and very complex. I highly recommend referring to the site mentioned at the end of this section, as it has some excellent information on the topic of closures.

Let's begin by looking at two simple examples of closures, shown in Listing 2-13.

Listing 2-13. *Two Examples of How Closures Can Improve the Clarity of Your Code*

```
// Find the element with an ID of 'main'
var obj = document.getElementById("main");

// Change it's border styling
obj.style.border = "1px solid red";

// Initialize a callback that will occur in one second
setTimeout(function(){
    // Which will hide the object
    obj.style.display = 'none';
}, 1000);

// A generic function for displaying a delayed alert message
function delayedAlert( msg, time ) {
    // Initialize an enclosed callback
    setTimeout(function(){
        // Which utilizes the msg passed in from the enclosing function
        alert( msg );
    }, time );
}
```

```
// Call the delayedAlert function with two arguments
delayedAlert( "Welcome!", 2000 );
```

The first function call to setTimeout shows a popular instance where new JavaScript developers have problems. It's not uncommon to see code like this in a new developer's program:

```
setTimeout("otherFunction()", 1000);
```

```
// or even…
setTimeout("otherFunction(" + num + "," + num2 + ")", 1000);
```

Using the concept of closures, it's entirely possible to circumnavigate this mess of code. The first example is simple; there is a setTimeout callback being called 1,000 milliseconds after when it's first called, but still referring to the obj variable (which is defined globally as the element with an ID of main). The second function defined, delayedAlert, shows a solution to the setTimeout mess that occurs, along with the ability to have closures within function scopes.

You should be able to find that when using simple closures such as these in your code, the clarity of what you're writing should increase instead of turning into a syntactical soup.

Let's look at a fun side effect of what's possible with closures. In some functional programming languages, there's the concept of currying. *Currying* is a way to, essentially, pre–fill in a number of arguments to a function, creating a new, simpler function. Listing 2-14 has a simple example of currying, creating a new function that pre–fills in an argument to another function.

Listing 2-14. *Example of Function Currying Using Closures*

```
// A function that generates a new function for adding numbers
function addGenerator( num ) {

    // Return a simple function for adding two numbers
    // with the first number borrowed from the generator
    return function( toAdd ) {
        return num + toAdd
    };

}

// addFive now contains a function that takes one argument,
// adds five to it, and returns the resulting number
var addFive = addGenerator( 5 );

// We can see here that the result of the addFive function is 9,
// when passed an argument of 4
alert( addFive( 4 ) == 9 );
```

There's another, common, JavaScript-coding problem that closures can solve. New JavaScript developers tend to accidentally leave a lot of extra variables sitting in the global scope. This is generally considered to be bad practice, as those extra variables could quietly interfere with other libraries, causing confusing problems to occur. Using a self-executing, anonymous function you can essentially hide all normally global variables from being seen by other code, as shown in Listing 2-15.

Listing 2-15. *Example of Using Anonymous Functions to Hide Variables from the Global Scope*

```
// Create a new anonymous function, to use as a wrapper
(function(){
    // The variable that would, normally, be global
    var msg = "Thanks for visiting!";

    // Binding a new function to a global object
    window.onunload = function(){
        // Which uses the 'hidden' variable
        alert( msg );
    };

// Close off the anonymous function and execute it
})();
```

Finally, let's look at one problem that occurs when using closures. Remember that closures allow you to reference variables that exist within the parent function. However, it does not provide the value of the variable at the time it is created; it provides the last value of the variable within the parent function. The most common issue under which you'll see this occur is during a for loop. There is one variable being used as the iterator (e.g., *i*). Inside of the for loop, new functions are being created that utilize the closure to reference the iterator again. The problem is that by the time the new closured functions are called, they will reference the last value of the iterator (i.e., the last position in an array), not the value that you would expect. Listing 2-16 shows an example of using anonymous functions to induce scope, to create an instance where expected closure is possible.

Listing 2-16. *Example of Using Anonymous Functions to Induce the Scope Needed to Create Multiple Closure-Using Functions*

```
// An element with an ID of main
var obj = document.getElementById("main");

// An array of items to bind to
var items = [ "click", "keypress" ];

// Iterate through each of the items
for ( var i = 0; i < items.length; i++ ) {
    // Use a self-executed anonymous function to induce scope
    (function(){
        // Remember the value within this scope
        var item = items[i];
```

```
            // Bind a function to the element
            obj[ "on" + item ] = function() {
                // item refers to a parent variable that has been successfully
                // scoped within the context of this for loop
                alert( "Thanks for your " + item );
            };
        })();
    }
```

The concept of closures is not a simple one to grasp; it took me a lot of time and effort to truly wrap my mind around how powerful closures are. Luckily, there exists an excellent resource for explaining how closures work in JavaScript: "JavaScript Closures" by Jim Jey at http://jibbering.com/faq/faq_notes/closures.html.

Finally, we're going to look at the concept of *context*, which is the building block upon which much of JavaScript's object-oriented functionality is built.

Context

Within JavaScript your code will always have some form on context (an object within which it is operating). This is a common feature of other object-oriented languages too, but without the extreme in which JavaScript takes it.

The way context works is through the this variable. The this variable will always refer to the object that the code is currently inside of. Remember that global objects are actually properties of the window object. This means that even in a global context, the this variable will still refer to an object. Context can be a powerful tool and is an essential one for object-oriented code. Listing 2-17 shows some simple examples of context.

Listing 2-17. *Examples of Using Functions Within Context and Then Switching Its Context to Another Variable*

```
var obj = {
    yes: function(){
        // this == obj
        this.val = true;
    },
    no: function(){
        this.val = false;
    }
};

// We see that there is no val property in the 'obj' object
alert( obj.val == null );

// We run the yes function and it changes the val property
// associated with the 'obj' object
obj.yes();
alert( obj.val == true );
```

```
// However, we now point window.no to the obj.no method and run it
window.no = obj.no;
window.no();

// This results in the obj object staying the same (as the context was
// switched to the window object)
alert( obj.val == true );

// and window val property getting updated.
alert( window.val == false );
```

You may have noticed in Listing 2-17 when we switched the context of the obj.no method to the window variable the clunky code needed to switch the context of a function. Luckily, JavaScript provides a couple methods that make this process much easier to understand and implement. Listing 2-18 shows two different methods, call and apply, that can be used to achieve just that.

Listing 2-18. *Examples of Changing the Context of Functions*

```
// A simple function that sets the color style of its context
function changeColor( color ) {
    this.style.color = color;
}

// Calling it on the window object, which fails, since it doesn't
// have a style object
changeColor( "white" );

// Find the element with an ID of main
var main = document.getElementById("main");

// Set its color to black, using the call method
// The call method sets the context with the first argument
// and passes all the other arguments as arguments to the function
changeColor.call( main, "black" );

// A function that sets the color on  the body element
function setBodyColor() {
    // The apply method sets the context to the body element
    // with the first argument, the second argument is an array
    // of arguments that gets passed to the function
    changeColor.apply( document.body, arguments );
}

// Set the background color of the body to black
setBodyColor( "black" );
```

While the usefulness of context may not be immediately apparent, it will become more visible when we look at object-oriented JavaScript in the next section.

Object-Oriented Basics

The phrase *object-oriented JavaScript* is somewhat redundant, as the JavaScript language is completely object-oriented and is impossible to use otherwise. However, a common shortcoming of most new programmers (JavaScript programmers included) is to write their code functionally without any context or grouping. To fully understand how to write optimal JavaScript code, you must understand how JavaScript objects work, how they're different from other languages, and how to use that to your advantage.

In the rest of this chapter we will go through the basics of writing object-oriented code in JavaScript, and then in upcoming chapters look at the practicality of writing code this way.

Objects

Objects are the foundation of JavaScript. Virtually everything within the language is an object. Much of the power of the language is derived from this fact. At their most basic level, objects exist as a collection of properties, almost like a hash construct that you see in other languages. Listing 2-19 shows two basic examples of the creation of an object with a set of properties.

Listing 2-19. *Two Examples of Creating a Simple Object and Setting Properties*

```
// Creates a new Object object and stores it in 'obj'
var obj = new Object();

// Set some properties of the object to different values
obj.val = 5;
obj.click = function(){
    alert( "hello" );
};

// Here is some equivalent code, using the {…} shorthand
// along with key-value pairs for defining properties
var obj = {

    // Set the property names and values use key/value pairs
    val: 5,
    click: function(){
        alert( "hello" );
    }

};
```

In reality there isn't much more to objects than that. Where things get tricky, however, is in the creation of new objects, especially ones that inherit the properties of other objects.

Object Creation

Unlike most other object-oriented languages, JavaScript doesn't actually have a concept of classes. In most other object-oriented languages you would instantiate an instance of a particular class, but that is not the case in JavaScript. In JavaScript, objects can create new objects, and objects can inherit from other objects. This whole concept is called *prototypal inheritance* and will be discussed more later in the "Public Methods" section.

Fundamentally, though, there still needs to be a way to create a new object, no matter what type of object scheme JavaScript uses. JavaScript makes it so that any function can also be instantiated as an object. In reality, it sounds a lot more confusing than it is. It's a lot like having a piece of dough (which is a raw object) that is molded using a cookie cutter (which is an object constructor, using an object's prototype).

Let's look at Listing 2-20 for an example of how this works.

Listing 2-20. *Creation and Usage of a Simple Object*

```
// A simple function which takes a name and saves
// it to the current context
function User( name ) {
    this.name = name;
}

// Create a new instance of that function, with the specified name
var me = new User( "My Name" );

// We can see that its name has been set as a property of itself
alert( me.name == "My Name" );

// And that it is an instance of the User object
alert( me.constructor == User );

// Now, since User() is just a function, what happens
// when we treat it as such?
User( "Test" );

// Since its 'this' context wasn't set, it defaults to the global 'window'
// object, meaning that window.name is equal to the name provided
alert( window.name == "Test" );
```

Listing 2-20 shows the use of the constructor property. This property exists on every object and will always point back to the function that created it. This way, you should be able to effectively duplicate the object, creating a new one of the same base class but not with the same properties. An example of this can be seen in Listing 2-21.

Listing 2-21. *An Example of Using the Constructor Property*

```
// Create a new, simple, User object
function User() {}

// Create a new User object
var me = new User();
```

```
// Also creates a new User object (from the
// constructor reference of  the first)
var you = new me.constructor();

// We can see that the constructors are, in fact, the same
alert( me.constructor == you.constructor );
```

Now that we know how to create simple objects, it's time to add on what makes objects so useful: contextual methods and properties.

Public Methods

Public methods are completely accessible by the end user within the context of the object. To achieve these public methods, which are available on every instance of a particular object, you need to learn about a property called *prototype*, which simply contains an object that will act as a base reference for all new copies of its parent object. Essentially, any property of the prototype will be available on every instance of that object. This creation/reference process gives us a cheap version of inheritance, which I discuss in Chapter 3.

Since an object prototype is just an object, you can attach new properties to them, just like any other object. Attaching new properties to a prototype will make them a part of every object instantiated from the original prototype, effectively making all the properties public (and accessible by all). Listing 2-22 shows an example of this.

Listing 2-22. *Example of an Object with Methods Attached Via the Prototype Object*

```
// Create a new User constructor
function User( name, age ){
    this.name = name;
    this.age = age;
}

// Add a new function to the object prototype
User.prototype.getName = function(){
    return this.name;
};

// And add another function to the prototype
// Notice that the context is going to be within
// the instantiated object
User.prototype.getAge = function(){
    return this.age;
};

// Instantiate a new User object
var user = new User( "Bob", 44 );
```

```
// We can see that the two methods we attached are with the
// object, with proper contexts
alert( user.getName() == "Bob" );
alert( user.getAge() == 44 );
```

Simple constructors and simple manipulation of the prototype object is as far as most JavaScript developers get when building new applications. In the rest of this section I'm going to explain a couple other techniques that you can use to get the most out of your object-oriented code.

Private Methods

Private methods and variables are only accessible to other private methods, private variables, and privileged methods (discussed in the next section). This is a way to define code that will only be accessible within the object itself, and not outside of it. This technique is based on the work of Douglas Crockford, whose web site provides numerous documents detailing how object-oriented JavaScript works and how it should be used:

- List of JavaScript articles: http://javascript.crockford.com/

- "Private Members in JavaScript" article: http://javascript.crockford.com/private.html

Let's now look at an example of how a private method could be used within an application, as shown in Listing 2-23.

Listing 2-23. *Example of a Private Method Only Usable by the Constructor Function*

```
// An Object constructor that represents a classroom
function Classroom( students, teacher ) {
    // A private method used for displaying all the students in the class
    function disp() {
        alert( this.names.join(", ") );
    }

    // Store the class data as public object properties
    this.students = students;
    this.teacher = teacher;

    // Call the private method to display the error
    disp();
}

// Create a new classroom object
var class = new Classroom( [ "John", "Bob" ], "Mr. Smith" );

// Fails, as disp is not a public property of the object
class.disp();
```

While simple, private methods and variables are important for keeping your code free of collisions while allowing greater control over what your users are able to see and use. Next, we're going to take a look at privileged methods, which are a combination of private and public methods that you can use in your objects.

Privileged Methods

Privileged methods is a term coined by Douglas Crockford to refer to methods that are able to view and manipulate private variables (within an object) while still being accessible to users as a public method. Listing 2-24 shows an example of using privileged methods.

Listing 2-24. *Example of Using Privileged Methods*

```
// Create a new User object constructor
function User( name, age ) {
    // Attempt to figure out the year that the user was born
    var year = (new Date()).getFullYear() - age;

    // Create a new Privileged method that has access to
    // the year variable, but is still publically available
    this.getYearBorn = function(){
        return year;
    };
}

// Create a new instance of the user object
var user = new User( "Bob", 44 );

// Verify that the year returned is correct
alert( user.getYearBorn() == 1962 );

// And notice that we're not able to access the private year
// property of the object

alert( user.year == null );
```

In essence, privileged methods are dynamically generated methods, because they're added to the object at runtime, rather than when the code is first compiled. While this technique is computationally more expensive than binding a simple method to the object prototype, it is also much more powerful and flexible. Listing 2-25 is an example of what can be accomplished using dynamically generated methods.

Listing 2-25. *Example of Dynamically Generated Methods That Are Created When a New Object Is Instantiated*

```
// Create a new user object that accepts an object of properties
function User( properties ) {
    // Iterate through the properties of the object, and make sure
    // that it's properly scoped (as discussed previously)
    for ( var i in properties ) { (function(){
        // Create a new getter for the property
        this[ "get" + i ] = function() {
            return properties[i];
        };

        // Create a new setter for the property
        this[ "set" + i ] = function(val) {
            properties[i] = val;
        };
    })(); }
}

// Create a new user object instance and pass in an object of
// properties to seed it with
var user = new User({
    name: "Bob",
    age: 44
});

// Just note that the name property does not exist, as it's private
// within the properties object
alert( user.name == null );

// However, we're able to access its value using the new getname()
// method, that was dynamically generated
alert( user.getname() == "Bob" );

// Finally, we can see that it's possible to set and get the age using
// the newly generated functions
user.setage( 22 );
alert( user.getage() == 22 );
```

The power of dynamically generated code cannot be understated. Being able to build code based on live variables is incredibly useful; it's what makes macros in other languages (such as Lisp) so powerful, but within the context of a modern programming language. Next we'll look at a method type that is useful purely for its organizational benefits.

Static Methods

The premise behind static methods is virtually identical to that of any other normal function. The primary difference, however, is that the functions exist as static properties of an object. As a property, they are not accessible within the context of an instance of that object; they are only available in the same context as the main object itself. For those familiar with traditional classlike inheritance, this is sort of like a static class method.

In reality, the only advantage to writing code this way is to keep object namespaces clean, a concept that I discuss more in Chapter 3. Listing 2-26 shows an example of a static method attached to an object.

Listing 2-26. *A Simple Example of a Static Method*

```
// A static method attached to the User object
User.cloneUser = function( user ) {
    // Create, and return, a new user
    return new User(
        // that is a clone of the other user object
        user.getName(),
        user.getAge()
    );
};
```

Static methods are the first methods that we've encountered whose purpose is purely organizationally related. This is an important segue to what we'll be discussing in the next chapter. A fundamental aspect of developing professional quality JavaScript is its ability to quickly, and quietly, interface with other pieces of code, while still being understandably accessible. This is an important goal to strive for, and one that we will look to achieve in the next chapter.

Summary

The importance of understanding the concepts outlined in this chapter cannot be understated. The first half of the chapter, giving you a good understanding of how the JavaScript language behaves and how it can be best used, is the starting point for fully grasping how to use JavaScript professionally. Simply understanding how objects act, references are handled, and scope is decided can unquestionably change how you write JavaScript code.

With the skill of knowledgeable JavaScript coding, the importance of writing clean object-oriented JavaScript code should become all the more apparent. In the second half of this chapter I covered how to go about writing a variety of object-oriented code to suit anyone coming from another programming language. It is this skill that much of modern JavaScript is based upon, giving you a substantial edge when developing new and innovative applications.

Creating Reusable Code

When developing code with other programmers, which is standard for most corporate or team projects, it becomes fundamentally important to maintain good authoring practices in order to maintain your sanity. As JavaScript has begun to come into its own in recent years, the amount of JavaScript code developed by professional programmers has increased dramatically. This shift in the perception and use of JavaScript has resulted in important advances in the development practices surrounding it.

In this chapter, we're going to look at a number of ways in which you can clean up your code, organize it better, and improve the quality so that others can use it.

Standardizing Object-Oriented Code

The first and most important step in writing reusable code is to write the code in a way that is standard across your entire application, object-oriented code especially. When you saw how object-oriented JavaScript behaved in the previous chapter, you saw that the JavaScript language is rather flexible, allowing you to simulate a number of different programming styles.

To start with, it is important to devise a system of writing object-oriented code and implementing object inheritance (cloning object properties into new objects) that best suits your needs. Seemingly, however, everyone who's ever written some object-oriented JavaScript has built their own scheme of doing this, which can be rather confusing. In this section, we're going to look at how inheritance works in JavaScript followed by a look at how a number of different, alternative helper methods work and how to use them in your application.

Prototypal Inheritance

JavaScript uses a unique form of object creation and inheritance called *prototypal inheritance*. The premise behind this method (as opposed to the classical class/object scheme that most programmers are familiar with) is that an object constructor can inherit methods from one other object, creating a *prototype* object from which all other new objects are built.

This entire process is facilitated by the *prototype property* (which exists as a property of every function, and since any function can be a constructor, it's a property of them, too). Prototypal inheritance is designed for single, not multiple, inheritance; however, there are ways that this can be worked around, which I'll discuss in the next section.

The part that makes this form of inheritance especially tricky to grasp is that prototypes do not inherit their properties from other prototypes or other constructors; they inherit them from physical objects. Listing 3-1 shows some examples of how exactly the prototype property is used for simple inheritance.

Listing 3-1. *Examples of Prototypal Inheritance*

```
// Create the constructor for a Person object
function Person( name ) {
    this.name = name;
}

// Add a new method to the Person object
Person.prototype.getName = function() {
    return this.name;
};

// Create a new User object constructor
function User( name, password ) {
    // Notice that this does not support graceful overloading/inheritance
    // e.g. being able to call the super class constructor
    this.name = name;
    this.password = password;
};

// The User object inherits all of the Person object's methods
User.prototype = new Person();

// We add a method of our own to the User object
User.prototype.getPassword = function() {
    return this.password;
};
```

The most important line in the previous example is `User.prototype = new Person();`. Let's look in depth at what exactly this means. `User` is a reference to the function constructor of the User object. `new Person()` creates a new Person object, using the Person constructor. You set the result of this as the value of the User constructor's prototype. This means that anytime you do `new User()`, the new User object will have all the methods that the Person object had when you did `new Person()`.

With this particular technique in mind, let's look at a number of different wrappers that developers have written to make the process of inheritance in JavaScript simpler.

Classical Inheritance

Classical inheritance is the form that most developers are familiar with. You have classes with methods that can be instantiated into objects. It's very typical for new object-oriented JavaScript programmers to attempt to emulate this style of program design, however few truly figure out how to do it correctly.

Thankfully, one of the masters of JavaScript, Douglas Crockford, set it as a goal of his to develop a simple set of methods that can be used to simulate classlike inheritance with JavaScript, as explained on his web site at http://javascript.crockford.com/ inheritance.html.

Listing 3-2 shows three functions that he built to create a comprehensive form of classical JavaScript inheritance. Each of the functions implement a different aspect of inheritance: inheriting a single function, inheriting everything from a single parent, and inheriting individual methods from multiple parents.

Listing 3-2. *Douglas Crockford's Three Functions for Simulating Classical-Style Inheritance Using JavaScript*

```
// A simple helper that allows you to bind new functions to the
// prototype of an object
Function.prototype.method = function(name, func) {
    this.prototype[name] = func;
    return this;
};

// A (rather complex) function that allows you to gracefully inherit
// functions from other objects and be able to still call the  'parent'
// object's function
Function.method('inherits', function(parent) {
    // Keep track of how many parent-levels deep we are
    var depth = 0;

    // Inherit the parent's methods
    var proto = this.prototype = new parent();

    // Create a new 'priveledged' function called 'uber', that when called
    // executes any function that has been written over in the inheritance
    this.method('uber', function uber(name) {

        var func; // The function to be execute
        var ret; // The return value of the function
        var v = parent.prototype; // The parent's prototype

        // If we're already within another 'uber' function
        if (depth) {
            // Go the necessary depth to find the orignal prototype
            for ( var i = d; i > 0; i += 1 ) {
                v = v.constructor.prototype;
            }

            // and get the function from that prototype
            func = v[name];
```

```
                    // Otherwise, this is the first 'uber' call
                    } else {
                        // Get the function to execute from the prototype
                        func = proto[name];

                        // If the function was a part of this prototype
                        if ( func == this[name] ) {
                            // Go to the parent's prototype instead
                            func = v[name];
                        }
                    }

                    // Keep track of how 'deep' we are in the inheritance stack
                    depth += 1;

                    // Call the function to execute with all the arguments but the first
                    // (which holds the name of the function that we're executing)
                    ret = func.apply(this, Array.prototype.slice.apply(arguments, [1]));

                    // Reset the stack depth
                    depth -= 1;

                    // Return the return value of the execute function
                    return ret;
                });

        return this;
});

// A function for inheriting only a couple functions from a parent object,
// not every function using new parent()
Function.method('swiss', function(parent) {
        // Go through all of the methods to inherit
        for (var i = 1; i < arguments.length; i += 1) {
            // The name of the method to import
            var name = arguments[i];

            // Import the method into this object's prototype
            this.prototype[name] = parent.prototype[name];
        }

        return this;
});
```

Let's look at what exactly these three functions provide us with and why we should use them instead of attempting to write our own prototypal inheritance model. The premise for the three functions is simple:

Function.prototype.method: This serves as a simple way of attaching a function to the prototype of a constructor. This particular clause works because all constructors are functions, and thus gain the new "method" method.

Function.prototyope.inherits: This function can be used to provide simple single-parent inheritance. The bulk of the code in this function centers around the ability to call `this.uber('methodName')` in any of your object methods, and have it execute the parent object's method that it's overwriting. This is one aspect that is not built into JavaScript's inheritance model.

Function.prototype.swiss: This is an advanced version of the .method() function which can be used to grab multiple methods from a single parent object. When used together with multiple parent objects, you can have a form of functional, multiple inheritance.

Now that you have a fair idea of what it is that these functions provide us with, Listing 3-3 revisits the Person/User example that you saw in Listing 3-1, only with this new classical-style form of inheritance. Additionally, you can see what additional functionality this library can provide, along with any improved clarity.

Listing 3-3. *Examples of Douglas Crockford's Classical Inheritance-Style JavaScript Functions*

```
// Create a new Person object constructor
function Person( name ) {
    this.name = name;
}

// Add a new method to the Person object
Person.method( 'getName', function(){
    return name;
});

// Create a new User object constructor
function User( name, password ) {
    this.name = name;
    this.password = password;
},

// Inherit all the methods from the Person object
User.inherits( Person );

// Add a new method to the User object
User.method( 'getPassword', function(){
    return this.password;
});
```

```
// Overwrite the method created by the Person object,
// but call it again using the uber function
User.method( 'getName', function(){
    return "My name is: " + this.uber('getName');
});
```

Now that you've had a taste for what is possible with a solid inheritance-enhancing JavaScript library, you should take a look at some of the other popular methods that are commonly used.

The Base Library

A recent addition to the space of JavaScript object creation and inheritance is the Base library developed by Dean Edwards. This particular library offers a number of different ways to extend the functionality of objects. Additionally, it even provides an intuitive means of object inheritance. Dean originally developed Base for use with some of his side projects, including the IE7 project, which serves as a complete set of upgrades to Internet Explorer. The examples listed on Dean's web site are rather comprehensive and really show the capabilities of the library quite well: `http://dean.edwards.name/weblog/2006/03/base/`. Additionally, you can find more examples in the Base source code directory: `http://dean.edwards.name/base/`.

While Base is rather long and quite complex, it deserves some additional comments for clarification (which are included in the code provided in the Source Code/Download section of the Apress web site, `http://www.apress.com`). It is highly recommended that, in addition to reading through the commented code, you look through the examples that Dean provides on his web site, as they can be quite helpful for clarifying common confusions.

As a starting point, however, I'm going to walk you through a couple important aspects of Base that can be very helpful to your development. Specifically, in Listing 3-4, there are examples of class creation, single-parent inheritance, and overriding parent functions.

Listing 3-4. *Examples of Dean Edwards's Base Library for Simple Class Creation and Inheritance*

```
// Create a new Person class
var Person = Base.extend({
    // The constructor of the Person class
    constructor: function( name ) {
        this.name = name;
    },

    A simple method of the Person class
    getName: function() {
        return this.name;
    }
});
```

```
// Create a new  User class that inherits from the Person class
var User = Person.extend({
    // Create the User class constructor
    constructor: function( name, password ) {
        // which, in turn calls the parent classes' constructor method
        this.base( name );
        this.password = password;
    },

    // Create another, simple, method for the User
    getPassword: function() {
        return this.password;
    }
});
```

Let's look at how it is that Base achieved the three goals outlined in Listing 3-4 to create a simple form of object creation and inheritance:

Base.extend(...);: This expression is used to create a new base constructor object. This function takes one property, a simple object containing properties and values, all of which are added to the object and used as its prototypal methods.

Person.extend(...);: This is an alternate version of the Base.extend() syntax. All constructors created using the .extend() method gain their own .extend() method, meaning that it's possible to inherit directly from them. In Listing 3-4 you create the User constructor by inheriting directly from the original Person constructor.

this.base();: Finally, the this.base() method is used to call a parent function that has been overridden. You'll notice that this is rather different from the this.uber() function that Crockford's classical library used, as you don't need to provide the name of the parent function (which can help to really clean up and clarify your code). Of all the object-oriented JavaScript libraries, Base's overridden parent method functionality is the best.

Personally, I find that Dean's Base library produces the most readable, functional, and understandable object-oriented JavaScript code. Ultimately, it is up to a developer to choose a library that best suits him. Next you're going to see how object-oriented code is implemented in the popular Prototype library.

The Prototype Library

Prototype is a JavaScript library that was developed to work in conjunction with the popular Ruby on Rails web framework. The name of the library shouldn't be confused with the prototype constructor property—it's just an unfortunate naming situation.

Naming aside, Prototype makes JavaScript look and behave a lot more like Ruby. To achieve this, Prototype's developers took advantage of JavaScript's object-oriented nature and attached a number of functions and properties to the core JavaScript objects. Unfortunately, the library itself isn't documented at all by its creator; fortunately it's written very clearly, and a number of its users have stepped in to write their own versions of the documentation. You can feel free to look through the entire code base on the Prototype web site: http://prototype.conio.net/. You can get Prototype documentation from the article "Painless JavaScript Using Prototype" at http://www.sitepoint.com/article/painless-javascript-prototype/.

In this section, we're going to only look at the specific functions and objects that Prototype uses to create its object-oriented structure and provide basic inheritance. Listing 3-5 has all the code that Prototype uses to achieve this goal.

Listing 3-5. *Two Functions Used by Prototype to Simulate Object-Oriented JavaScript Code*

```
// Create a global object named 'Class'
var Class = {
    // it has a single function that creates a new object constructor
    create: function() {

        // Create an anonymous object constructor
        return function() {
            // This calls its own initialization method
            this.initialize.apply(this, arguments);
        }

    }
}

// Add a static method to the Object object which copies
// properties from one object to another
Object.extend = function(destination, source) {
    // Go through all of the properties to extend
    for (property in source) {
        // and add them to the destination object
        destination[property] = source[property];
    }

    // return the modified object
    return destination;
}
```

Prototype really only uses two distinct functions to create and manipulate its whole object-oriented structure. You may notice, simply from looking at the code, that it is also decidedly less powerful than Base or Crockford's classical method. The premises for the two functions are simple:

Class.create(): This function simply returns an anonymous function wrapper that can be used as a constructor. This simple constructor does one thing: it calls and executes the initialize property of the object. This means that there should be, at the very least, an initialize property containing a function on your object; otherwise, the code will throw an exception.

Object.extend(): This simply copies all properties from one object into another. When you use the prototype property of constructors you can devise a simpler form of inheritance (simpler than the default prototypal inheritance that's available in JavaScript).

Now that you know how the underlying code works in Prototype, Listing 3-6 shows some examples of how it's used in Prototype itself to extend native JavaScript objects with additional layers of functionality.

Listing 3-6. *Examples of How Prototype Uses Object-Oriented Functions to Extend the Default Operations of a String in JavaScript*

```
// Add additional methods to the String prototype
Object.extend(String.prototype, {
    // A new Strip Tags function that removes all HTML tags from the string
    stripTags: function() {
        return this.replace(/<\/?[^>]+>/gi, '');
    },

    // Converts a string to an array of characters
    toArray: function() {
        return this.split('');
    },

    // Converts "foo-bar" text to "fooBar" 'camel' text
    camelize: function() {
        // Break up the string on dashes
        var oStringList = this.split('-');

        // Return early if there are no dashes
        if (oStringList.length == 1)
            return oStringList[0];

        // Optionally camelize the start of the string
        var camelizedString = this.indexOf('-') == 0
            ? oStringList[0].charAt(0).toUpperCase() + oStringList[0].substring(1)
            : oStringList[0];

        // Capitalize each subsequent portion
        for (var i = 1, len = oStringList.length; i < len; i++) {
            var s = oStringList[i];
            camelizedString += s.charAt(0).toUpperCase() + s.substring(1);
        }
```

```
                // and return the modified string
                return camelizedString;
        }
});

// An example of the stripTags() method
// You can see that it removes all the HTML from the string
// and leaves us with a clean text-only string
"<b><i>Hello</i>, world!".stripTags() == "Hello, world!"

// An example of toArray() method
// We get the fourth character in the string
"abcdefg".toArray()[3] == "d"

// An example of the camelize() method
// It converts the old string to the new format.
"background-color".camelize() == "backgroundColor"
```

Next let's revisit the example that I've been using in this chapter of having a Person and User object with the User object inheriting from the Person object. This code, using Prototype's object-oriented style, is shown in Listing 3-7.

Listing 3-7. *Prototype's Helper Functions for Creating Classes and Implementing Simple Inheritance*

```
// Create a new Person object with dummy constructor
var Person = Class.create();

// Copy the following functions into the Person prototype
Object.extend( Person.prototype, {

    // The function called immediately by the Person constructor
    initialize: function( name ) {
        this.name = name;
    },

    // A simple function for the Person object
    getName: function() {
        return this.name;
    }

});

// Create a new User object with a dummy constructor
var User = Class.create();
```

```
// The User object inherits all the functions of its parent class
User.prototype = Object.extend( new Person(), {

    // Overwrite the old initialize function with the new one
    initialize: function( name, password ) {
        this.name = name;
        this.password = password;
    },

    // and add a new function to the object
    getPassword: function() {
        return this.password;
    }

});
```

While the object-oriented techniques proposed by the Prototype library aren't revolutionary, they are powerful enough to help a developer create simpler, easier-to-write code. Ultimately, however, if you're writing a significant amount of object-oriented code, you'll most likely want to choose a library such as Base to help your writing efforts.

Next we're going to look at how you can take your object-oriented code and get it ready for other developers and libraries to use and interact with it.

Packaging

After (or during, if you're smart) you finish writing your beautiful object-oriented, JavaScript code, it comes time to improve it such that it will play nicely with other JavaScript libraries. Additionally, it becomes important to realize that your code will need to be used by other developers and users whose requirements may be different than yours. Writing the cleanest code possible can help with this, but so can learning from what others have done.

In this section you're going to see a couple, large libraries that are used by thousands of developers daily. Each of these libraries provides unique ways of managing their structure that make it easy to use and learn. Additionally you're going to look at some ways in which you can clean up your code, to provide the best possible experience for others.

Namespacing

An important but simple technique that you can use to clean up and simplify your code is the concept of *namespacing*. JavaScript currently does not support namespacing by default (unlike Java or Python, for example), so we have to make do with an adequate but similar technique.

In reality, there is no such thing as proper namespacing in JavaScript. However, using the premise that in JavaScript, all objects can have properties, which can in turn contain other objects, you can create something that appears and works very similarly to the namespacing that you're used to in other languages. Using this technique, you can create unique structures like those shown in Listing 3-8.

Listing 3-8. *Namespacing in JavaScript and How It's Implemented*

```
// Create a default, global, namespace
var YAHOO = {};

// Setup some child namespaces, using objects
YAHOO.util = {};

// Create the final namespace, which contains a property with a function
YAHOO.util.Event = {
    addEventListener: function(){ … }
};

// Call the function within that particular namespace
YAHOO.util.Event.addEventListener( … )
```

Let's look at some examples of namespacing used within some different, popular libraries and how that plays into a solid, expandable, plug-in architecture.

Dojo

Dojo is an incredibly popular framework that provides everything that a developer needs to build a full web application. This means that there are a lot of sublibraries that need to be included and evaluated individually, otherwise the whole library would simply be too large to handle gracefully. More information about Dojo can be found on its project site: http://dojotoolkit.org/.

Dojo has an entire package system built around JavaScript namespacing. You can import new packages dynamically, upon which they're automatically executed and ready for use. Listing 3-9 shows an example of the namespacing that is used within Dojo.

Listing 3-9. *Packaging and Namespacing in Dojo*

```
<html>
<head>
    <title>Accordion Widget Demo</title>
    <!-- Include the Dojo Framework -->
    <script type="text/javascript" src="dojo.js"></script>
    <!-- Include the different Dojo Packages -->
    <script type="text/javascript">
        // Two different packages are imported and used to create
        // an Accordian Container widget
        dojo.require("dojo.widget.AccordionContainer");
        dojo.require("dojo.widget.ContentPane");
    </script>
</head>
```

```
<body>
<div dojoType="AccordionContainer" labelNodeClass="label">
    <div dojoType="ContentPane" open="true" label="Pane 1">
        <h2>Pane 1</h2>
        <p>Nunc consequat nisi vitae quam. Suspendisse sed nunc. Proin…</p>
    </div>
    <div dojoType="ContentPane" label="Pane 2">
        <h2>Pane 2</h2>
        <p>Nunc consequat nisi vitae quam. Suspendisse sed nunc. Proin…</p>
    </div>
    <div dojoType="ContentPane" label="Pane 3">
        <h2>Pane 3</h2>
        <p>Nunc consequat nisi vitae quam. Suspendisse sed nunc. Proin…</p>
    </div>
</div>
</body>
</html>
```

Dojo's package architecture is very powerful and deserves a look if you're interested in attempts at maintaining large code bases with JavaScript. Additionally, considering the sheer vastness of the library, you're bound to find some functionality that can benefit you.

YUI

Another library that maintains a large namespaced package architecture is the JavaScript library Yahoo UI library (http://developer.yahoo.com/yui/). This library is designed to implement and provide solutions to a number of common web application idioms (such as dragging and dropping). All of these UI elements are broken up and distributed among the hierarchy. The documentation for the Yahoo UI library is quite good and deserves some attention for its completeness and detail.

Much like Dojo, Yahoo UI uses the deep namespace hierarchy to organize its functions and features. However, unlike Dojo, any "importing" of external code is done expressly by you, and not through an import statement. Listing 3-10 shows an example of how namespacing looks and operates within the Yahoo UI library.

Listing 3-10. *Packaging and Namespacing Within the Yahoo UI Library*

```
<html>
<head>
    <title>Yahoo! UI Demo</title>
    <!-- Import the main Yahoo UI library -->
    <script type="text/javascript" src="YAHOO.js"></script>

    <!-- Import the events package -->
    <script type="text/javascript" src="event.js"></script>
```

```
    <!-- Use the imported Yahoo UI library -->
    <script type="text/javascript">
        // All Yahoo events and utilities are contained within the YAHOO
        // namespace, and subdivided into smaller namespaces (like 'util')
        YAHOO.util.Event.addListener( 'button', 'click', function() {
            alert( "Thanks for clicking the button!" );
        });
    </script>
</head>

<body>
    <input type="button" id="button" value="Click Me!"/>
</body>
</html>
```

Both Dojo and Yahoo UI do a very good job of organizing and maintaining a lot of code within a single large package. Understanding how they accomplish this with JavaScript namespacing can be extremely helpful when it comes time to implement a package architecture of your own.

Cleaning Up Your Code

Before I get to the topic of debugging or writing test cases (which I'll be doing in the next chapter) it's important to first look at how you write your code, getting it ready for others to use. If you want your code to survive the use and modification of other developers, you're going to need to make sure that there are no statements that could be misconstrued or used wrongly. While you could go through and clear things up by hand, it's often more efficient to use a tool to help spot tricky pieces of code that could be troublesome later. This is where JSLint comes in. JSLint has a set of built-in rules that spot pieces of code that could cause you or others problems later. There is a full analyzer available on the JSLint web site: http://www.jslint.com/. Additionally, all of JSLint's rules and settings can be found here: http://www.jslint.com/lint.html.

JSLint is another tool developed by Douglas Crockford and it's written to embody his style of coding, so if you don't enjoy or particularly believe in some of the changes that he requires, then simply don't follow them. However, some of the rules make particularly good sense, so I'm going to cover them here for additional clarification.

Variable Declaration

One smart requirement that JSLint puts forth is that all variables used in your program must be declared before they are used. While JavaScript does not explicitly require you to declare variables, not doing so can cause confusion as to its actual scope. For example, if you were to set a value to an undeclared variable inside of a function, would the variable be scoped within the function or within the global scope? That isn't immediately apparent just by looking at the code and is a good item to clarify. An example of JSLint's variable declaration practice is shown in Listing 3-11.

Listing 3-11. *Variable Delcaration That JSLint Requires*

```
// Incorrect variable use
foo = 'bar';

// Correct variable delcaration
var foo;
…
foo = 'bar';
```

!= and == vs. !== and ===

A common mistake that developers are susceptible to is the lack of understanding of false values in JavaScript. In JavaScript, null, 0, '', false, and undefined are all equal (==) to each other, since they all evaluate to false. This means that if you use the code test == false, it will evaluate true if test is also undefined or equal to null, which may not be what you want.

This is where !== and === become useful. Both of these operators look at the explicit value of the variable (such as null), not just what it is equivalent to (such as false). JSLint requires that anytime you use != or == against a falselike value, you must use !== or === instead. Listing 3-12 shows some examples of how these operators differ.

Listing 3-12. *Examples of How != and == Differ from !== and ===*

```
// Both of these are true
null == false
0 == undefined

// You should use !== or === instead
null !== false
false === false
```

Blocks and Brackets

This is a clause that I have some difficulty accepting, but nonetheless, it does make sense to follow if you're in a shared code environment. The premise behind this rule is that single-line blocks cannot be used. When you have a clause (such as if (dog == cat)) and there's only one statement inside of it (dog = false;) you can leave off the brackets that the clause would normally require. The same is true for while() and for() blocks. While this is a great shortcut that JavaScript provides, leaving off the brackets in your code can cause some strange consequences for those who don't realize which code is under the block and which code is not. Listing 3-13 explains this situation quite well.

Listing 3-13. *Improperly Indented Single-Statement Code Blocks*

```
// This code is legal, normal, Javascript
if ( dog == cat )
if ( cat == mouse )
mouse = "cheese";
```

```
// JSLint requires that it be written like this:
if ( dog == cat ) {
    if ( cat == mouse ) {
        mouse = "cheese";
    }
}
```

Semicolons

This last point will prove to be most useful in the next section, when we look at code compression. In JavaScript, semicolons on the end of statements are optional, if you have one statement per line. Leaving semicolons off of your uncompressed code may seem fine, but once you begin removing end lines to cut down your file size, problems begin to occur. To avoid this, you should always remember to include semicolons at the end of all your statements, as shown in Listing 3-14.

Listing 3-14. *Statements That Need to Have Semicolons*

```
// Be sure to include semicolons at the end of all statements, if you plan on
// compressing your Javascript code
var foo = 'bar';
var bar = function(){
    alert('hello');
};
bar();
```

Finally, this last point will help to carry us over to the concept of JavaScript compression. Whereas using JSLint to write clean code is beneficial for other developers, and for yourself, compression is ultimately most useful for your users, such that they will be able to begin using your site faster.

Compression

An essential aspect of JavaScript library distribution is the use of code compressors to save on bandwidth. Compression should be used as the final step, just before putting your code into production, as your code will frequently become obfuscated beyond recognition. There are three types of JavaScript compressors:

- Compressors that simply remove all extraneous white space and comments, leaving nothing but the essential code.

- Compressors that remove the white space and comments but also change all variable names to be smaller.

- Compressors that do the previous, but also minimize the size of all words in your code, not just variable names.

I'm going to discuss two separate libraries: JSMin and Packer. JSMin falls under the first compressor classification (extraneous noncode removal) while Packer falls under the third (complete compression of all words).

JSMin

The premise behind JSMin is simple. It goes through a block of JavaScript code and removes all nonessential characters, leaving only the purely functional code. JSMin does this by simply removing all extraneous white-space characters (this includes tabs and end lines) and all comments. An online version of the compressor can be found here: `http://www.crockford.com/javascript/jsmin.html`.

To get a feel for what happens to the code once it's been passed through JSMin, we're going to take a sample block of code (shown in Listing 3-15), pass it through the minifier, and see its resulting output in Listing 3-16.

Listing 3-15. *Code for Determining a User's Browser*

```
// (c) 2001 Douglas Crockford
// 2001 June 3
// The -is- object is used to identify the browser.  Every browser edition
// identifies itself, but there is no standard way of doing it, and some of
// the identification is deceptive. This is because the authors of web
// browsers are liars. For example, Microsoft's IE browsers claim to be
// Mozilla 4. Netscape 6 claims to be version 5.

var is = {
    ie:      navigator.appName == 'Microsoft Internet Explorer',
    java:    navigator.javaEnabled(),
    ns:      navigator.appName == 'Netscape',
    ua:      navigator.userAgent.toLowerCase(),
    version: parseFloat(navigator.appVersion.substr(21)) ||
             parseFloat(navigator.appVersion),
    win:     navigator.platform == 'Win32'
}
is.mac = is.ua.indexOf('mac') >= 0;
if (is.ua.indexOf('opera') >= 0) {
    is.ie = is.ns = false;
    is.opera = true;
}
if (is.ua.indexOf('gecko') >= 0) {
    is.ie = is.ns = false;
    is.gecko = true;
}
```

Listing 3-16. *A Compressed Copy of the Code in Listing 3-15*

```
// Compressed code
var is={ie:navigator.appName=='Microsoft Internet Explorer',java:
navigator.javaEnabled(),ns:navigator.appName=='Netscape',ua:
navigator.userAgent.toLowerCase(),version:parseFloat(
navigator.appVersion.substr(21))||parseFloat(navigator.appVersion),win:
```

```
navigator.platform=='Win32'} is.mac=is.ua.indexOf('mac')>=0;if(
is.ua.indexOf('opera')>=0){is.ie=is.ns=false;is.opera=true;}
if(is.ua.indexOf('gecko')>=0){is.ie=is.ns=false;is.gecko=true;}
```

Notice that all of the white space and comments have been removed, dramatically cutting down on the overall size of the code.

JSMin is perhaps the simplest JavaScript compression utility. It's a great way to get started using compression within your production code. When you're ready to save additional bandwidth, however, you'll want to graduate to using Packer, which is a formidable and extremely powerful JavaScript compression library.

Packer

Packer is by far the most powerful JavaScript compressor available. Developed by Dean Edwards, it serves as a way to completely reduce the size of your code and expand and execute it again on the fly. By using this technique, Packer creates the optimally smallest code possible. You can think of it as a self-extracting ZIP file for JavaScript code. An online version of the script is available at http://dean.edwards.name/packer/.

The Packer script is quite large and very complicated, so it's recommended that you not try to implement this on your own. Additionally, the code that it generates has a couple hundred bytes of overhead (in order to be able to extract itself), so it's not perfect for extremely small code (JSMin would be better for that). However, for large files, it is absolutely perfect. Listing 3-17 shows an extract of the self-extracting code that is generated by Packer.

Listing 3-17. *Portion of Code Compressed Using Packer*

```
eval(function(p,a,c,k,e,d){e=function(c){return c.toString(36)};if(!''.replace(/^/,
String)){while(c--){d[c.toString(a)]=k[c]||c.toString(a)}k=[(function(e){return
d[e]})];e=(function(){return'\\w+'});c=1};while(c--){if(k[c]){p=p.replace(new
RegExp('\\b'+e(c)+'\\b','g'),k[c])}}return p}('u 1={5:2.f==\'t s
r\',h:2.j(),4:2.f==\'k\',3:2.l.m(),n:7(2.d.o(p))||7(2.d),q:2.g==\'i\'}1.
b=1.3.6(\'b\')>=0;a(1.3.6(\'c\')>=0){1.5=1.4=9;1.c=e}a(1.3.6(\'8\')>=0){1.5=
1.4=9;1.8=e}',31,31,'|is|navigator|ua|ns|ie….
```

The usefulness of compressing your code, and especially of using Packer to do so, cannot be understated. Depending on how your code is written, you'll frequently be able to reduce its size by more than 50%, which can result in improved page load times for your users, which should be a top goal for any JavaScript application.

Distribution

The final step of the JavaScript writing process is an optional one and depends mostly upon your particular situation. If you're simply writing code for yourself or a company, you'll most likely be simply distributing your code to other developers or uploading it to your web site for use.

However, if you develop an interesting piece of code and wish to let the world use it however they wish, this is where a service such as the JavaScript Archive Network (JSAN) comes into play. JSAN was started by a couple of Perl developers who enjoyed the functionality and usefulness of CPAN (Comprehensive Perl Archive Network). More information about JSAN can be found on its site: http://openjsan.org/.

JSAN asks that all modules submitted be written in a nicely formatted object-oriented style, conforming to its particular module architecture. JSAN, in addition to its central repository of code, has a means through which you can import external JSAN module dependencies, which are required by your code. This can make it extremely simple to write interdependent applications without worrying about which modules the user already has installed. To understand how a typical JSAN module works, let's look at a simple one, DOM.Insert, which is available here: http://openjsan.org/doc/r/rk/rkinyon/DOM/Insert/0.02/lib/DOM/Insert.html.

This particular module takes an HTML string and inserts it into a web page at a particular point. In addition to it being nicely object-oriented, this module also requires and loads two other JSAN modules, both of which are shown in Listing 3-18.

Listing 3-18. *A Sample JSAN Module (DOM.Insert)*

```
// We're going to try and include some other modules using JSAN
try {
    // Load in the two required JSAN libraries
    JSAN.use( 'Class' )
    JSAN.use( 'DOM.Utils' )

// If JSAN isn't loaded, it will throw an exception
} catch (e) {
    throw "DOM.Insert requires JSAN to be loaded";
}

// Make sure that the DOM namespace exists
if ( typeof DOM == 'undefined' )
    DOM = {};

// Create a new DOM.Insert constructor, which inherits from 'Object'
DOM.Insert = Class.create( 'DOM.Insert', Object, {
    // The constructor which takes two arguments
    initialize: function(element, content) {
        // An element to insert HTML into
        this.element = $(element);

        // The HTML string to insert
        this.content = content;

        // Try inserting the HTML using the Internet Explorer way
        if (this.adjacency && this.element.insertAdjacentHTML) {
            this.element.insertAdjacentHTML(this.adjacency, this.content);
```

```
        // Otherwise, try it the W3C way
        } else {
            this.range = this.element.ownerDocument.createRange();
            if (this.initializeRange) this.initializeRange();
            this.fragment = this.range.createContextualFragment(this.content);
            this.insertContent();
        }
    }
});
```

The power of having cleanly written object-oriented, easily intractable JavaScript code should be the hallmark of development for you, or any other web developer. It is through this means that we are going to build upon and explore the rest of the JavaScript language. As JavaScript continues to come into its own, the importance of this style of writing will only increase and become more useful and prevalent.

Summary

In this chapter you saw different ways of building reusable code structures. Using the object-oriented techniques that you learned in the previous chapter, you were able to apply them and create clean data structures that are perfectly suited to multideveloper environments. Additionally, you saw the best ways to create maintainable code, reduce JavaScript file size, and package code for distribution. Knowing how to write nicely formatted, maintainable code will save you countless hours of frustration.

CHAPTER 4

■ ■ ■

Tools for Debugging and Testing

Perhaps the most time-consuming process when developing in any programming language is that of testing and debugging your code. With professional-grade code it becomes of the utmost importance to make sure that what you create is fully tested, verifiable, and bug-free. One aspect that makes JavaScript so different from other programming languages is that it isn't owned or backed by any one company or organization (unlike C#, PHP, Perl, Python, or Java). This difference can make it challenging to have a consistent base with which you can test and debug your code.

To cut down on the amount of stress and work that you may have to endure, when catching JavaScript bugs, any one of a number of powerful development tools can be used. There exist tools (often in varying quality) for every modern browser. Using them makes JavaScript development become a much more consistent picture, and one that seems much more promising.

In this chapter I discuss the different tools that can be used to debug your JavaScript code, then build solid, reusable testing suites with which to verify future developments.

Debugging

Testing and debugging are two processes that go hand in hand. While you should be building comprehensive test cases for your code, you'll most definitely hit strange errors that require more attention. This is where the debugging process comes in. By knowing how to use the best tools available, to find and fix bugs in your code, you can get your code back up and working faster.

Error Console

The most accessible tool that's available in all modern browsers is some form of an error console. The quality of the console, the accessibility of the interface, and the quality of the error messages all vary from browser to browser. Ultimately, you'll probably find it best to begin your debugging process with a single browser whose error console (or other debugging extension) is best suited for developers.

Internet Explorer

Having the most popular browser does not imply a correlation between that and having the best debugging tools. Unfortunately, Internet Explorer's error console is quite lacking. Among other issues, the console is disabled by default, making the hunt for errors all the more confusing if you don't use Internet Explorer as your default browser (and it's doubtful that any self-respecting JavaScript developer would).

Beyond the aforementioned usability issue, the most troubling problems with the Internet Explorer error console are the following:

- Only one error is displayed at a time; you must toggle through the menu system to find other error messages.

- Error messages are particularly cryptic, making little logical sense. They very infrequently give an accurate description of the problem that's occurring.

- The line that an error is reported as being on is always "off by one," meaning that the actual error line is really one less than the reported line. Combining this with the cryptic error messages, you may be in for quite a bug hunt.

An example of an error occurring in the Internet Explorer error console can be seen in Figure 4-1.

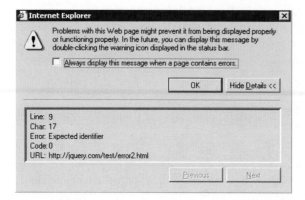

Figure 4-1. *The JavaScript error console in Internet Explorer*

As I mentioned at the beginning of this section, it'll probably be a very good idea to begin your JavaScript debugging process in another browser (one that isn't Internet Explorer). Once you've completely eliminated all bugs in that browser you should have an easier time locating the strange intricacies of Internet Explorer.

Firefox

The Firefox web browser has made many great UI advancements in the past couple years, helping web developers develop better web sites with greater ease. The JavaScript error console has gone through a number of revisions, resulting in something that is quite usable. A couple points to consider about the Firefox error console are the following:

- The console allows you to enter arbitrary JavaScript commands. This can be extremely useful to figure out what the value of a variable is after page load.

- The console gives you the ability to sort messages based upon the type of message that they are, for example, errors, warnings, or messages.

- The latest version of the console provides additional style-sheet warnings and errors along with the JavaScript errors. This can provide an unnecessary flood of error messages on poorly designed sites, but is generally helpful for finding strange layout bugs on your own.

- One drawback of the console is that it does not filter based on what page you're currently looking at, meaning that you'll have a mixture of errors from different pages. (The Firebug extension, which I discuss in the next section, solves this.)

A screenshot of the Firefox error console is shown in Figure 4-2. Notice the different buttons you can use to toggle between the different message types.

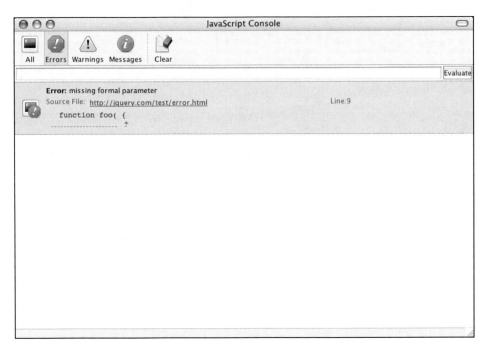

Figure 4-2. *The JavaScript error console in Firefox*

While the Firefox error console is quite good, it isn't perfect. It is for this reason that developers tend to turn to various Firefox extensions to better debug their applications. I discuss some of these extensions later in this debugging section.

Safari

The Safari browser is one of the newest browsers on the market, and also one that's grown quite fast. With that growth, JavaScript support (both in development and in execution) has been rather shaky at times. Due to this fact, the JavaScript console is not easily accessible within the browser. It isn't even an option that can be easily enabled. It is completely hidden away in a secret debug menu that is unavailable to the average user.

To enable the debug menu (and, therefore, the JavaScript console) you'll need to execute the command shown in Listing 4-1 inside of a terminal (while Safari isn't running).

Listing 4-1. *The Command for Safari to Reveal the Debug Menu*

```
defaults write com.apple.Safari IncludeDebugMenu 1
```

The next time you open Safari, you'll have a new debug menu option that will include a JavaScript console.

As you can probably imagine from its obscure location, the console is still in a very poor state. A couple points to consider about the console are the following:

- Error messages are frequently quite cryptic, about on the same level of quality as Internet Explorer's errors.

- Line numbers are present for the errors but frequently will just reset to zero, leaving you back where you started.

- There is no filtering of error messages by page, but all messages have the script that threw the error listed next to them.

A screenshot of the error console running in Safari 2.0 is shown in Figure 4-3.

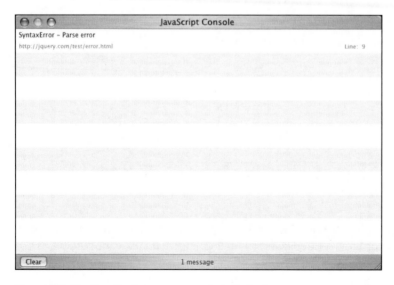

Figure 4-3. *The JavaScript error console in Safari*

As a web development platform, Safari is still rather far behind. However, the WebKit development team (those who develop the rendering engine for Safari) has been making good progress bringing the browser up to speed. Look for many new developments in the browser in the upcoming months and years.

Opera

The last error console that we're going to look at is the one contained within the Opera browser. Thankfully Opera put a lot of time and effort into making it quite functional and useful. In addition to all the features available in the Firefox error console, it additionally provides the following:

- Descriptive error messages, giving you a good understanding of what the problem is.

- Inline code snippets, showing you where the problem is in the code itself.

- Error messages filterable by type (e.g., JavaScript, CSS, etc.).

Unfortunately, the console lacks the ability to execute JavaScript commands, which is a shame, as it's such a useful feature. All of this together, however, provides you with an excellent error console. Figure 4-4 shows a screenshot of the console in Opera 9.0.

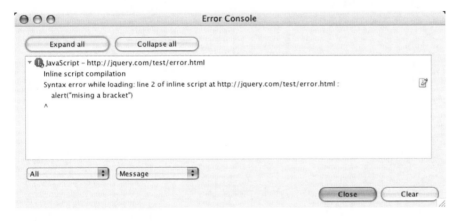

Figure 4-4. *The JavaScript error console in Opera*

Opera has long taken web development seriously. With a large number of active, avid developers and specification authors on its development team, its platform has strived to serve web developers well.

Next I will show you a couple JavaScript-related browser extensions that are very powerful and capable of improving your development abilities.

DOM Inspectors

DOM inspection is one of the most useful but underused tools available to a JavaScript developer. DOM inspection can be thought of as an advanced version of viewing a page's source code, allowing you to see the current state of a page after your code has already modified its contents.

Different DOM inspectors behave differently in each browser, some providing you with additional functionality, allowing you to peer deeper into what you're manipulating. I discuss three inspectors in this section and what makes them so different from each other.

Firefox DOM Inspector

The Firefox DOM Inspector is a Firefox extension that comes prepackaged with all installations of Firefox (but disabled in the installer by default). This extension allows you to navigate the HTML document after it's already been built and manipulated. A screenshot of the extension is shown in Figure 4-5.

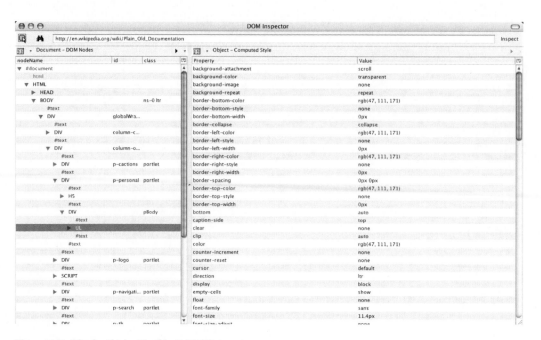

Figure 4-5. *The built-in Firefox DOM Inspector*

When navigating a document, not only do you get to see the structure of the modified HTML elements, but you can also see each element's style properties along with their physical object properties. This helps you to know exactly what the web page looks and feels like after you modify it. The result is a tool that is completely indispensable.

Safari Web Inspector

Safari has a new DOM inspector included with the latest builds of its browser. In some ways it's better than Firefox DOM Inspector, in that you can right-click any element of the page and have it instantly navigate to the element in the inspector. A screenshot of the (quite elegantly designed) Safari DOM inspector can be seen in Figure 4-6.

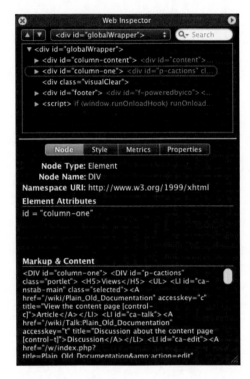

Figure 4-6. *The built-in DOM inspector in Safari*

While this extension is included in the latest builds of Safari, it's even more of a hassle to enable than the aforementioned JavaScript console. It's rather mind-boggling as to why the Safari team put so much effort into writing and adding these components and then hiding them from developers who wish to use them. Regardless, to enable the DOM inspector, you must execute the statement shown in Listing 4-2.

Listing 4-2. *Enabling the Safari DOM Inspector*

```
defaults write com.apple.Safari WebKitDeveloperExtras -bool true
```

The Safari DOM inspector still has a lot of room to grow and improve, which is good, as the Safari development team is quite talented. However, for now, you'd most likely be better off starting with Firefox as your base for development until Safari is completely finished and properly released.

View Rendered Source

Finally, I'd like to introduce the most accessible DOM inspector available to web developers. The View Rendered Source Firefox extension provides you with an alternate menu item, below the normal View Source option, providing you with a complete representation of the new HTML document, presented in an intuitive and accessible manner. More information about the extension can be found on its web site: http://jennifermadden.com/scripts/ViewRenderedSource.html.

In addition to providing a view of the source code that feels and looks very natural, it additionally provides hierarchical color coding for each level of the document, giving you a better feel as to where exactly you are in the code, as shown in Figure 4-7.

Figure 4-7. *The View Rendered Source extension for Firefox*

The View Rendered Source extension should be standard in every web developer's toolkit; its basic usefulness far exceeds anything presented by the basic View Source while still allowing a graceful graduation to the more complicated DOM inspector extension in Firefox.

Firebug

Firebug is one of the most important JavaScript development extensions to come along in recent history. Created by Joe Hewitt, this extension serves as a complete package for a JavaScript developer. It has an error console, a debugger, and a DOM inspector. More information about the extension can be found on its web site: `http://www.joehewitt.com/software/firebug/`.

The primary advantage of having so many tools integrated together is that you can get a better understanding of where problems are occurring. For example, when clicking an error message you are presented with the JavaScript file and line where the error occurred. From there you have the ability to set stop points, which can be used to allow you to step through the execution of a script, getting a better feel for where errors occur. A screenshot of the extension can be seen in Figure 4-8.

Figure 4-8. *The Firebug debugging extension*

As far as modern tools go, there is none better than Firebug. I highly recommend that you choose Firefox as your base JavaScript programming platform, combined with the Firebug extension.

Venkman

The last piece of the JavaScript development puzzle is the Venkman extension. Originating as a part of the Mozilla browser, Venkman is the code name for the JavaScript debugger project started by Mozilla. More information about the project and the renovated Firefox extension can be found at the following web sites:

- *Mozilla Venkman project*: `http://www.mozilla.org/projects/venkman/`

- *Venkman for Firefox*: `https://addons.mozilla.org/firefox/216/`

- *Venkman tutorial*: `http://www.mozilla.org/projects/venkman/venkman-walkthrough.html`

The importance of using an extension like this, over the Firebug extension, is that since it's integrated deep into the JavaScript engine itself, it's able to give you advanced controls over what exactly your code is doing. A screenshot of the Venkman extension for Firefox can be seen in Figure 4-9.

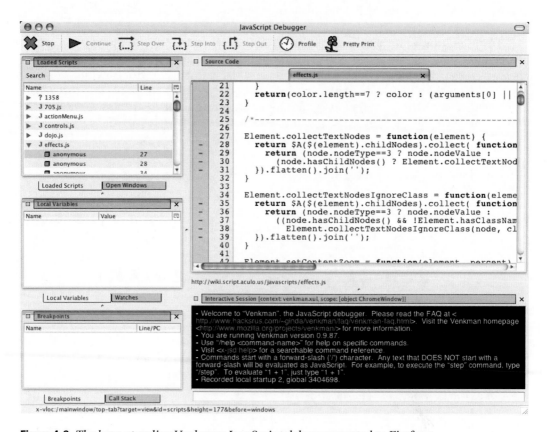

Figure 4-9. *The long-standing Venkman JavaScript debugger ported to Firefox*

With all the additional controls presented in this extension, you can know exactly what variables are available to you in a certain scope and the exact information about the state of properties or variables, in addition to being able to step through your code and analyze its progress.

Testing

Personally I see the process of testing and building test cases as "future-proofing" your code. When you create reliable test cases for your code base or libraries, you can save yourself countless hours of debugging, trying to find that one weird bug, or even worse, unknowingly introducing bugs into your code.

By having a solid set of test cases, a common practice in most modern programming environments, you can help not only yourself, but others who use your code base, add new features, and fix bugs.

In this section I introduce three different libraries that can be used to build suites of JavaScript test cases, all of which can be executed in a cross-browser, automated manner.

JSUnit

JSUnit has long been something of a gold standard for JavaScript unit testing. It bases most of its functionality on the popular JUnit package for Java, meaning that if you're familiar with how JUnit works with Java you'll have an easy time with this library. There's plenty of information and documentation (http://www.jsunit.net/documentation/) available on its web site: http://www.jsunit.net/.

As is the case with most unit testing suites (or at least all the ones I discuss in this section), this particular one has three basic components:

Test runner: This portion of the suite provides a nice graphical output of how far along in the tests the full operation is. It provides the ability to load test suites and execute their contents, logging all the output that they provide.

Test suite: This is a collection of test cases (sometimes split among multiple web pages).

Test cases: These are individual commands that evaluate to a simple true/false expression, giving you a quantifiable result to determine whether your code is operating properly. Alone, a test case may not be entirely useful, but when used together with a test runner you can get a useful interactive experience.

All of these together create the full, automated test suite that can be used to run and add further tests. An example of a simple test suite is shown in Listing 4-3, and a set of test cases are shown in Listing 4-4.

Listing 4-3. *A Test Suite Built Using JSUnit*

```
<html>
<head>
    <title>JsUnit Test Suite</title>
    <script src="../app/jsUnitCore.js"></script>
    <script>
        function suite() {
            var newsuite = new top.jsUnitTestSuite();
            newsuite.addTestPage("jsUnitTests.html");
            return newsuite;
        }
    </script>
</head>
<body></body>
</html>
```

Listing 4-4. *Various Test Cases That Can Be Used in a Typical Test Page in JSUnit*

```html
<html>
<head>
<title>JsUnit Assertion Tests</title>
<script src="../app/jsUnitCore.js"></script>
<script>
// Test that an expression is  true
function testAssertTrue() {
    assertTrue("true should be true", true);
    assertTrue(true);
}

// Test that an expression is false
function testAssertFalse() {
    assertFalse("false should be false", false);
    assertFalse(false);
}

// Tests to see if two arguments are equal to each other
function testAssertEquals() {
    assertEquals("1 should equal 1", 1, 1);
    assertEquals(1, 1);
}

// Tests to see if they're not equal to each other
function testAssertNotEquals() {
    assertNotEquals("1 should not equal 2", 1, 2);
    assertNotEquals(1, 2);
}
// Tests to see if the argument is equal to null
function testAssertNull() {
    assertNull("null should be null", null);
    assertNull(null);
}

// Of is not equal to null
function testAssertNotNull() {
    assertNotNull("1 should not be null", 1);
    assertNotNull(1);
}

// plus many many more…
</script>
</head>
<body></body>
</html>
```

The documentation for JSUnit is quite good, and since it's been around for quite a while, you're quite likely to find good examples of it in use.

J3Unit

J3Unit is a newcomer to the world of JavaScript unit testing. What this particular library provides over JSUnit is that it can be integrated directly with a server-side testing suite, such as JUnit or Jetty. For Java developers, this can be immensely useful, as they can quickly go through all of their test cases for both their client- and server-side code. However, since not everyone uses Java, J3Unit also provides a *static* mode that can be executed in your browser like other unit testing libraries. More information about J3Unit can be found on its web site: http:// j3unit.sourceforge.net/.

Since hooking the client-side test cases in with server-side code is rather a rare example, let's take a look at how the static client-side unit tests work in J3Unit. Thankfully, they behave virtually identically to other test suites, making the switch quite simple, as shown by the code in Listing 4-5.

Listing 4-5. *A Simple Test Performed Using J3Unit*

```
<html>
<head>
<title>Sample Test</title>
<script src="js/unittest.js" type="text/javascript"></script>
<script src="js/suiterunner.js" type="text/javascript"></script>
</head>
<body>
<p id="title">Sample Test</p>
<script type="text/javascript">
new Test.Unit.Runner({
    // Test hiding and showing an element
    testToggle: function() {with(this) {
        var title = document.getElementById("title");
        title.style.display = 'none';
        assertNotVisible(title, "title should be invisible");
        element.style.display = 'block';
        assertVisible(title, "title should be visible");
    }},

    // Test appending an element to another
    testAppend: function() {with(this) {
        var title = document.getElementById("title");
        var p = document.createElement("p");
        title.appendChild( p );
```

```
        assertNotNull( title.lastChild );
        assertEqual( title.lastChild, p );
    }}
});
</script>
</body>
</html>
```

J3Unit, while relatively new, shows a lot of promise for a unit-testing framework. If you're interested in its object-oriented style, I recommend that you check it out.

Test.Simple

The last sample of JavaScript unit testing is another relative newcomer. Test.Simple was introduced with the creation of JSAN as a way to standardize the testing of all the Java-Script modules submitted. Due to its broad use, Test.Simple has a lot of documentation and a lot of examples of it in use, both of which are very important aspects when using a testing framework. More information about Test.Simple (and Test.More, its companion library) can be found here:

- *Test.Simple*: http://openjsan.org/doc/t/th/theory/Test/Simple/

- *Test.Simple documentation*: http://openjsan.org/doc/t/th/theory/Test/Simple/0.21/ lib/Test/Simple.html

- *Test.More documentation*: http://openjsan.org/doc/t/th/theory/Test/Simple/0.21/ lib/Test/More.html

The Test.Simple library provides a large number of methods to test with along with a full test runner to provide automated test execution. An example of a sample Test.Simple test suite is shown in Listing 4-6.

Listing 4-6. *Using Test.Simple and Test.More to Perform Tests*

```
// Load the Test More module (to test itself!)
new JSAN('../lib').use('Test.More');

// Plan for six tests to occur (to know when something goes wrong)
plan({tests: 6});

// Test three simple cases
ok( 2 == 2,            'two is two is two is two' );
is( "foo", "foo",      'foo is foo' );
isnt( "foo", "bar",    'foo isnt bar');

// Test using regular expressions
like("fooble", /^foo/,   'foo is like fooble');
like("FooBle", /foo/i,   'foo is like FooBle');
like("/usr/local/", '^\/usr\/local', 'regexes with slashes in like' );
```

Personally, I enjoy the simplicity of Test.Simple and Test.More, as they don't provide much overhead and help to keep your code simple. Ultimately, however, it is up to you to decide upon a test suite that suits you best, as having a test suite for your code is far too important a topic to ignore.

Summary

While nothing presented in this chapter should be particularly new for a seasoned programmer, combining these concepts with the use of JavaScript ultimately improves JavaScript's usability and stature as a professional programming language. I highly recommend that you give the debugging and testing process a try. I'm sure it'll only help you write better, clearer JavaScript code.

## PART 3

Unobtrusive JavaScript

■ ■ ■

## CHAPTER 5

The Document Object Model

Of all the advances made in web development during the past decade, DOM (Document Object Model) scripting is one of the most important techniques that a developer can use to improve the quality of experience for his users.

Using DOM scripting to add *unobtrusive* JavaScript to a page (meaning that it doesn't interfere with unsupported browsers nor people who have JavaScript disabled) you will be able to provide all sorts of modern enhancements that your users will be able to enjoy without harming those who are unable to utilize them. A side effect of doing this is that all of your code ends up being nicely separated and easier to manage—all thanks to DOM scripting.

Thankfully, all modern browsers support the DOM and additionally support a built-in DOM representation of the current HTML document. All of this is easily accessible via JavaScript, which gives a huge advantage to modern web developers. Understanding how to use this technology and how to best wield it can give you a head start toward developing your next web application.

In this chapter I discuss a number of topics relating to the DOM. In case you're new to the DOM, I'll be starting out with the basics and moving through all the important concepts. For those of you already familiar with the DOM, I make sure to provide a number of cool techniques that I'm sure you'll enjoy and start using in your own web pages.

An Introduction to the Document Object Model

The DOM is a standard way of representing XML documents (instituted by the W3C). It is not necessarily the fastest, lightest, or easiest to use, but it is the most ubiquitous, with an implementation existing in most web development programming languages (such as Java, Perl, PHP, Ruby, Python, and JavaScript). The DOM was constructed to provide an intuitive way for developers to navigate an XML hierarchy. Even if you're not completely familiar with XML, you will get great satisfaction knowing that all HTML documents (which are, in the eyes of the browser, XML documents) have a DOM representation that is ready to use.

Navigating the DOM

The way that the XML structure is represented in the DOM is as a navigable tree. All the terminology used is akin to that of a genealogical tree (parents, children, siblings, etc.). Unlike a typical family tree, all XML documents start with a single root node (called the *document element*), which contains pointers to its children. Each child node then contains pointers back to its parent, its fellow siblings, and its children.

The DOM uses some special terminology to refer to the different objects within the XML tree. Every object in a DOM tree is a *node*. Each node can have a different *type*, such as element, text, or document. In order to continue, we need to know how a DOM document looks and how to navigate it once it's been constructed. Let's examine how this DOM construction works by looking at a simple HTML snippet:

```
<p><strong>Hello</strong> how are you doing?</p>
```

Each portion of this snippet breaks down into a DOM node with pointers from each node pointing to its direct relatives (parents, children, siblings). If you were to completely map out the relations that exist, it would look something like Figure 5-1. Each portion of the snippet (rounded boxes represent elements, regular boxes represent text nodes) is displayed along with its available references.

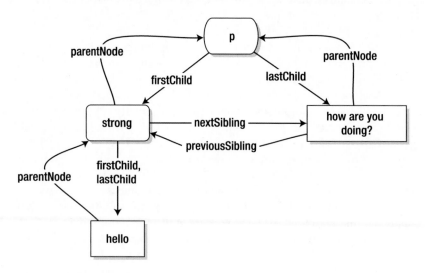

Figure 5-1. *Relationships between nodes*

Every single DOM node contains a collection of pointers that it can use to refer to its relatives. You'll be using these pointers to learn how to navigate the DOM. All the available pointers are displayed in Figure 5-2. Each of these properties, available on every DOM node, is a pointer to another DOM element (or null if one doesn't exist).

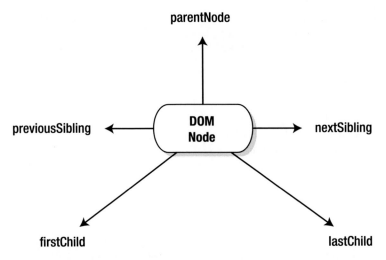

Figure 5-2. *Navigating the DOM tree using pointers*

Using nothing but the different pointers, it's possible to navigate to any element or text block on a page. The best way to understand how this would work in a practical setting is to take a look at a common HTML page, as shown in Listing 5-1.

Listing 5-1. *A Simple HTML Web Page, Which Doubles As a Simple XML Document*

```
<html>
<head>
    <title>Introduction to the DOM</title>
</head>
<body>
    <h1>Introduction to the DOM</h1>
    <p class="test">There are a number of reasons why the
        DOM is awesome, here are some:</p>
    <ul>
        <li id="everywhere">It can be found everywhere.</li>
        <li class="test">It's easy to use.</li>
        <li class="test">It can help you to find what you want, really quickly.</li>
    </ul>
</body>
</html>
```

In the example document, the root element is the <html> element. Accessing this root element is trivial in JavaScript:

```
document.documentElement
```

The root node has all the pointers used for navigation, just like any other DOM node. Using these pointers you have the ability to start browsing the entire document, navigating to any element that you desire. For example, to get the <h1> element, you could use the following:

```
// Does not work!
document.documentElement.firstChild.nextSibling.firstChild
```

But we've just hit our first snag: The DOM pointers can point to both text nodes and elements. Well, the previous statement doesn't actually point to the <h1> element; it points to the <title> element instead. Why did this happen? It happened due to one of the stickiest and most-debated aspects of XML: white space. If you'll notice, in between the <html> and <head> elements there is actually an end line, which is considered white space, which means that there's actually a text node first, not the <head> element. There are three things that we can learn from this:

- Writing nice, clean HTML markup can actually make things very confusing when attempting to browse the DOM using nothing but pointers.

- Using nothing but DOM pointers to navigate a document can be very verbose and impractical.

- Frequently, you don't need to access text nodes directly, only the elements that surround them.

This leads us to the question: Is there a better way to find elements in a document? Yes, there is! With a couple helpful functions in your toolbox, you can easily improve upon the existing methods and make DOM navigation much simpler.

Handling White Space in the DOM

Let's go back to our example HTML document. Previously, you attempted to locate the single <h1> element and had difficulties due to the extraneous text nodes. This may be fine for one single element, but what if you want to find the next element after the <h1> element? You still hit the infamous white space bug causing you to have to do `.nextSibling.nextSibling` to skip past the end lines between the <h1> and the <p> elements. All is not lost though. There is one technique that can act as a workaround for the white-space bug, shown in Listing 5-2. This particular technique removes all white space–only text nodes from a DOM document, making it easier to traverse. Doing this will have no noticeable effects on how your HTML renders, but it will make it easier for you to navigate by hand. It should be noted that the results of this function are not permanent and will need to be re-run every time the HTML document is loaded.

Listing 5-2. *A Workaround for the White-Space Bug in XML Documents*

```
function cleanWhitespace( element ) {
    // If no element is provided, do the whole HTML document
    element = element || document;
    // Use the first child as a starting point
    var cur = element.firstChild;

    // Go until there are no more child nodes
    while ( cur != null ) {

        // If the node is a text node, and it contains nothing but whitespace
        if ( cur.nodeType == 3 && ! /\S/.test(cur.nodeValue) ) {
            // Remove the text node
            element.removeChild( cur );

        // Otherwise, if it's an element
        } else if ( cur.nodeType == 1 ) {
            // Recurse down through the document
            cleanWhitespace( cur );
        }

        cur = cur.nextSibling; // Move through the child nodes
    }
}
```

Let's say that you want to use this function in your example document to find the element after the first <h1> element. The code to do so would look something like this:

```
cleanWhitespace();

// Find the H1 Element
document.documentElement
    .firstChild          // Find the Head Element
    .nextSibling     // Find the <body> Element
    .firstChild        // Get the H1 Element
    .nextSibling     // Get the adjacent Paragraph
```

This technique has both advantages and disadvantages. The greatest advantage is that you get to maintain some level of sanity when trying to navigate your DOM document. However, this technique is particularly slow, considering that you have to traverse every single DOM element and text node looking for the text nodes that contain nothing but white space. If you have a document with a lot of content in it, it could significantly slow down the loading of your site. Additionally, every time you inject new HTML into your document, you'll need to rescan that portion of the DOM, making sure that no additional space-filled text nodes were added.

One important aspect in this function is the use of node types. A node's type can be determined by checking its nodeType property for a particular value. There are a number of possible values, but the three that you'll encounter the most are the following:

Element (nodeType = 1): This matches most elements in an XML file. For example, <li>, <a>, <p>, and <body> elements all have a nodeType of 1.

Text (nodeType = 3): This matches all text segments within your document. When navigating through a DOM structure using previousSibling and nextSibling you'll frequently encounter pieces of text inside and in between elements.

Document (nodeType = 9): This matches the root element of a document. For example, in an HTML document it's the <html> element.

Additionally, you can use constants to refer to the different DOM node types (but only in non-IE browsers). For example, instead of having to remember 1, 3, or 9, you could just use document.ELEMENT_NODE, document.TEXT_NODE, or document.DOCUMENT_NODE. Since constantly cleaning the DOM's white space has the potential to be cumbersome, you should explore other ways to navigate a DOM structure.

Simple DOM Navigation

Using the principle of pure DOM navigation (having pointers in every navigable direction) you can develop functions that might better suit you when navigating an HTML DOM document. This particular principle is based around the fact that most web developers only need to navigate around DOM elements and very rarely navigate through sibling text nodes. To aid you, there are a number of helpful functions that can be used in place of the standard previousSibling, nextSibling, firstChild, lastChild, and parentNode. Listing 5-3 shows a function that returns the element previous to the current element, or null if no previous element is found, similar to the previousSibling element property.

Listing 5-3. *A Function for Finding the Previous Sibling Element in Relation to an Element*

```
function prev( elem ) {
    do {
        elem = elem.previousSibling;
    } while ( elem && elem.nodeType != 1 );
    return elem;
}
```

Listing 5-4 shows a function that returns the element next to the current element, or null if no next element is found, similar to the nextSibling element property.

Listing 5-4. *A Function for Finding the Next Sibling Element in Relation to an Element*

```
function next( elem ) {
    do {
        elem = elem.nextSibling;
    } while ( elem && elem.nodeType != 1 );
    return elem;
}
```

Listing 5-5 shows a function that returns the first element child of an element, similar to the firstChild element property.

Listing 5-5. *A Function for Finding the First Child Element of an Element*

```
function first( elem ) {
    elem = elem.firstChild;
    return elem && elem.nodeType != 1 ?
        next ( elem ) : elem;
}
```

Listing 5-6 shows a function that returns the last element child of an element, similar to the lastChild element property.

Listing 5-6. *A Function for Finding the Last Child Element of an Element*

```
function last( elem ) {
    elem = elem.lastChild;
    return elem && elem.nodeType != 1 ?
        prev ( elem ) : elem;
}
```

Listing 5-7 shows a function that returns the parent element of an element, similar to the parentNode element property. You can optionally provide a number to navigate up multiple parents at a time—for example, parent(elem,2) is equivalent to parent(parent(elem)).

Listing 5-7. *A Function for Finding the Parent of an Element*

```
function parent( elem, num ) {
    num = num || 1;
    for ( var i = 0; i < num; i++ )
        if ( elem != null ) elem = elem.parentNode;
    return elem;
}
```

Using these new functions you can quickly browse through a DOM document without having to worry about the text in between each element. For example, to find the element next to the <h1> element, like before, you can now do the following:

```
// Find the Element next to the <h1> Element
next( first( document.body ) )
```

You should notice two things with this code. One, there is a new reference: document.body. All modern browsers provide a reference to the <body> element inside the body parameter of an HTML DOM document. You can use this to make your code shorter and more understandable. The other thing you might notice is that the way the functions are written is very counterintuitive. Normally, when you think of navigating you might say, "Start at the <body> element, get the first element, then get the next element," but with the way it's physically written, it seems backward. To work around this, I'll now discuss some ways to make your custom navigation code clearer.

Binding to Every HTML Element

In Firefox and Opera there is a powerful object prototype that's available named HTMLElement, which allows you to attach functions and data to every single HTML DOM element. The functions described in the previous section are particularly obtuse and could stand for some cleaning up. One perfect way to do this is to attach your functions directly to the HTMLElement prototype, thus attaching your function to every individual HTML DOM element directly. There are three changes that you have to make to the functions that you created in the previous section in order for this to work:

1. You need to add a single line to the top of the functions to refer to the element as *this*, as opposed to retrieving it from the list of arguments.

2. You need to remove the element argument that you are no longer using.

3. You need to bind the function to the HTMLElement prototype, so that you can use it on every HTML element in the DOM.

For example, the new next function looks something like Listing 5-8.

Listing 5-8. *Dynamically Binding a New DOM Navigation Function to All HTML DOM Elements*

```
HTMLElement.prototype.next = function() {
    var elem = this;
    do {
        elem = elem.nextSibling;
    } while ( elem && elem.nodeType != 1 );
    return elem;
};
```

Now you can use the next function (and all the other functions, after the previous tweaking) like this:

```
// A simple example - gets the first <p> element
document.body.first().next()
```

This makes your code much cleaner and easier to understand. Now that you can write your code in the order in which you naturally think, your JavaScript as a whole becomes much more understandable. If this style of writing interests you, I highly recommend that you check into the jQuery JavaScript library (`http://jquery.com`), which makes great use of this technique.

■**Note** Since the HTMLElement only exists in three of the modern browsers (Firefox, Safari, and Opera) you need to take special precautions to make it work in Internet Explorer. There is a particularly handy library available written by Jason Karl Davis (`http://browserland.org`) that provides access to the HTMLElement (among other features) in the two unsupported browsers. More information about this library can be found here: `http://www.browserland.org/scripts/htmlelement/`.

Standard DOM Methods

All modern DOM implementations contain a couple methods that make life more sane. Using these together with some custom functions, navigating the DOM can become a much smoother experience. To start with, let's look at two powerful methods included with the JavaScript DOM:

getElementById("everywhere"): This method, which can only be run on the document object, finds all elements that have an ID equal to *everywhere*. This is a very powerful function and is the fastest way to immediately access an element.

getElementsByTagName("li"): This method, which can be run on any element, finds all descendant elements that have a tag name of li and returns them as a NodeList (which is nearly identical to an array).

■**Caution** getElementById works as you would imagine with HTML documents: it looks through all elements and finds the one single element that has an attribute named id with the specified value. However, if you are loading in a remote XML document and using getElementById (or using a DOM implementation in any other language besides JavaScript), it doesn't use the id attribute by default. This is by design; an XML document must explicitly specify what the id attribute is, generally using an XML definition or a schema.

■**Caution** getElementsByTagName returns a NodeList. This structure looks and behaves a lot like a normal JavaScript array, with an important exception: it does not have any of the normal .push(), .pop(), .shift(), and so on, methods that come with normal JavaScript arrays. Simply keep this in mind when working with getElementsByTagName; it will save you from a lot of confusion.

These three methods are available in all modern browsers and can be immensely helpful for locating specific elements. Going back to the previous example where we tried to find the <h1> element, we can now do the following:

```
document.getElementsByTagName("h1")[0]
```

This code is guaranteed to work and will always return the first <h1> element in the document. Going back to the example document, let's say that you want to get all the <li> elements and add a border to them:

```
var li = document.getElementsByTagName("li");
for ( var j = 0; j < li.length; j++ ) {
    li[j].style.border = "1px solid #000";
}
```

Finally, let's say that you want to make text in the first <li> element bold, which just so happens to have a convenient ID associated with it:

```
document.getElementById("everywhere").style.fontWeight = 'bold';
```

You might've noticed by now that the process of getting a single element with a specific ID requires a lot of overhead text, as does retrieving elements by tag name. To work around this, you can create a wrapper function to simplify the retrieval process:

```
function id(name) {
    return document.getElementById(name);
}
```

Listing 5-9 shows a simple function for locating elements by tag name within an HTML DOM document. The function takes one to two arguments. If one argument is provided, and it's a tag name, the entire HTML document will be searched. Otherwise you can provide a DOM element as context as the optional first argument.

Listing 5-9. *A Function for Locating Elements by Tag Name Within an HTML DOM Document*

```
function tag(name, elem) {
    // If the context element is not provided, search the whole document
    return (elem || document).getElementsByTagName(name);
}
```

Once again, let's revisit the problem of finding the element after the first <h1> element. Thankfully, the code to do this can be shortened even more:

```
// Find the element after the first <h1> Element
next( tag("h1")[0] );
```

These functions provide you with the power needed to quickly get to the elements that you need to work with in a DOM document. Before you learn about using this power to modify the DOM, you need to quickly look at the problem of the DOM loading after your scripts first execute.

Waiting for the HTML DOM to Load

One of the difficulties that exist when working with HTML DOM documents is that your JavaScript code is able to execute before the DOM is completely loaded, potentially causing a number of problems in your code. The order of operation inside a browser looks something like this:

- HTML is parsed.

- External scripts/style sheets are loaded.

- Scripts are executed as they are parsed in the document.

- HTML DOM is fully constructed.

- Images and external content are loaded.

- The page is finished loading.

Scripts that are in the header and loaded from an external file are executed before the HTML DOM is actually constructed. As mentioned previously, this is a significant problem because all script executed in those two places won't have access to the DOM. However, thankfully, there exist a number of workarounds for this problem.

Waiting for the Page to Load

By far, the most common technique is simply waiting for the entire page to load before performing any DOM operations. This technique can be utilized by simply attaching a function, to be fired on page load, to the load event of the window object. I'll discuss *events* in greater detail in Chapter 6. Listing 5-10 shows an example of executing DOM-related code after the page has finished loading.

Listing 5-10. *The addEvent Function for Attaching a Callback onto the window.onload Property*

```
// Wait until the page is loaded
// (Uses addEvent, described in the next chapter)
addEvent(window, "load", function() {
    // Perform HTML DOM operations
    next(  id("everywhere") ).style.background = 'blue';
});
```

While this operation may be the simplest, it will always be the slowest. From the order of loading operations, you'll notice that the page being loaded is the absolute last step taken. This means that if you have a significant amount of images, videos, and so on, on your page, your users might be waiting quite a while until the JavaScript finally executes.

Waiting for Most of the DOM to Load

The second technique is particularly devious and isn't completely recommended. If you'll remember, in the previous section I say that inline scripts are executed after the DOM is constructed. This is a half-truth. The scripts are actually executed as they're encountered, when the DOM is constructed. This means that if you have an inline script embedded in your page, halfway through, that script would only have immediate access to the first half of the DOM. However, embedding a script as the very last element in the page means that you will effectively have access to all the previous elements in the DOM, giving you a fake way to simulate the DOM loading. An implementation of this method typically looks something like the document presented in Listing 5-11.

Listing 5-11. *Determining Whether the DOM Is Loaded by Injecting a <script> Tag (Containing a Function Call) at the End of Your HTML DOM*

```
<html>
<head>
    <title>Testing DOM Loading</title>
    <script type="text/javascript">
        function init() {
            alert( "The DOM is loaded!" );
            tag("h1")[0].style.border = "4px solid black";
        }
    </script>
</head>
<body>
    <h1>Testing DOM Loading</h1>
    <!--Lots of HTML goes here -->
    <script type="text/javascript">init();</script>
</body>
</html>
```

In this sample you have the inline script as the last element in the DOM; it will be the last thing to be parsed and executed. The only thing that it's executing is the init function, which should contain any DOM-related code that you want handled. The biggest problem that exists with this solution is that it's messy: you've now added extraneous markup to your HTML only for the sake of determining whether the DOM is loaded. This technique is generally considered to be messy since you're adding additional, unnecessary code to your web page just to check its load state.

Figuring Out When the DOM Is Loaded

The final technique, which can be used for watching the DOM load, is probably the most complex (from an implementation standpoint) but also the most effective. You get the simplicity of binding to the window load event combined with the speed of the inline script technique.

This technique works by checking as fast as physically possible without blocking the browser to see if the HTML DOM document has the features that you need. There are a few things to test for to see if the HTML document is ready to be worked with:

1. *document*: You need to see whether the DOM document even exists yet. If you check it quickly enough, chances are good that it will simply be undefined.

2. *document.getElementsByTagName and document.getElementById*: Check to see whether the document has the frequently used getElementsByTagName and getElementById functions; these functions will exist when they're ready to be used.

3. *document.body*: For good measure, check to see whether the <body> element has been fully loaded. Theoretically the previous check should've caught it, but I've found instances where that check wasn't good enough.

Using these checks you're able to get a *good enough* picture of when the DOM will be ready for use (*good enough* in that you might be off by a few milliseconds). This method is nearly flawless. Using the previous checks alone, the script should run relatively well in all modern browsers. Recently, however, with some recent caching improvements implemented by Firefox, the window load event is actually capable of firing before your script is able to determine whether the DOM is ready. To account for this advantage, I also attach the check to the window load event, hoping to gain some extra speed.

Finally, the domReady function has been collecting references to all the functions that need to be run whenever the DOM is ready. Whenever the DOM is deemed to be ready, run through all of these references and execute them one by one. Listing 5-12 shows a function that can be used to watch for when the DOM has completely loaded.

Listing 5-12. *A Function for Watching the DOM Until It's Ready*

```
function domReady( f ) {
    // If the DOM is already loaded, execute the function right away
    if ( domReady.done ) return f();

    // If we've already added a function
    if ( domReady.timer ) {
        // Add it to the list of functions to execute
        domReady.ready.push( f );
    } else {
        // Attach an event for when the page finishes loading,
        // just in case it finishes first. Uses addEvent.
        addEvent( window, "load", isDOMReady );

        // Initialize the array of functions to execute
        domReady.ready = [ f ];

        //  Check to see if the DOM is ready as quickly as possible
        domReady.timer = setInterval( isDOMReady, 13 );
    }
}
```

```
// Checks to see if the DOM is ready for navigation
function isDOMReady() {
    // If we already figured out that the page is ready, ignore
    if ( domReady.done ) return false;

    // Check to see if a number of functions and elements are
    // able to be accessed
    if ( document && document.getElementsByTagName &&
            document.getElementById && document.body ) {

        // If they're ready, we can stop checking
        clearInterval( domReady.timer );
        domReady.timer = null;

        // Execute all the functions that were waiting
        for ( var i = 0; i < domReady.ready.length; i++ )
            domReady.ready[i]();

        // Remember that we're now done
        domReady.ready = null;
        domReady.done = true;
    }
}
```

We should now look at how this might look in an HTML document. The domReady function should be used just as if you were using the addEvent function (discussed in Chapter 6), binding your particular function to be fired when the document is ready for navigation and manipulation. For this sample I've placed the domReady function in an external JavaScript file named domready.js. Listing 5-13 shows how you can use your new domReady function to watch for when the DOM has loaded.

Listing 5-13. *Using the domReady Function to Determine When the DOM Is Ready to Navigate and Modify*

```
<html>
<head>
    <title>Testing DOM Loading</title>
    <script type="text/javascript" src="domready.js"></script>
    <script type="text/javascript">
        function tag(name, elem) {
            // If the context element is not provided, search the whole document
            return (elem || document).getElementsByTagName(name);
        }
```

```
        domReady(function() {
            alert( "The DOM is loaded!" );
            tag("h1")[0].style.border = "4px solid black";
        });
    </script>
</head>
<body>
    <h1>Testing DOM Loading</h1>
    <!--Lots of HTML goes here -->
</body>
</html>
```

Now that you know a couple ways to navigate a generic XML DOM document and how to work around the difficulties of a loading HTML DOM document, the question should be posed: Are there better ways to find elements in an HTML document? Thankfully, the answer to this is a resounding yes.

Finding Elements in an HTML Document

How you would want to find elements in an HTML document is often very different from how you would in an XML document. This seems like an oxymoron, considering that modern HTML is virtually a subset of XML; however HTML documents contain a number of fundamental differences that can be used to your advantage.

The two most important advantages to the JavaScript/HTML developer are the uses of classes and the knowledge of CSS selectors. With this in mind, there are a number of powerful functions that you can create to make DOM navigation simpler and more understandable.

Finding Elements by Class Name

Locating elements by their class name is a widespread technique popularized by Simon Willison (http://simon.incutio.com) in 2003 and originally written by Andrew Hayward (http://www.mooncalf.me.uk). The technique is pretty straightforward: you search through all elements (or a subset of all elements) looking for any that have the specified class. A possible implementation is shown in Listing 5-14.

Listing 5-14. *A Function That Searches for All Elements That Have a Particular Class Name*

```
function hasClass(name,type) {
    var r = [];
    // Locate the class name (allows for multiple class names)
    var re = new RegExp("(^|\\s)" + name + "(\\s|$)");
```

```
        // Limit search by type, or look through all elements
        var e = document.getElementsByTagName(type || "*");
        for ( var j = 0; j < e.length; j++ )
            // If the element has the class, add it for return
            if ( re.test(e[j]) ) r.push( e[j] );

        // Return the list of matched elements
        return r;
}
```

You can now use this function to quickly find any element, or any element of a specific type (e.g., <li> or <p>), with a specified class name. Specifying a tag name to search for will always be faster than searching for everything (*), as there will be fewer elements to hunt through to find the correct ones. For example, in our HTML document, if you want to find all elements that have a class of test you could do the following:

```
hasClass("test"")
```

If you want to find only the <li> elements that have a class of test, do this:

```
hasClass("test","li")
```

Finally, if you want to find the first <li> with a class of test you could do the following:

```
hasClass("test","li")[0]
```

This function alone is very powerful. But when combined with getElementById and getElementsByTagName, you can have a very powerful set of tools that could be used to get most tricky DOM jobs done.

Finding Elements by CSS Selector

As a web developer, you already know of a way to select HTML elements: *CSS selectors*. A CSS selector is the expression used to apply CSS styles to a set of elements. With each revision of the CSS standard (1, 2, and 3) more features have been added to the selector specification, allowing developers to more easily locate the exact elements that they desire. Unfortunately, browsers have been incredibly slow to provide full implementations of CSS 2 and 3 selectors, meaning that you may not know of some of the cool new features that they provide. If you're interested in all the cool new features in CSS, I recommend exploring the W3C's pages on the subject:

- *CSS 1 selectors*: http://www.w3.org/TR/REC-CSS1#basic-concepts/

- *CSS 2 selectors*: http://www.w3.org/TR/REC-CSS2/selector.html

- *CSS 3 selectors*: http://www.w3.org/TR/2005/WD-css3-selectors-20051215/

The features that are available from each CSS selector specification are generally similar, in that each subsequent release contains all the features from the past ones, too. However, with each release a number of new features are added. As a sample, CSS 2 contains attribute and child selectors while CSS 3 provides additional language support, selecting by attribute type, and negation. For example, all of these are valid CSS selectors:

#main <div> p: This expression finds an element with an ID of main, all <div> element descendants, and then all <p> element descendants. All of this is a proper CSS 1 selector.

div.items > p: This expression finds all <div> elements that have a class of items, then locates all child <p> elements. This is a valid CSS 2 selector.

div:not(.items): This locates all <div> elements that do not have a class of items. This is a valid CSS 3 selector.

Now, you may be wondering why I'm discussing CSS selectors if you can't actually use them to locate elements (only to apply CSS styles). This is where a number of enterprising developers have stepped up to the plate and created CSS selector implementations that are capable of handling CSS 1 all the way up to full CSS 3. Using these libraries you'll be able to quickly and easily select any element and perform operations on them.

cssQuery

The first publicly available library with full CSS 1–3 support was called cssQuery, created by Dean Edwards (dean.edwards.name). The premise behind it is simple: you provide a CSS selector and cssQuery finds all matching elements. Additionally, cssQuery is broken down into multiple sublibraries, one for each CSS selector stage, meaning that you can optionally exclude CSS 3 support if you don't need it. This particular library is completely comprehensive and works in all modern browsers (Dean is a stickler for cross-browser support). To use this library you need to provide a selector and, optionally, a context element to search within. The following are samples:

```
// Find all <p> children of <div> elements
cssQuery("div > p");

// Find all <div>s, <p>s, and <form>s
cssQuery("div,p,form");

// Find all <p>s and <div>s then find all <a>s inside of them
var p = cssQuery("p,div");
cssQuery("a",p);
```

Executing the cssQuery function returns an array of matched elements. You can now perform operations against it as if you had just done a getElementsByTagName. For example, to add a border around all links to Google, you can do the following:

```
// Add a border around all links to Google
var g = cssQuery("a[href^='google.com']");
for ( var i = 0; i < g.length; i++ ) {
    g[i].style.border = "1px dashed red";
}
```

More information about cssQuery can be found on Dean Edwards's site, along with a download of the complete source code: http://dean.edwards.name/my/cssQuery/.

Tip Dean Edwards is a JavaScript wizard; his code is absolutely amazing. I highly recommend poking around in his cssQuery library, at the very least, to see how great extensible JavaScript code is written.

jQuery

This is a recent entrant into the world of JavaScript libraries, but provides some significantly new ways of writing JavaScript code. I first wrote it to be a "simple" CSS selector library, much like cssQuery, until Dean Edwards released his excellent cssQuery library, forcing this code in a different direction. The library provides full CSS 1-3 support along with some basic XPath functionality. On top of this, it additionally provides the ability to do further DOM navigation and manipulation. Like cssQuery, jQuery has complete support for modern web browsers. Here are some examples of how to select elements using jQuery's custom blend of CSS and XPath:

```
// Find all <div>s that have a class of 'links' and a <p> element inside of them
$("div.links[p]")

// Find all descendants of all <p>s and <div>s
$("p,div").find("*")

// Find every other link that points to Google
$("a[@href^='google.com']:even")
```

Now, to use the results from jQuery, you have two options. First, you can do $("expression").get() to get an array of matched elements—the same exact result as cssQuery. The second thing that you can do is use jQuery's special built-in functions for manipulating CSS and the DOM. So, going back to the example with cssQuery of adding a border to all Google links you could do the following:

```
// Add a border around all links to Google
$("a[@href^=google.com]").css("border","1px dashed red");
```

A lot of examples, demos, and documentation can be found on the jQuery project site, in addition to a customizable download: http://jquery.com/.

Note It should be stated that neither cssQuery nor jQuery actually require the use of an HTML document for navigation; they may be used on any XML document. For a pure XML form of navigation, read the next section on XPath.

XPath

XPath expressions are an incredibly powerful way of navigating XML documents. Having existed now for quite a few years, it's almost assumed that where there's a DOM implementation, XPath is soon behind. XPath expressions are much more powerful than anything that can be written using a CSS selector, even though they are more verbose. Table 5-1 shows a side-by-side comparison between some different CSS selectors and XPath expressions.

Table 5-1. *Comparision of CSS 3 Selectors and XPath Expressions*

Goal	CSS 3	XPath
All elements	*	//*
All <p> elements	p	//p
All child elements	p > *	//p/*
Element by ID	#foo	//*[@id='foo']
Element by class	.foo	//*[contains(@class,'foo')]
Element with attribute	*[title]	//*[@title]
First child of all <p>	p > *:first-child	//p/*[0]
All <p> with an A child	Not possible	//p[a]
Next element	p + *	//p/following-sibling::*[0]

If the previous expressions have sparked your interest, I recommend browsing through the two XPath specifications (however, XPath 1.0 is generally the only one fully supported in modern browsers) to get a feel for how the expressions work:

- *XPath 1.0*: http://www.w3.org/TR/xpath/

- *XPath 2.0*: http://www.w3.org/TR/xpath20/

If you're looking to really dive into the topic, I recommend that you pick up O'Reilly's *XML in a Nutshell* by Elliotte Harold and Scott Means (2004), or Apress' *Beginning XSLT 2.0: From Novice to Professional* by Jeni Tennison (2005). Additionally, there are some excellent tutorials that will help you get started using XPath:

- *W3Schools XPath Tutorial*: http://w3schools.com/xpath/

- *ZVON XPath Tutorial*: http://zvon.org/xxl/XPathTutorial/General/examples.html

Currently, XPath support in browsers is spotty; IE and Mozilla both have full (albeit, different) XPath implementations, while Safari and Opera both have versions in development. To get around this, there are a couple of XPath implementations written completely in JavaScript. They're generally slow (in comparison to browser-based XPath implementations), but will work consistently in all modern browsers:

- *XML for Script*: http://xmljs.sf.net/

- *Google AJAXSLT*: http://goog-ajaxslt.sf.net/

Additionally, a project named Sarissa (`http://sarissa.sf.net/`) aims to create a common wrapper around each browser implementation. This can give you the ability to write your XML-accessing code once, but still get all the speed benefits of having browser-supported XML parsing. The largest problem with this technique is that it's still lacking support for XPath in the Opera and Safari browsers, something that the previous XPath implementations fix.

Using in-browser XPath is generally considered to be an experimental technique when compared to pure JavaScript solutions, which are widely supported. However, the use and popularity of XPath is only rising and it should definitely be considered as a strong contender to the CSS selector throne.

Since you have the knowledge and tools necessary to locate any DOM element, or even a set of DOM elements, we should now discuss what you could do with that power. Everything is possible, from manipulation of attributes to the adding and removing of DOM elements.

Getting the Contents of an Element

All DOM elements can contain one of three things: text, more elements, or a mixture of text and elements. Generally speaking, the most common situations are the first and last. In this section you're going to see the common ways that exist for retrieving the contents of an element.

Getting the Text Inside an Element

Getting the text inside an element is probably the most confusing task for those who are new to the DOM. However, it is also a task that works in HTML DOM documents and XML DOM documents, so knowing how to do this will suit you well. In the example DOM structure shown in Figure 5-3, there is a root <p> element that contains a <strong> element and a block of text. The <strong> element itself also contains a block of text.

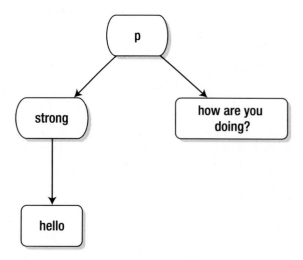

Figure 5-3. *A sample DOM structure containing both elements and text*

Let's look at how get the text of each of these elements. The <strong> element is the easiest to start with, since it only contains one text node and nothing else.

It should be noted that there exists a property called innerText that captures the text inside an element in all non-Mozilla-based browsers. It's incredibly handy, in that respect. Unfortunately, since it doesn't work in a noticeable portion of the browser market, and it doesn't work in XML DOM documents, you still need to explore viable alternatives.

The trick with getting the text contents of an element is that you need to remember that text is not contained within the element directly; it's contained within the child text node, which may seem a little bit strange. It is assumed that the variable strongElem contains a reference to the <strong> element. Listing 5-15 shows how to extract text from inside of an element using the DOM.

Listing 5-15. *Getting the Text Contents of the <strong> Element*

```
// Non-Mozilla Browsers:
strongElem.innerText

// All platforms:
strongElem.firstChild.nodeValue
```

Now that you know how to get the text contents of a single element, you need to look at how to get the combined text contents of the <p> element. In doing so, you might as well develop a generic function to get the text contents of any element, regardless of what they actually contain, as shown in Listing 5-16. Calling text(Element) will return a string containing the combined text contents of the element and all child elements that it contains.

Listing 5-16. *A Generic Function for Retreiving the Text Contents of an Element*

```
function text(e) {
    var t = "";

    // If an element was passed, get its children,
    // otherwise assume it's an array
    e = e.childNodes || e;

    // Look through all child nodes
    for ( var j = 0; j < e.length; j++ ) {
        // If it's not an element, append its text value
        // Otherwise, recurse through all the element's children
        t += e[j].nodeType != 1 ?
            e[j].nodeValue : text(e[j].childNodes);
    }

    // Return the matched text
    return t;
}
```

With a function that can be used to get the text contents of any element, you can retrieve the text contents of the <p> element, used in the previous example. The code to do so would look something like this:

```
// Get the text contents of the <p> Element
text( pElem );
```

The particularly nice thing about this function is that it's guaranteed to work in both HTML and XML DOM documents, meaning that you now have a consistent way of retrieving the text contents of any element.

Getting the HTML Inside an Element

As opposed to getting the text inside an element, getting the HTML inside of an element is one of the easiest DOM tasks that can be performed. Thankfully, due to a feature developed by the Internet Explorer team, all modern browsers now include an extra property on every HTML DOM element: innerHTML. With this property you can get all the HTML and text inside of an element. Additionally, using the innerHTML property is very fast—often times much faster than doing a recursive search to find all the text contents of an element. However, it isn't all roses. It's up to the browser to figure out how to implement the innerHTML property, and since there's no true standard for this, the browser can return whatever contents it deems worthy. For example, here are some of the weird bugs you can look forward to when using the innerHTML property:

- Mozilla-based browsers don't return the <style> elements in an innerHTML statement.

- Internet Explorer returns its elements in all caps, which if you're looking for consistency can be frustrating.

- The innerHTML property is only consistently available as a property on elements of HTML DOM documents; trying to use it on XML DOM documents will result in retrieving null values.

Using the innerHTML property is straightforward; accessing the property gives you a string containing the HTML contents of the element. If the element doesn't contain any subelements and only text, the returned string will only contain the text. To look at how it works, we're going to examine the two elements shown in Figure 5-2:

```
// Get the innerHTML of the <strong> element
// Should return "Hello"
strongElem.innerHTML

// Get the innerHTML of  the <p> element
// Should return "<strong>Hello</strong> how are you doing?"
pElem.innerHTML
```

If you're certain that your element contains nothing but text, this method could serve as a super simple replacement to the complexities of getting the element text. On the other hand, being able to retrieve the HTML contents of an element means that you can now build some cool dynamic applications that take advantage of in-place editing—more on this topic can be found in Chapter 10.

Working with Element Attributes

Next to retrieving the contents of an element, getting and setting the value of an element's attribute is one of the most frequently completed operations. Typically, the list of attributes that an element has is preloaded with information collected from the XML representation of the element itself and stored in an associative array for later access, as in this example of an HTML snippet inside a web page:

```
<form name="myForm" action="/test.cgi" method="POST">
    ...
</form>
```

Once loaded into the DOM, and the variable formElem, the HTML form element would have an associative array from which you could collect name/value attribute pairs. The result of this would look something like this:

```
formElem.attributes = {
    name: "myForm",
    action: "/test.cgi",
    method: "POST"
};
```

Figuring out whether an element's attribute exists should be absolutely trivial using the attributes array, but there's one problem: for whatever reason Safari doesn't support this. On top of that, the potentially useful hasAttribute function isn't supported in Internet Explorer. So how are you supposed to find out if an attribute exists? One possible way is to use the getAttribute function (which I talk about in the next section) and test to see whether the return value is null, as shown in Listing 5-17.

Listing 5-17. *Determining Whether an Element Has a Certain Attribute*

```
function hasAttribute( elem, name ) {
    return elem.getAttribute(name) != null;
}
```

With this function in hand, and knowing how attributes are used, you are now ready to begin retrieving and setting attribute values.

Getting and Setting an Attribute Value

To retrieve attribute data from an element, two different methods exist, depending on the type of DOM document you're using. If you wish to be safe and always use generic XML DOM–compatible methods, there are getAttribute and setAttribute. They can be used in this manner:

```
// Get an attribute
id("everywhere").getAttribute("id")

// Set an attribute value
tag("input")[0].setAttribute("value","Your Name");
```

In addition to this standard getAttribute/setAttribute pair, HTML DOM documents have an extra set of properties that act as quick getters/setters for your attributes. These are universally available in modern DOM implementations (but only guaranteed for HTML DOM documents), so using them can give you a big advantage when writing short code. The following code shows how you can use DOM properties to both access and set DOM attributes:

```
// Quick get an attribute
tag("input")[0].value

// Quick set an attribute
tag("div")[0].id = "main";
```

There are a couple strange cases with attributes that you should be aware of. The one that's most frequently encountered is that of accessing the class name attribute. To work with class names consistently in all browsers you must access the className attribute using elem.className, instead of using the more appropriately named getAttribute("class"). This problem is also the case for the for attribute, which gets renamed to htmlFor. Additionally, this is also the case with a couple CSS attributes: cssFloat and cssText. This particular naming convention arose due to the fact that words such as *class*, *for*, *float*, and *text* are all reserved words in JavaScript.

To work around all these strange cases and simplify the whole process of dealing with getting and setting the right attributes, you should use a function that will take care of all those particulars for you. Listing 5-18 shows a function for getting and setting the values of element attributes. Calling the function with two parameters, for example attr(element, id), returns that value of that attribute. Calling the function with three parameters, such as attr(element, class, test), will set the value of the attribute and return its new value.

Listing 5-18. *Getting and Setting the Values of Element Attributes*

```
function attr(elem, name, value) {
    // Make sure that a valid name was provided
    if ( !name || name.constructor != String ) return '';

    // Figure out if the name is one of the weird naming cases
    name = { 'for': 'htmlFor', 'class': 'className' }[name] || name;

    // If the user is setting a value, also
    if ( typeof value != 'undefined' ) {
        // Set the quick way first
        elem[name] = value;

        // If we can, use setAttribute
        if ( elem.setAttribute )
            elem.setAttribute(name,value);
    }
```

```
    // Return the value of the attribute
    return elem[name] || elem.getAttribute(name) || '';
}
```

Having a standard way to both access and change attributes, regardless of their implementation, is a powerful tool. Listing 5-19 shows some examples of how you could use the attr
function in a number of common situations to simplify the process of dealing with attributes.

Listing 5-19. *Using the attr Function to Set and Retreive Attribute Values from DOM Elements*

```
// Set the class for the first <h1> Element
attr( tag("h1")[0], "class", "header" );

// Set the value for each <input> element
var input = tag("input");
for ( var i = 0; i < input.length; i++ ) {
    attr( input[i], "value", "" );
}

// Add a border to the <input> Element that has a name of 'invalid'
var input = tag("input");
for ( var i = 0; i < input.length; i++ ) {
    if ( attr( input[i], "name" ) == 'invalid' ) {
        input[i].style.border = "2px solid red";
    }
}
```

Up until now, I've only discussed getting/setting attributes that are commonly used in
the DOM (e.g., ID, class, name, etc.). However, a very handy technique is to set and get nontraditional attributes. For example, you could add a new attribute (which can only be seen
by accessing the DOM version of an element) and then retrieve it again later, all without
modifying the physical properties of the document. For example, let's say that you want to
have a definition list of items, and whenever a term is clicked have the definition expand.
The HTML for this setup would look something like Listing 5-20.

Listing 5-20. *An HTML Document with a Definition List, with the Definitions Hidden*

```
<html>
<head>
    <title>Expandable Definition List</title>
    <style>dd { display: none; }</style>
</head>
<body>
    <h1>Expandable Definition List</h1>
```

```
    <dl>
        <dt>Cats</dt>
        <dd>A furry, friendly, creature.</dd>
        <dt>Dog</dt>
        <dd>Like to play and run around.</dd>
        <dt>Mice</dt>
        <dd>Cats like to eat  them.</dd>
    </dl>
</body>
</html>
```

I'll be talking more about the particulars of events in Chapter 6, but for now I'll try to keep our event code simple enough. What follows is a quick script that allows you to click the definition terms and show (or hide) the definitions themselves. This script should be included in the header of your page or included from an external file. Listing 5-21 shows the code required to build an expandable definition list.

Listing 5-21. *Allowing for Dynamic Toggling to the Definitions*

```
// Wait until the DOM is Ready
domReady(function(){

    // Find all the definition terms
    var dt = tag("dt");
    for ( var i = 0; i < dt.length; i++ ) {

        // Watch for a user click on the term
        addEvent( dt[i], "click", function() {

            // See if the definition is already open, or not
            var open = attr( this, "open" );

            // Toggle the display of the definition
            next( this ).style.display = open ? 'none' : 'block';

            // Remember if the defnition is open
            attr( this, "open", open ? '' : 'yes' );
        });
    }
});
```

Now that you know how to traverse the DOM and how to examine and modify attributes, you need to learn how to create new DOM elements, insert them where you desire, and remove elements that you no longer need.

Modifying the DOM

By knowing how to modify the DOM, you can do anything from creating custom XML documents on the fly to building dynamic forms that adapt to user input; the possibilities are nearly limitless. Modifying the DOM comes in three steps: first you need to learn how to create a new element, then you need to learn how to insert it into the DOM, then you need to learn how to remove it again.

Creating Nodes Using the DOM

The primary method behind modifying the DOM is the createElement function, which gives you the ability to create new elements on the fly. However, this new element is not immediately inserted into the DOM when you create it (a common point of confusion for people just starting with the DOM). First, I'll focus on creating a DOM element.

The createElement method takes one parameter, the tag name of the element, and returns the virtual DOM representation of that element—no attributes or styling included. If you're developing applications that use XSLT-generated XHTML pages (or are XHTML pages served with an accurate content type), you have to remember that you're actually using an XML document and that your elements need to have the correct XML namespace associated with them. To seamlessly work around this, you can have a simple function that quietly tests to see whether the HTML DOM document that you're using has the ability to create new elements with a namespace (a feature of XHTML DOM documents). If this is the case, you must create a new DOM element with the correct XHTML namespace, as shown in Listing 5-22.

Listing 5-22. *A Generic Function for Creating a New DOM Element*

```
function create( elem ) {
    return document.createElementNS ?
        document.createElementNS( 'http://www.w3.org/1999/xhtml', elem ) :
        document.createElement( elem );
}
```

For example, using the previous function you can create a simple <div> element and attach some additional information to it:

```
var div = create("div");
div.className = "items";
div.id = "all";
```

Additionally, it should be noted that there is a DOM method for creating new text nodes called createTextNode. It takes a single argument, the text that you want inside the node, and it returns the created text node.

Using the newly created DOM elements and text nodes, you can now insert them into your DOM document right where you need them.

Inserting into the DOM

Inserting into the DOM is very confusing and can feel very clumsy at times, even for those experienced with the DOM. You have two functions in your arsenal that you can use to get the job done.

The first function, insertBefore, allows you to insert an element before another child element. When you use the function, it looks something like this:

```
parentOfBeforeNode.insertBefore( nodeToInsert, beforeNode );
```

The mnemonic that I use to remember the order of the arguments is the phrase "You're *insert*ing the first element, *before* the second." I'll show you an easier way of remembering this in just a minute.

Now that you have a function to insert nodes (this includes both elements and text nodes) before other nodes, you should be asking yourself: "How do I insert a node as the last child of a parent?" There is another function that you can use called appendChild that allows you to do just that. appendChild is called on an element, appending the specified node to the end of the list of child nodes. Using the function looks something like this:

```
parentElem.appendChild( nodeToInsert );
```

To help you avoid having to remember the particular order of the arguments to insertBefore and appendChild, you can use two helper functions that I created to solve this problem: Using the new functions shown in Listings 5-23 and 5-24, the arguments are always called in the order of the element/node you're inserting in relation to and then the element/node that you're inserting. Additionally, the before function allows you to optionally provide the parent element, potentially saving you some code. Finally, both of these functions allow you to pass in a string to be inserted/appended and it will automatically be converted into a text node for you. It is recommended that you provide a parent element as reference (in case elem happens to be null).

Listing 5-23. *A Function for Inserting an Element Before Another Element*

```
function before( parent, before, elem ) {
    // Check to see if no parent node was provided
    if ( elem == null ) {
        elem = before;
        before = parent;
        parent  = before.parentNode;
    }
    parent.insertBefore( checkElem( elem ), before );
}
```

Listing 5-24. *A Function for Appending an Element As a Child of Another Element*

```
function append( parent, elem ) {
    parent.appendChild( checkElem( elem ) );
}
```

The helper function in Listing 5-25 allows you to easily insert both elements and text (which is automatically converted to its proper text node).

Listing 5-25. *A Helper Function for the before and append() Functions*

```
function checkElem( elem ) {
    // If only a string was provided, convert it into a Text Node
    return elem && elem.constructor == String ?
        document.createTextNode( elem ) : elem;
}
```

Now, using the before and append() functions, and by creating new DOM elements, you can add more information into the DOM for the user to view, as shown in Listing 5-26.

Listing 5-26. *Using the append and before Functions*

```
// Create a new <li> element
var li = create("li");
attr( li, "class", "new" );

// Create some new text contents and add it to the <li>
append( li, "Thanks for visiting!" );

// Add the <li> onto the top of the first Ordered List
before( first( tag("ol")[0] ), li );

// Running these statements will convert an empty <ol>
<ol></ol>

// Into the following:
<ol>
    <li class='new'>Thanks for visiting!</li>
</ol>
```

The instant you "insert" this information into the DOM (either with insertBefore or appendChild) it will be immediately rendered and seen by the user. Because of this, you can use it to provide instantaneous feedback. This is especially helpful in interactive applications that require user input.

Now that you've seen how to create and insert nodes using nothing but DOM-based methods, it should be especially beneficial to look at alternative methods of injecting content into the DOM.

Injecting HTML into the DOM

A technique that is even more popular than creating normal DOM elements and inserting them into the DOM is that of injecting HTML straight into the document. The simplest method for achieving this is by using the previously discussed innerHTML method. In addition to it being a way to retrieve the HTML inside of an element, it is also a way to set the HTML inside of an element. As an example of its simplicity, let's assume that you have an empty <ol> element and you want to add some <li>s to it; the code to do so would look like this:

```
// Add some LIs to an OL element
tag("ol")[0].innerHTML = "<li>Cats.</li><li>Dogs.</li><li>Mice.</li>";
```

Isn't that so much simpler than obsessively creating a number of DOM elements and their associated text nodes? You'll be happy to know that (according to http://www. quirksmode.org) it's much faster than using the DOM methods, too. It's not all perfect, however—there are a number of tricky problems that exist with using the innerHTML injection method:

- As mentioned previously, the innerHTML method doesn't exist in XML DOM documents, meaning that you'll have to continue to use the traditional DOM creation methods.

- XHTML documents that are created using client-side XSLT don't have an innerHTML method, as they too are a pure XML document.

- innerHTML completely removes any nodes that already exist inside of the element, meaning that there's no way to conveniently append or insert before, as with the pure DOM methods.

The last point is especially troublesome, as inserting before another element or appending onto the end of a child list is a particularly useful feature. Spinning some DOM magic, however, you can adapt your append and before methods to work with regular HTML strings, in addition to regular DOM elements. The transition comes in two steps. First you create a new checkElem function, which is capable of handling HTML strings, DOM elements, and arrays of DOM elements, as shown in Listing 5-27.

Listing 5-27. *Converting an Array of Mixed DOM Node/HTML String Arguments into a Pure Array of DOM Nodes*

```
function checkElem(a) {
    var r = [];
    // Force the argument into an array, if it isn't already
    if ( a.constructor != Array ) a = [ a ];

    for ( var i = 0; i < a.length; i++ ) {
        // If there's a String
        if ( a[i].constructor == String ) {
            // Create a temporary element to house the HTML
            var div = document.createElement("div");

            // Inject the HTML, to convert it into a DOM structure
            div.innerHTML = a[i];
```

```
            // Extract the DOM structure back out of the temp DIV
            for ( var j = 0; j < div.childNodes.length; j++ )
                r[r.length] = div.childNodes[j];
        } else if ( a[i].length ) { // If it's an array
            // Assume that it's an array of DOM Nodes
            for ( var j = 0; j < a[i].length; j++ )
                r[r.length] = a[i][j];
        } else { // Otherwise, assume it's a DOM Node
            r[r.length] = a[i];
        }
    }
    return r;
}
```

Second, you need to adapt the two insertion functions to work with this modified check-
Elem, accepting arrays of elements, as shown in Listing 5-28.

Listing 5-28. *Enhanced Functions for Inserting and Appending into the DOM*

```
function before( parent, before, elem ) {
    // Check to see if no parent node was provided
    if ( elem == null ) {
        elem = before;
        before = parent;
        parent  = before.parentNode;
    }

    // Get the new array of elements
    var elems = checkElem( elem );

    // Move through the array backwards,
    // because we're prepending elements
    for ( var i = elems.length - 1; i >= 0; i-- ) {
        parent.insertBefore( elems[i], before );
    }
}

function append( parent, elem ) {
    // Get the array of elements
    var elems = checkElem( elem );

    // Append them all to the element
    for ( var i = 0; i <= elems.length; i++ ) {
        parent.appendChild( elems[i] );
    }
}
```

Now, using these new functions, appending an <li> onto an ordered list can become an incredibly simple task:

```
append( tag("ol")[0], "<li>Mouse trap.</li>" );
```

```
// Running that simple line could add append HTML onto this <ol>
<ol>
    <li>Cats.</li>
    <li>Dogs.</li>
    <li>Mice.</li>
</ol>
```

```
// Turning it into the following:
<ol>
    <li>Cats.</li>
    <li>Dogs.</li>
    <li>Mice.</li>
    <li>Mouse trap.</li>
</ol>
```

```
// And running a similar statement for the before() function
before( last( tag("ol")[0] ), "<li>Zebra.</li>" );
```

```
// Would instead turn the <ol> into:
<ol>
    <li>Cats.</li>
    <li>Dogs.</li>
    <li>Zebra.</li>
    <li>Mice.</li>
</ol>
```

This really helps to make your code phenomenally shorter, and saner to develop. However, what if you want to move the other way and remove nodes from the DOM? As always, there's another method to handle that, too.

Removing Nodes from the DOM

Removing nodes from the DOM is nearly as frequent as the create and insert counterparts. When creating a dynamic form asking for an unlimited number of items (for example), it becomes important to allow the user to be able to remove portions of the page that they no longer wish to deal with. The ability to remove a node is encapsulated into one function: removeChild. It's used just like appendChild, but has the opposite effect. The function in action looks something like this:

```
NodeParent.removeChild( NodeToRemove );
```

With this in mind, you can create two separate functions to quickly remove Nodes, as shown in Listing 5-29.

Listing 5-29. *Function for Removing a Node from the DOM*

```
// Remove a single Node from the DOM
function remove( elem ) {
    if ( elem ) elem.parentNode.removeChild( elem );
}
```

Listing 5-30 shows a function for removing all child nodes from an element, using only a reference to the DOM element.

Listing 5-30. *A Function for Removing All Child Nodes from an Element*

```
// Remove all of an Element's children from the DOM
function empty( elem ) {
    while ( elem.firstChild )
        remove( elem.firstChild );
}
```

As an example, let's say you want to remove an <li> that you added in a previous section, assuming that you've already given the user enough time to view the <li> and that it can be removed without implication. The following code shows the JavaScript code that you can use to perform such an action, creating a desirable result:

```
// Remove the last <li> from an <ol>
remove( last( tag("ol")[0] ) )

// The above will convert this:
<ol>
    <li>Learn Javascript.</li>
    <li>???</li>
    <li>Profit!</li>
</ol>

// Into this:
<ol>
    <li>Learn Javascript.</li>
    <li>???</li>
</ol>

// If we were to run the empty() function instead of remove()
empty( last( tag("ol")[0] ) )

// It would simply empty out our <ol>, leaving:
<ol></ol>
```

Having learned the ability to remove a node from the DOM, you have completed your lesson on how the Document Object Model works, and how to make the most out of it.

Summary

In this chapter I discussed a lot relating to the Document Object Model. Unfortunately, some of the topics are more complex than others, such as waiting for the DOM to load, and will continue to be into the foreseeable future. However, using what you've learned, you'll be able to build just about any dynamic web application.

If you'd like to see some examples of DOM scripting in action, look at Appendix A, as it includes plenty of additional code through which to browse. Additionally, more DOM scripting examples can be found online on the book's web site, `http://jspro.org`, or in the Source Code/Download section of the Apress web site, `http://www.apress.com`. Next, I'm going to turn your attention to the next component of unobtrusive DOM scripting: events.

CHAPTER 6

■ ■ ■

Events

The most important aspect to unobtrusive DOM scripting is the use of dynamically bound *events*. The ultimate goal of writing usable JavaScript code is to have a web page that will work for the users, no matter what browser they're using or what platform they're on. To accomplish this, you set a goal of the features that you want to use, and exclude any browsers that do not support them. For the unsupported browsers, you then give them a functional, albeit less interactive, version of the site. The benefits to writing JavaScript and HTML interactions in this manner include cleaner code, more accessible web pages, and better user interactions. All of this is accomplished by using DOM events to improve the interaction that occurs in web applications.

The concept of events in JavaScript has advanced through the years—to the reliable, semiusable plateau where we now stand. Thankfully, due to the general similarities that exist, you can develop some excellent tools to help you build powerful, cleanly written web applications.

In this chapter I'm going to start with an introduction to how events work in JavaScript and how it compares to event models in other languages. Then you're going to look at what information the event model provides you with and how you can best control it. After looking at binding events to DOM elements and the different types of events that are available, I conclude by showing how to integrate some effective unobtrusive scripting techniques into any web page.

Introduction to JavaScript Events

If you look at the core of any JavaScript code, you'll see that events are the glue that holds everything together. In a nicely designed JavaScript application, you're going to have your data source and its visual representation (inside of the HTML DOM). In order to synchronize these two aspects, you're going to have to look for user interactions and attempt to update your web site accordingly. The combination of using the DOM and JavaScript events is the fundamental union that makes all modern web applications what they are.

Asynchronous Events vs. Threads

The event system in JavaScript is rather unique. It operates completely asynchronously using no threads at all. This means that all code in your application will be reliant upon other actions—such as a user's click or a page loading—triggering your code.

The fundamental difference between threaded program design and asynchronous program design is in how you wait for things to happen. In a threaded program you would keep checking over and over whether your condition has been met. Whereas in an asynchronous program you would simply register a callback function with an event handler, and then whenever that event occurs, the handler would let you know by executing your callback function. Let's explore how a JavaScript program could be written if it used threads, and how a JavaScript program is written using asynchronous callbacks.

JavaScript Threads

As it stands today, JavaScript threads do not exist. The closest that you can get is by using a setTimeout() callback, but even then, it's less than ideal. If JavaScript were a traditional threaded programming language, something like the code shown in Listing 6-1 would work. It is a mock piece of code in which you're waiting until the page has completely loaded. If JavaScript were a threaded programming language, you would have to do something like this. Thankfully, that is not the case.

Listing 6-1. *Mock JavaScript Code for Simulating a Thread*

```
// NOTE: This code DOES NOT work!
// Wait until the page is loaded, checking constantly
while ( ! window.loaded() ) { }

// The page is loaded now, so start doing stuff
document.getElementById("body").style.border = "1px solid #000";
```

If you'll notice, in this code there is a loop that's continually checking to see if window.loaded() returns true or not. Regardless of the fact that there's no loaded() function on the window object, having a loop like that doesn't work in JavaScript. This is due to the fact that all loops in JavaScript are blocking (this means that nothing else can happen until they finish running). If JavaScript were able to handle threads, you would see something like Figure 6-1. In the figure, the while loop in your code continually checks to see if the window is loaded. This does not work in JavaScript due to the fact that all loops are blocking (in that no other operations can be executed while the loop is operating).

while (! window.loaded()) {}

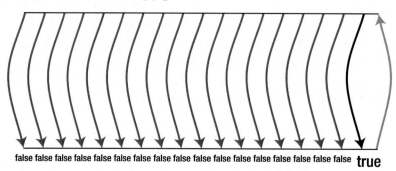

false false false false false false false false false false false false false false false false false **true**

Figure 6-1. *What you'd see if JavaScript were able to handle threads*

In reality, since our while loop continues running and blocking the normal flow of the application, it'll never reach a true value. The result is that the user's browser will hang and stall and possibly crash. The lesson that you can take away from this is that if you ever see anyone claiming that using a while loop to wait for an action works (in JavaScript), they're probably lying or very confused.

Asynchronous Callbacks

The programmatic alternative to using threads to constantly check for updates is to use asynchronous callbacks, which is what JavaScript uses. Using plain terminology, you tell a DOM element that anytime an event of a specific type is called, you want a function to be called to handle it. This means that you can provide a reference to the code that you wish to be executed when needed and the browser takes care of all the details. A sample piece of code using event handlers and callbacks is shown in Listing 6-2. You see the actual code required to bind a function to an event handler (window.onload) in JavaScript. window.onload() will be called whenever the page has been loaded. This is also the case for other common events such as click, mousemove, and submit.

Listing 6-2. *Asynchronous Callbacks in JavaScript*

```
// Register a function to be called whenever the page is loaded
window.onload = loaded;

// The function to call whenever the page is loaded.
function loaded() {
    // The page is loaded now, so start doing stuff
    document.getElementById("body").style.border = "1px solid #000";
}
```

Comparing the code in Listing 6-2 to the code shown in Listing 6-1, you see a distinct difference. The only code that is executed right away is the binding of the event handler (the loaded function) to the event listener (the onload property). The browser, whenever the page is completely loaded, calls the function associated with window.onload and executes it. The flow of the JavaScript code looks something like what's shown in Figure 6-2. The figure shows a representation of using callbacks to wait for the page to load in JavaScript. Since it's actually impossible to wait for something, you register a callback (loaded) with a handler (window.onload), which will be called whenever the page is fully loaded.

One point that isn't immediately apparent with our simple event listener and handler is that the order of events can vary and can be handled differently depending on the type of event and where in the DOM the element exists. We'll look at the two different phases of events in the next section and what makes them so different.

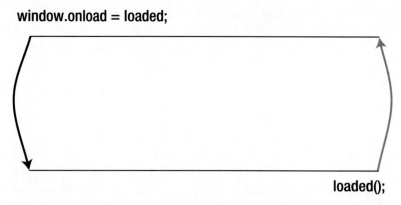

window.onload = loaded;

loaded();

Figure 6-2. *A representation of using callbacks to wait for the page to load*

Event Phases

JavaScript events are executed in two phases called the *capturing* and *bubbling* phases. What this means is that when an event is fired from an element (e.g., the user clicking a link causing the click event to fire), the elements that are allowed to handle it, and in what order, vary. You can see an example of the execution order in Figure 6-3. The figure shows what event handlers are fired, in what order, whenever a user clicks the first <a> element on the page.

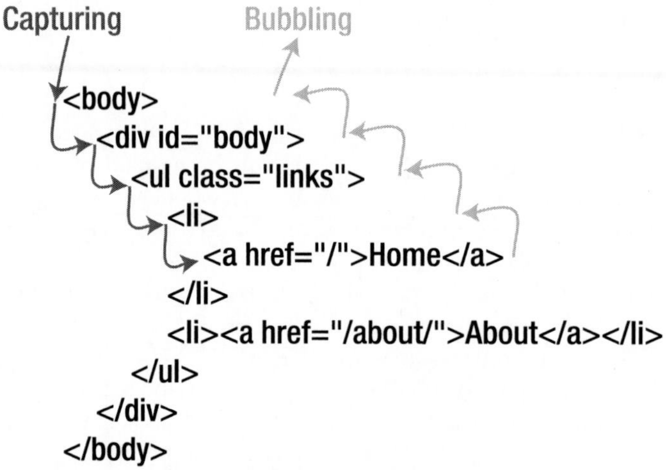

Capturing   Bubbling

```
<body>
    <div id="body">
        <ul class="links">
            <li>
                <a href="/">Home</a>
            </li>
            <li><a href="/about/">About</a></li>
        </ul>
    </div>
</body>
```

Figure 6-3. *The two phases of event handling*

Looking at a simple example of someone clicking a link (in Figure 6-3), you can see the order of execution for an event. Pretending that the user clicked the <a> element, the click handler for the document is fired first, then the <body>'s handler, then the <div>'s handler, and so on, down to the <a> element; this is called the *capturing* phase. Once that finishes, it moves back up the tree again, and the <li>, <ul>, <div>, <body>, and document event handlers are all fired, in that order.

There are very specific reasons why event handling is built this way, and it works very well. Let's look at a simple example. Say you want each of the <li> elements to change its background color whenever a user moves his mouse over them, and change back again when the mouse moves off—a common need for most menus. The code shown in Listing 6-3 does exactly this.

Listing 6-3. *A Tabbed-Navigation Scenario with Hovering Effects*

```
// Find all the <li> elements, to attach the event handlers to them
var li = document.getElementsByTagName("li");
for ( var i = 0; i < li.length; i++ ) {

    // Attach a mouseover event handler to the <li> element,
    // which changes the <li>s background to blue.
    li[i].onmouseover = function() {
        this.style.backgroundColor = 'blue';
    };

    // Attach a mouseout event handler to the <li> element
    // which changes the <li>s background back to its default white
    li[i].onmouseout = function() {
        this.style.backgroundColor = 'white';
    };

}
```

This code behaves exactly as you'd imagine: you mouse over an <li> element and its background color is changed; you move your mouse off of it, and the color goes back. However, what you don't realize is that you're actually toggling two different elements every time you move your mouse over the <li>. Since the <li> element also contains an <a> element, you're moving your mouse over it, instead of just the <li>. Let's look at the exact flow of the event calls:

1. *<li> mouseover:* You move your mouse over the <li> element.

2. *<li> mouseout:* You move from the <li> to the <a> contained inside of it.

3. *<a> mouseover:* Your mouse is now over the <a> element.

4. *<li> mouseover:* The <a> mouseover event bubbles up to the <li> mouseover.

You may notice from the way that you're calling the events, that you're completely ignoring the capturing event phase; don't worry, I haven't forgotten about it. The way that you're binding the event listeners is by using an old "traditional" means of binding events by setting the onevent property of an element, which only supports event bubbling, not capturing. This way of event binding, and others, is discussed in the next section.

In addition to the strange order of event calls, you may have noticed two unexpected actions: the mouseout of the <li> element and the <a> to <li> mouseover bubbling. Let's look at those in detail.

The first mouseout event occurs because, as far as the browser is concerned, you've left the realm of the parent <li> element and have moved into another element. This is due to the fact that whichever element is currently on top of the elements beneath them (as the <a> element is to its <li> parent) receives the immediate focus of the mouse.

The <a> mouseover bubbling to the parent <li> element ends up becoming our saving grace in this piece of code. Since you haven't actually bound any sort of listener to the <a> element, the event simply continues on up the DOM tree, looking for another element that is listening. The first element that it encounters in its bubbling process is the <li> element, which is listening for incoming mouseover events (and which is exactly what you want).

One point that you should consider is, what if you did bind an event handler to the <a> element's mouseover event? Is there any way that you could stop the bubbling of the event? This is an important and useful topic that I will be covering next.

Common Event Features

A great aspect of JavaScript events is that they have a number of relatively consistent features that give you more power and control when developing. The simplest and oldest concept is that of the event object, which provides you with a set of metadata and contextual functions to allow you to deal with things such as mouse events and keyboard presses. Additionally, there are functions that can be used to modify the normal capture/bubbling flow of an event. Learning these features inside and out can make your life much simpler.

The Event Object

One standard feature of event handlers is some way to access an event object, which contains contextual information about the current event. This object serves as a very valuable resource for certain events. For example, when handling keyboard presses you can access the keyCode property of the object to get the specific key that is pressed. More details concerning the specifics of the event object can be found in Appendix B.

The tricky part of the event object, however, is that Internet Explorer's implementation is different from the W3C's specification. Internet Explorer has a single global event object (which can be reliably found in the global variable property window.event), whereas every other browser has a single argument passed to it, containing the event object. An example of reliably using the event object is shown in Listing 6-4. The listing is an example of modifying a common <textarea> element to behave differently. Typically, users can hit the Enter key inside of a textarea, causing there to be extra end lines. But what if you don't want that and instead only want a large text box? This function provides just that.

Listing 6-4. *Overriding Functionality Using DOM Events*

```
// Find the first <textarea> on the page and bind a keypress listener
document.getElementsByTagName("textarea")[0].onkeypress = function(e){
    // If no event object exists, then grab the global (IE-only) one
    e = e || window.event;

    // If the Enter key is pressed, return false (causing it to do nothing)
    return e.keyCode != 13;
};
```

There are a lot of attributes and functions contained within the event object, and what they're named or how they behave varies from browser to browser. I won't go into the particulars right now, but I highly recommend that you read Appendix B, which has a large list of all the event object features, how to use them, and examples of them in use.

The this Keyword

The this keyword (as discussed in Chapter 2) serves as a way to access the current object within the scope of a function. Modern browsers give all event handlers some context using the this keyword. As usual, only some of them (and only some methods) play nice and set it equal to the current element; this will be discussed in depth in a minute. For example, in Listing 6-5, I can take advantage of this fact by only creating one generic function for handling clicks but using the this keyword to determine which element is currently being affected. The listing shows an example of using only one function to handle a click event, but since it uses the this keyword to reference the element, it will work as intended.

Listing 6-5. *Changing the Background and Foreground Color of All <li> Elements Whenever They Are Clicked*

```
// Find all <li> elements and bind the click handler to each of them
var li = document.getElementsByTagName("li");
for ( var i = 0; i < li.length; i++ ) {
    li[i].onclick = handleClick;
}

// The click handler – when called it changes the background and
// foreground color of  the specified element
function handleClick() {
    this.style.backgroundColor = "blue";
    this.style.color = "white";
}
```

The this keyword really is nothing more than a convenience, however, I think you'll find that it can greatly reduce the complexity of your JavaScript code when using it properly. I try to write all the event-related code in this book using the this keyword.

Canceling Event Bubbling

Since you know how event capturing/bubbling works, let's explore how you can take control of it. An important point brought up in the previous example is that if you want an event to only occur on its target and not its parent elements, you have no way to stop it. Stopping the flow of an event bubble would cause an occurrence similar to what is shown in Figure 6-4, which shows the result of an event being captured by the first <a> element and the subsequent bubbling being canceled.

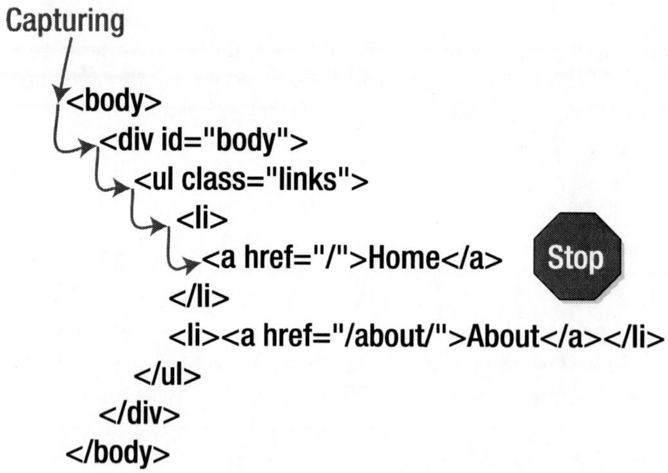

Capturing

```
<body>
  <div id="body">
    <ul class="links">
      <li>
        <a href="/">Home</a>        Stop
      </li>
      <li><a href="/about/">About</a></li>
    </ul>
  </div>
</body>
```

Figure 6-4. *The result of an event being captured by the first <a> element*

Stopping the bubbling (or capturing) of an event can prove immensely useful in complex applications. Unfortunately, Internet Explorer offers a different way than all other browsers to stop an event from bubbling. A generic function to cancel event bubbling can be found in Listing 6-6. The function takes a single argument: the event object passed into an event handler. The function handles the two different ways of canceling the event bubbling: the standard W3C way, and the nonstandard Internet Explorer way.

Listing 6-6. *A Generic Function for Stopping Event Bubbling*

```
function stopBubble(e) {
    // If an event object is provided, then this is a non-IE browser
    if ( e && e.stopPropagation )
        // and therefore it supports the W3C stopPropagation() method
        e.stopPropagation();
    else
        // Otherwise, we need to use the Internet Explorer
        // way of cancelling event bubbling
        window.event.cancelBubble = true;
}
```

What you're probably wondering now is, when would I want to stop the bubble of events? Honestly, the majority of the time you'll probably never have to worry about it. The need for it begins to arise when you start developing dynamic applications (especially ones that deal with the keyboard or mouse).

Listing 6-7 shows a brief snippet that adds a red border around the current element that you're hovered over. You do this by adding a mouseover and a mouseout event handler to every DOM element. If you don't stop the event bubbling, every time you move your mouse over an element, the element and all of its parent elements will have the red border, which isn't what you want.

Listing 6-7. *Using stopBubble() to Create an Interactive Set of Elements*

```
// Locate, and traverse, all the elements in the DOM
var all = document.getElementsByTagName("*");
for ( var i = 0; i < all.length; i++ ) {

    // Watch for when the user moves his mouse over the element
    // and add a red border around the element
    all[i].onmouseover = function(e) {
        this.style.border = "1px solid red";
        stopBubble( e );
    };

    // Watch for when the user moves back out of the element
    // and remove the border that we added
    all[i].onmouseout = function(e) {
        this.style.border = "0px";
        stopBubble( e );
    };

}
```

With the ability to stop the event bubbling, you now have complete control over which elements get to see and handle an event. This is a fundamental tool necessary for exploring the development of dynamic web applications. The final aspect is to cancel the default action of the browser, allowing you to completely override what the browser does and implement new functionality instead.

Overriding the Browser's Default Action

For most events that take place, the browser has some default action that will always occur. For example, clicking an <a> element will take you to its associated web page; this is a default action in the browser. This action will always occur after both the capturing and the bubbling event phases, as shown in Figure 6-5. This particular example shows the results of a user clicking an <a> element in a web page. The event begins by traveling through the DOM in both a capturing and bubbling phase (as discussed previously). However, once the event has finished traversing, the browser attempts to execute the default action for that event and element. In this case, it's visiting the / web page.

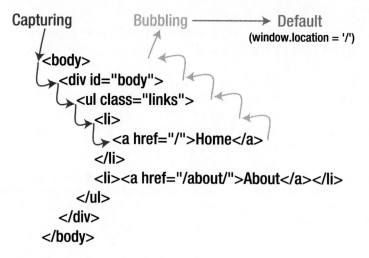

Figure 6-5. *The full life cycle of an event*

Default actions can be summarized as anything that the browser does that you do not explicitly tell it to do. Here's a sampling of the different types of default actions that occur, and on what events:

- Clicking an <a> element will redirect you to a URL provided in its href attribute.

- Using your keyboard and pressing Ctrl+S, the browser will attempt to save a physical representation of the site.

- Submitting an HTML <form> will submit the query data to the specified URL and redirect the browser to that location.

- Moving your mouse over an <img> with an alt or a title attribute (depending on the browser) will cause a tool tip to appear, providing a description of the <img>.

All of the previous actions are executed by the browser even if you stop the event bubbling or if you have no event handler bound at all. This can lead to significant problems in your scripts. What if you want your submitted forms to behave differently? Or what if you want <a> elements to behave differently than their intended purpose? Since canceling event bubbling isn't enough to prevent the default action, you need some specific code to handle that directly. As with canceling event bubbling, there are two ways of stopping the default action from occurring: the IE-specific way and the W3C way. Both ways are shown in Listing 6-8. The function shown takes a single argument: the event object that's passed in to the event handler. This function should be used at the very end of your event handler, like so: `return stopDefault( e );`—as your handler needs to also return false (which is, itself, returned from stopDefault for you).

Listing 6-8. *A Generic Function for Preventing the Default Browser Action from Occurring*

```
function stopDefault( e ) {
    // Prevent the default browser action (W3C)
    if ( e && e.preventDefault )
        e.preventDefault();

    // A shortcut for stoping the browser action in IE
    else
        window.event.returnValue = false;

    return false;
}
```

Using the stopDefault function, you can now stop any default action presented by the browser. This allows you to script some neat interactions for the user, such as the one shown in Listing 6-9. The code makes all the links on a page load in a self-contained <iframe>, rather than opening up a whole new page. Doing this allows you to keep the user on the page, and for possibly a more interactive experience.

Note Preventing a default action works for 95% of all cases in which you will want to use it. Things start to get really tricky when you move from browser to browser, due to the fact that it's up to the browser to prevent the default action (which they don't always do correctly), especially when working with preventing actions from key presses in text areas and preventing actions inside <iframe>s; other than that, things should be pretty sane though.

Listing 6-9. *Using stopDefault() to Override Browser Functionality*

```
// Let's assume that we already have an IFrame in the page
// with an ID of 'iframe'
var iframe = document.getElementById("iframe");

// Locate all <a> elements on the page
var a = document.getElementsByTagName("a");
for ( var i = 0; i < a.length; i++ ) {

    // Bind a click handler to the <a>
    a[i].onclick = function(e) {
        // Set the IFrame's location
        iframe.src = this.href;
```

```
        // Prevent the browser from ever visiting the web site pointed to from
        // the <a> (which is the default action)
        return stopDefault( e );
    };

}
```

Overriding default events is at the absolute crux of the DOM and events, which come together to form unobtrusive DOM scripting. I'll talk more about how this works, in a functional sense, in the section "Unobtrusive DOM Scripting" later in this chapter. However, it's not all perfect; a major point of contention arrives when it comes time to actually bind your event handlers to a DOM element. There are actually three different ways of binding events, some of which are better than others, all of which are discussed in the next section.

Binding Event Listeners

How to bind event handlers to elements has been a constantly evolving quest in JavaScript. It began with browsers forcing users to write their event handler code inline, in their HTML document. Thankfully that technique has since become much less popular (which is good, considering that it goes against the data abstraction principles of unobtrusive DOM scripting).

When Netscape and Internet Explorer were actively competing with each other, they each developed two separate, but very similar, event registration models. In the end, Netscape's model was modified to become a W3C standard, and Internet Explorer's stayed the same.

Today, there remain three ways of reliably registering events. The traditional method is an offshoot of the old inline way of attaching event handlers, but it's reliable and works consistently. The other methods are the IE and W3C ways of registering events. Finally, I present a reliable set of methods that developers can use to register and remove events and no longer worry about what browser is lying underneath.

Traditional Binding

The traditional way of binding events is the one that I've been using up until now in this chapter. It is by far the simplest, most compatible way of binding event handlers. To use this particular method, you attach a function as a property to the DOM element that you wish to watch. Some samples of attaching events using the traditional method are shown in Listing 6-10.

Listing 6-10. *Attaching Events Using the Traditional Method of Event Binding*

```
// Find the first <form> element and attach a 'submit' event handler to it
document.getElementsByTagName("form")[0].onsubmit = function(e){
    // Stop all form submission attempts
    return stopDefault( e );
};
```

```
// Attach a keypress event handler to the <body> element of the document
document.body.onkeypress = myKeyPressHandler;

// Attach an load event hanlder to the page
window.onload = function(){ … };
```

This particular technique has a number of advantages and disadvantages, which you must be aware of when using them.

Advantages of Traditional Binding

The following are the advantages of using the traditional method:

- The biggest advantage of using the traditional method is that it's incredibly simple and consistent, in that you're pretty much guaranteed that it'll work the same no matter what browser you use it in.

- When handling an event, the this keyword refers to the current element, which can be very useful (as demonstrated in Listing 6-5).

Disadvantages of Traditional Binding

The disadvantages of the traditional method are as follows:

- The traditional method only works with event bubbling, not capturing and bubbling.

- It's only possible to bind one event handler to an element at a time. This has the potential to cause confusing results when working with the popular window.onload property (effectively overwriting other pieces of code that have used the same method of binding events). An example of this problem is shown in Listing 6-11, where an event handler overwrites an old event handler.

- The event object argument is only available in non-Internet Explorer browsers.

Listing 6-11. *Event Handlers Overwriting Each Other*

```
// Bind your initial load handler
window.onload = myFirstHandler;

// somewhere, in another library that you've included,
// your first handler is overwritten
// only 'mySecondHandler' is called when the page finishes loading
window.onload = mySecondHandler;
```

Knowing that it's possible to blindly override other events, you should probably opt to only use the traditional means of event binding in simple situations, where you can trust all the other code that is running alongside yours. One way to get around this troublesome mess, however, is to use the modern event binding methods provided by browsers.

DOM Binding: W3C

The W3C's method of binding event handlers to DOM elements is the only truly standardized means of doing so. With that in mind, every modern browser supports this way of attaching events except for Internet Explorer.

The code for attaching a new handler function is simple. It exists as a function of every DOM element (named addEventListener) and takes three parameters: the name of the event (e.g., click), the function that will handle the event, and a Boolean flag to enable or disable event capturing. An example of addEventListener in use is shown in Listing 6-12.

Listing 6-12. *Sample Pieces of Code That Use the W3C Way of Binding Event Handlers*

```
// Find the first <form> element and attach a 'submit' event handler to it
document.getElementsByTagName("form")[0].addEventListener('submit',function(e){
    // Stop all form submission attempts
    return stopDefault( e );
}, false);

// Attach a keypress event handler to the <body> element of the document
document.body.addEventListener('keypress', myKeyPressHandler, false);

// Attach an load event hanlder to the page
window.addEventListener('load', function(){ … }, false);
```

Advantages of W3C Binding

The advantages to the W3C event-binding method are the following:

- This method supports both the capturing and bubbling phases of event handling. The event phase is toggled by setting the last parameter of addEventListener to false (for bubbling) or true (for capturing).

- Inside of the event handler function, the this keyword refers to the current element.

- The event object is always available in the first argument of the handling function.

- You can bind as many events to an element as you wish, with none overwriting previously bound handlers.

Disadvantage of W3C Binding

The disadvantage to the W3C event-binding method is the following:

- It does not work in Internet Explorer; you must use IE's attachEvent function instead.

If Internet Explorer utilized the W3C's method of attaching event handlers, this chapter would be much shorter than it is now, as there would be virtually no need to discuss alternative methods of binding events. Until that day, however, the W3C's event-binding methods are still the most comprehensive and easy to use.

DOM Binding: IE

In a lot of ways, the Internet Explorer way of binding events appears to be very similar to the W3C's. However, when you get down to the details, it begins to differ in some very significant ways. Some examples of attaching event handlers in Internet Explorer can be found in Listing 6-13.

Listing 6-13. *Samples of Attaching Event Handlers to Elements Using the Internet Explorer Way of Binding Events*

```
// Find the first <form> element and attach a 'submit' event handler to it
document.getElementsByTagName("form")[0].attachEvent('onsubmit',function(){
    // Stop all form submission attempts
    return stopDefault();
},);

// Attach a keypress event handler to the <body> element of the document
document.body.attachEvent('onkeypress', myKeyPressHandler);

// Attach an load event hanlder to the page
window.attachEvent('onload', function(){ … });
```

Advantage of IE Binding

The advantage to Internet Explorer's event-binding method is the following:

- You can bind as many events to an element as you desire, with none overwriting previously bound handlers.

Disadvantages of IE Binding

The disadvantages to Internet Explorer's event-binding method are the following:

- Internet Explorer only supports the bubbling phase of event capturing.

- The this keyword inside of event listener functions points to the window object, not the current element (a huge drawback of IE).

- The event object is only available in the window.event parameter.

- The name of the event must be named as ontype—for example, onclick instead of just requiring click.

- It only works in Internet Explorer. You must use the W3C's addEventListener for non-IE browsers.

As far as semistandard event features go, Internet Explorer's event-binding implementation is sorely lacking. Due to its many shortcomings, workarounds will continue to have to exist to force it to behave reasonably. However, all is not lost: A standard function for adding events to the DOM does exist and it will greatly ease our pain.

addEvent and removeEvent

In a contest run by Peter-Paul Koch (of http://quirksmode.org) in late 2005, he asked the general JavaScript-coding public to develop a new pair of functions, addEvent and removeEvent, which would provide a reliable way for users to add and remove events onto a DOM element. I ended up winning that contest with a very concise piece of code that worked well enough. However, afterward, one of the judges (Dean Edwards) then came out with another version of the functions that far surpassed what I wrote. His implementation uses the traditional means of attaching event handlers, completely ignoring the modern methods. Due to this fact, his implementation is able to work in a large number of browsers, while still providing all the necessary event niceties (such as the this keyword and standard event object). Listing 6-14 shows a sample piece of code, using all of the different aspects of event handling, which makes great use of the new addEvent function, including the prevention of the default browser event, the inclusion of the correct event object, and the inclusion of the correct this keyword.

Listing 6-14. *A Sample Piece of Code Using the addEvent Function*

```
// Wait for the page to finish loading
addEvent( window, "load", function(){

    // Watch for any keypresses done by the user
    addEvent( document.body, "keypress", function(e){
        // If the user hits the Spacebar + Ctrl key
        if ( e.keyCode == 32 && e.ctrlKey ) {

            // Display our special form
            this.getElementsByTagName("form")[0].style.display = 'block';

            // Make sure that nothing strange happens
            e.preventDefault();

        }
    });

});
```

The addEvent function provides an incredibly simple but powerful way of working with DOM events. Just looking at the advantages and disadvantages, it becomes quite clear that this function can serve as a consistent and reliable way to deal with events. The full source code to it can be found in Listing 6-15, which works in all browsers, doesn't leak any memory, handles the this keyword and the event object, and normalizes common event object functions.

Listing 6-15. *The addEvent/removeEvent Library Written by Dean Edwards*

```
// addEvent/removeEvent written by Dean Edwards, 2005
// with input from Tino Zijdel
// http://dean.edwards.name/weblog/2005/10/add-event/

function addEvent(element, type, handler) {
    // assign each event handler a unique ID
    if (!handler.$$guid) handler.$$guid = addEvent.guid++;

    // create a hash table of event types for the element
    if (!element.events) element.events = {};

    // create a hash table of event handlers for each element/event pair
    var handlers = element.events[type];
    if (!handlers) {
        handlers = element.events[type] = {};

        // store the existing event handler (if there is one)
        if (element["on" + type]) {
            handlers[0] = element["on" + type];
        }

    }

    // store the event handler in the hash table
    handlers[handler.$$guid] = handler;

    // assign a global event handler to do all the work
    element["on" + type] = handleEvent;
};

// a counter used to create unique IDs
addEvent.guid = 1;

function removeEvent(element, type, handler) {
    // delete the event handler from the hash table
    if (element.events && element.events[type]) {
        delete element.events[type][handler.$$guid];
    }
};

function handleEvent(event) {
    var returnValue = true;

    // grab the event object (IE uses a global event object)
    event = event || fixEvent(window.event);
```

```
        // get a reference to the hash table of event handlers
        var handlers = this.events[event.type];

        // execute each event handler
        for (var i in handlers) {
            this.$$handleEvent = handlers[i];
            if (this.$$handleEvent(event) === false) {
                returnValue = false;
            }
        }

        return returnValue;
};

// Add some "missing" methods to IE's event object
function fixEvent(event) {
    // add W3C standard event methods
    event.preventDefault = fixEvent.preventDefault;
    event.stopPropagation = fixEvent.stopPropagation;
    return event;
};

fixEvent.preventDefault = function() {
    this.returnValue = false;
};

fixEvent.stopPropagation = function() {
    this.cancelBubble = true;
};
```

Advantages of addEvent

The advantages of Dean Edwards's addEvent event-binding method are the following:

- It works in all browsers, even older unsupported browsers.

- The this keyword is available in all bound functions, pointing to the current element.

- All browser-specific functions for preventing the default browser action and for stopping event bubbling are neutralized.

- The event object is always passed in as the first argument, regardless of the browser type.

Disadvantage of addEvent

The disadvantage of Dean Edwards's addEvent event-binding method is the following:

- It only works during the bubbling phase (since it uses the traditional method of event binding under the hood).

Considering just how powerful the addEvent/removeEvent functions are, there is absolutely no reason not to use them in your code. On top of what's shown in Dean's default code, it's really trivial to add things such as better event object normalization, event triggering, and bulk event removal, all things that are very difficult to do with the normal event structure.

Types of Events

Common JavaScript events can be classified into a couple different categories. Probably the most commonly used category is that of mouse interaction, followed closely by keyboard and form events. The following list provides a broad overview of the different classes of events that exist and can be handled in a web application. For a lot of examples of the events in action, please refer to Appendix B.

Mouse events: These fall into two categories: events that track where the mouse is currently located (mouseover, mouseout), and events that track where the mouse is clicking (mouseup, mousedown, click).

Keyboard events: These are responsible for tracking when keyboard keys are pressed and within what context—for example, tracking keyboard presses inside of form elements as opposed to key presses that occur within the entire page. As with the mouse, three event types are used to track the keyboard: keyup, keydown, and keypress.

UI events: These are used to track when users are utilizing one aspect of the page over another. With this you can reliably know when a user has begun input into a form element, for example. The two events used to track this are focus and blur (for when an object losses focus).

Form events: These relate directly to interactions that only occur with forms and form input elements. The submit event is used to track when a form is submitted; the change event watches for user input into an element; and the select event fires when a <select> element has been updated.

Loading and error events: The final class of events are those that relate to the *page* itself, observing its load state. They are tied to when the user first loads the page (the load event) and when the user finally leaves the page (the unload and beforeunload events). Additionally, JavaScript errors are tracked using the error event, giving you the ability to handle errors individually.

With these general classes of events in mind, I recommend that you actively look over the material in Appendix B where I dissect all the popular events, how they work, and how they behave in different browsers, and describe all the intricacies needed to make them do what you want.

Unobtrusive DOM Scripting

Everything that you've learned up to this point comes to one incredibly important goal: writing your JavaScript so that it interacts with your users unobtrusively and naturally. The driving force behind this style of scripting is that you can now focus your energy on writing good code that will work in modern browsers while failing gracefully for older (unsupported) browsers.

To achieve this, you could combine three techniques that you've learned to make an application unobtrusively scripted:

1. All functionality in your application should be verified. For example, if you wish to access the HTML DOM you need to verify that it exists and has all the functions that you need to use it (e.g., `if ( document && document.getElementById )`). This technique is discussed in Chapter 2.

2. Use the DOM to quickly and uniformly access elements in your document. Since you already know that the browser supports DOM functions, you can feel free to write your code simply and without hacks or kludges.

3. Finally, you dynamically bind all events to the document using the DOM and your addEvent function. Nowhere must you have something such as this: `<a href="#" onclick="doStuff();">…</a>`. This is very bad in the eyes of coding unobtrusively, as that code will effectively do nothing if JavaScript is turned off or if the user has an old version of a browser that you don't support. Since you're just pointing the user to a nonsensical URL, it will give no interaction to users who are unable to support your scripting functionality.

If it isn't apparent already, you need to pretend that the user does not have JavaScript installed at all, or that his browser may be inferior in some way. Go ahead, open your browser, visit your favorite web page, and turn off JavaScript; does it still work? How about all CSS; can you still navigate to where you need to go? Finally, is it possible to use your site without a mouse? All of these should be part of the ultimate goal for your web site. Thankfully, since you've built up an excellent understanding of how to code really efficient JavaScript code, the cost of this transition is negligible and can be done with minimal effort.

Anticipating JavaScript Being Disabled

The first goal that you should achieve is the complete removal of all inline event binding inside your HTML documents. There are a couple problem areas that you can look for in your document that frequently arise:

- If you disable JavaScript on your page and click any/all links, do they take you to a web page? Frequently developers will have URLs such as `href=""` or `href="#"`, meaning that they're working some additional JavaScript voodoo to get the users their results.

- If you disable JavaScript, do all of your forms work and submit properly? A common problem occurs when using `<select>`s as dynamic menus (that only work with JavaScript enabled).

Using these important lessons, you now have a web page that is completely usable for people who have JavaScript disabled and who continue to use unsupported browsers.

Making Sure Links Don't Rely on JavaScript

Now that the user can perform all the actions on the page, you need to make sure that the user is provided with adequate notice before any action is performed. When Google released Google Accelerator, which goes through all the links of a page and caches them for you, users found that their e-mail, posts, and messages were magically being deleted for no apparent reason. This was due to the fact that developers were putting links in their pages to delete a message (for example), and then popping up a confirmation box (using JavaScript) to confirm the deletion. But Google Accelerator completely ignored that pop-up, as it should, and traversed the link anyway.

This scenario is an elaborate way of pointing you toward the HTTP specification, which is used to transport all documents and files over the Web. Most simply, a GET request occurs when you click a link; a POST occurs when you submit a form. In the specification it is stated that no GET request should have damaging side effects (such as deleting a message), which is why the Google Accelerator did what it did. It wasn't due to bad programming on Google's part, but on the part of the web application developers who created the links in the first place.

In a nutshell, all links on your site must be nondestructive. If by clicking a link you are able to delete, edit, or modify any user-owned data, you should probably be using a form to achieve that goal instead.

Watching for When CSS Is Disabled

One particularly sticky situation is the intersection between old and new browsers: browsers that are too old to support modern JavaScript techniques but are new enough to support CSS styling. A popular DHTML technique is to have an element start off as *hidden* (either with display set to none, or visibility set to hidden) and then have it fade in (using JavaScript) when the user first visits the page. However, if the user does not have JavaScript enabled, he will never see that element. A solution to this problem is shown in Listing 6-16.

Listing 6-16. *Providing a Fade-in-on-Load Technique Without Failing if JavaScript Is Disabled*

```
<!DOCTYPE html PUBLIC "-//W3C//DTD XHTML 1.0 Transitional//EN"
        "http://www.w3.org/TR/xhtml1/DTD/xhtml1-transitional.dtd">
<html xmlns="http://www.w3.org/1999/xhtml">
<head>
    <meta http-equiv="Content-Type" content="text/html;charset=utf-8" />

    <!--The instant the script is run, a new class is attached to the <html> element
            giving us the ability to know if JavaScript is enabled, or not.-->
    <script>document.documentElement.className = "js";</script>

    <!--If JavaScript is enabled, hide the block of text,
        which we will fade in later.-->
    <style>.js #fadein { display: none }</style>
</head>
<body>
    <div id="fadein">Block of stuff to fade in...</div>
</body>
</html>
```

This technique goes way beyond simple fade-in DHTML, however. The ability to know whether JavaScript is disabled/enabled and to apply styles is a huge win for careful web developers.

Event Accessibility

The final piece to take into consideration when developing a purely unobtrusive web application is to make sure that your events will work even without the use of a mouse. By doing this, you help two groups of people: those in need of accessibility assistance (vision-impaired users), and people who don't like to use a mouse. (Sit down one day, disconnect your mouse from your computer, and learn how to navigate the Web using only a mouse. It's a real eye-opening experience.)

To make your JavaScript events more accessible, anytime you use the click, mouseover, and mouseout events, you need to strongly consider providing alternative nonmouse bindings. Thankfully there are easy ways to quickly remedy this situation:

Click event: One smart move on the part of browser developers was to make the click event work whenever the Enter key is pressed. This completely removes the need to provide an alternative to this event. One point to note, however, is that some developers like to bind click handlers to submit buttons in forms to watch for when a user submits a web page. Instead of using that event, the developer should bind to the submit event on the form object, a smart alternative that works reliably.

Mouseover event: When navigating a web page using a keyboard, you're actually changing the focus to different elements. By attaching event handlers to both the mouseover and focus events you can make sure that you'll have a comparable solution for both keyboard and mouse users.

Mouseout event: Like the focus event for the mouseover event, the blur event occurs whenever the user's focus moves away from an element. You can then use the blur event as a way to simulate the mouseout event with the keyboard.

Now that you know which event pairs behave the way you want them to, you can revisit Listing 6-3 to build a hoverlike effect that works, even without a mouse, as shown in Listing 6-17.

Listing 6-17. *Attaching Pairs of Events to Elements to Allow for Accessible Web Page Use*

```
// Find all the <a> elements, to attach the event handlers to them
var li = document.getElementsByTagName("a");
for ( var i = 0; i < a.length; i++ ) {

    // Attach a mouseover and focus event handler to the <a> element,
    // which changes the <a>s background to blue when the user either
    // mouses over the link, or focuses on it (using the keyboard)
    a[i].onmouseover = a[i].onfocus = function() {
        this.style.backgroundColor = 'blue';
    };
```

```
// Attach a mouseout and blur event handler to the <a> element
// which changes the <li>s background back to its default white
// when the user moves away from the link
a[i].onmouseout = a[i].onblur = function() {
    this.style.backgroundColor = 'white';
};

}
```

In reality, adding the ability to handle keyboard events, in addition to typical mouse events, is completely trivial. If nothing else, this can help to serve as a way to help keyboard-dependant users better use your site, which is a huge win for everyone.

Summary

Now that you know how to traverse the DOM, and bind event handlers to DOM elements, and you know about the benefits of writing your JavaScript code unobtrusively, you can begin to tackle some larger applications and cooler effects.

In this chapter I started with an introduction to how events work in JavaScript and compared them to event models in other languages. Then you saw what information the event model provides and how you can best control it. We then explored binding events to DOM elements, and the different types of events that are available. I concluded by showing how to integrate some effective unobtrusive scripting techniques into any web page.

Next you're going to look at how to perform a number of dynamic effects and interactions, which make great use of the techniques that you just learned.

■ ■ ■

JavaScript and CSS

The interaction between JavaScript and CSS is a mainstay of modern JavaScript programming. It is virtually a requirement that all modern web applications use at least some form of dynamic interaction. When they do, the user is able to move faster and waste less time waiting for pages to load. Combining dynamic techniques with the ideas presented in Chapter 6 on events is fundamental to creating a seamless and powerful user experience.

Cascading style sheets are the de facto standard for styling and laying out usable, attractive web pages that still afford you (the developer) the greatest amount of power while providing your users with the least amount of difficulties. Interestingly, when you combine that power with JavaScript, you are then able to build powerful interfaces, including such things as animations, widgets, or dynamic displays.

Accessing Style Information

The combination of JavaScript and CSS is all about the resulting interaction that occurs. Understanding what is available to you is very important to achieving the exact set of interactions that you want.

Your primary tool for both setting and getting the CSS properties of an element is its style property. For example, if you want to get the height of an element you could write the following code: `elem.style.height`. And if you want to set the height of the element to a certain dimension you would execute the following code: `elem.style.height = '100px'`.

There are two problems that you encounter when working with CSS properties on DOM elements, since they behave unlike how you would expect. First, JavaScript requires that you specify the unit of size for setting any dimensional property (such as what you did for the height property previously). While at the same time, any dimensional property also returns a string representation of the element's style property instead of a number (e.g., 100px instead of 100).

Second, if an element is 100 pixels high, and you attempt to retrieve its current height, you would expect to receive 100px from the style property, but that won't necessarily be the case. This is due to the fact that any style information that you've preset using style sheets or inline CSS will not be reliably reflected in your style property.

This brings us to an important function for dealing with CSS in JavaScript: a method for retrieving the actual, current style properties of an element, giving you an exact, expected value. To handle the problem of computed style values there exists a fairly reliable set of methods that you can use to get the actual, computed style properties of a DOM element. When calling these methods (which come in W3C- and IE-specific varieties) you receive the actual computed style value of an element. This takes into account all past style sheets and element-specific properties along with your current JavaScript modifications. Using these methods can be immensely helpful when developing an accurate view of the elements that you're working with.

It's also important to take into account the numerous differences that exist between browsers when getting the computed style value of an element. As with most things, Internet Explorer has one means of getting the current computed style of an element, while all other browsers use the W3C-defined way of doing so.

A function for finding the computed style value of an element is shown in Listing 7-1, and an example of your new function in action is shown in Listing 7-2.

Listing 7-1. *A Function for Finding the Actual Computed Value of a CSS Style Property on an Element*

```
// Get a style property (name) of a specific element (elem)
function getStyle( elem, name ) {
    // If the property exists in style[], then it's been set
    // recently (and is current)
    if (elem.style[name])
        return elem.style[name];

    // Otherwise, try to use IE's method
    else if (elem.currentStyle)
        return elem.currentStyle[name];

    // Or the W3C's method, if it exists
    else if (document.defaultView && document.defaultView.getComputedStyle) {
        // It uses the traditional 'text-align' style of rule writing,
        // instead of textAlign
        name = name.replace(/([A-Z])/g,"-$1");
        name = name.toLowerCase();

        // Get the style object and get the value of the property (if it exists)
        var s = document.defaultView.getComputedStyle(elem,"");
        return s && s.getPropertyValue(name);

    // Otherwise, we're using some other browser
    } else
        return null;
}
```

Listing 7-2. *A Situation Where the Computed Value of an Element's CSS Is Not Necessarily the Same As the Values Made Available in the Style Object*

```html
<html>
<head>
    <style>p { height: 100px; }</style>
    <script>
    window.onload = function(){
        // Locate the paragraph to check the height of
        var p = document.getElementsByTagName("p")[0];

        // Check the height the traditional way
        alert( p.style.height + " should be null" );

        // Check the computed value of the height
        alert( getStyle( p, "height" ) + " should be 100px" );
    };
    </script>
</head>
<body>
    <p>I should be 100 pixels tall.</p>
</body>
</html>
```

Listing 7-2 shows how you can get the actual computed value of a CSS property on a DOM element. In this case you get an actual height of an element in pixels, even though that height is set via a CSS in the header of the file. It's important to note that your function ignores alternative units of measurement (such as using percentages). So while this solution isn't completely foolproof, it does make for an excellent starting point.

With this tool in hand you can now look at how to get and set the properties that you need to build some basic DHTML interactions.

Dynamic Elements

The premise behind a dynamic element is that it's an element that is manipulated using JavaScript and CSS to create nonstatic effects (a simple example is a check box indicating you're interested in a newsletter, and an e-mail input area pops up).

Fundamentally, there are three critical properties that are used to create dynamic effects: position, size, and visibility. Using these three properties you can simulate most common user interactions in a modern web browser.

An Element's Position

Working with the position of an element is an important building block for developing interactive elements within a page. Accessing and modifying the CSS position properties lets you effectively simulate a number of popular animations and interactions (such as dragging and dropping).

An important step to working with element positioning is to know how the positioning system works in CSS, which you'll be using extensively. In CSS, elements are positioned using offsets. The measurement used is the amount of offset from the top-left corner of an element's parent. An example of the coordinate system used in CSS is shown in Figure 7-1.

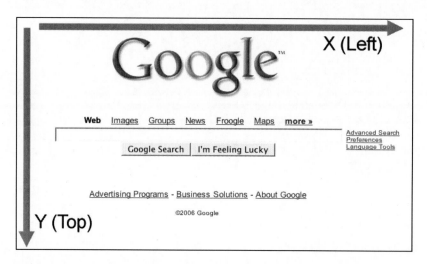

Figure 7-1. *An example of the coordinate system on a web page using CSS*

All elements on a page have some form of a *top* (vertical coordinate) and a *left* (horizontal coordinate) offset. Generally speaking, most elements are simply positioned statically in relation to the elements surrounding them. An element can have a number of different positioning schemes, as proposed by the CSS standard. To understand this better, take a look at the simple HTML web page shown in Listing 7-3.

Listing 7-3. *An HTML Web Page You Can Use to Show Differences in Positioning*

```html
<html>
<head>
<style>
p {
    border: 3px solid red;
    padding: 10px;
    width: 400px;
    background: #FFF;
}
```

```
p.odd {
    /* Positioning information goes in here */
    position: static;
    top: 0px;
    left: 0px;
}
</style>
</head>
<body>
    <p>Lorem ipsum dolor sit amet, consectetuer adipiscing elit. Etiam …p>
    <p class='odd'>Phasellus dictum dignissim justo. Duis nec risus id nunc…p>
    <p>Sed vel leo. Nulla iaculis, tortor non laoreet dictum, turpis diam …</p>
</body>
</html>
```

With your simple HTML page all set up, let's look at how changing the positioning of the second paragraph results in different layouts for the site:

Static positioning: This is the default way that an element is positioned; it simply follows the normal flow of the document. The top and left properties have no effect when an element has static positioning. Figure 7-2 shows a paragraph that has CSS positioning of `position: static; top: 0px; left: 0px;`.

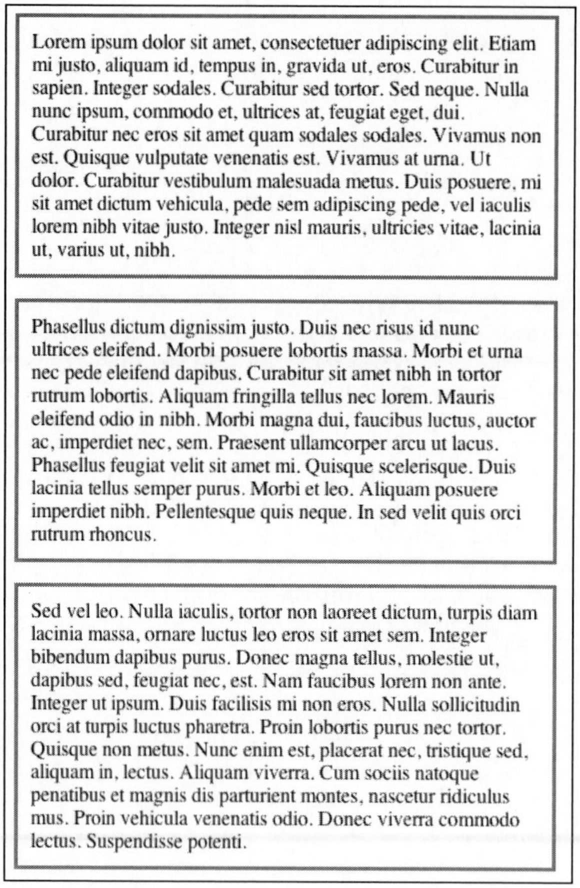

Lorem ipsum dolor sit amet, consectetuer adipiscing elit. Etiam mi justo, aliquam id, tempus in, gravida ut, eros. Curabitur in sapien. Integer sodales. Curabitur sed tortor. Sed neque. Nulla nunc ipsum, commodo et, ultrices at, feugiat eget, dui. Curabitur nec eros sit amet quam sodales sodales. Vivamus non est. Quisque vulputate venenatis est. Vivamus at urna. Ut dolor. Curabitur vestibulum malesuada metus. Duis posuere, mi sit amet dictum vehicula, pede sem adipiscing pede, vel iaculis lorem nibh vitae justo. Integer nisl mauris, ultricies vitae, lacinia ut, varius ut, nibh.

Phasellus dictum dignissim justo. Duis nec risus id nunc ultrices eleifend. Morbi posuere lobortis massa. Morbi et urna nec pede eleifend dapibus. Curabitur sit amet nibh in tortor rutrum lobortis. Aliquam fringilla tellus nec lorem. Mauris eleifend odio in nibh. Morbi magna dui, faucibus luctus, auctor ac, imperdiet nec, sem. Praesent ullamcorper arcu ut lacus. Phasellus feugiat velit sit amet mi. Quisque scelerisque. Duis lacinia tellus semper purus. Morbi et leo. Aliquam posuere imperdiet nibh. Pellentesque quis neque. In sed velit quis orci rutrum rhoncus.

Sed vel leo. Nulla iaculis, tortor non laoreet dictum, turpis diam lacinia massa, ornare luctus leo eros sit amet sem. Integer bibendum dapibus purus. Donec magna tellus, molestie ut, dapibus sed, feugiat nec, est. Nam faucibus lorem non ante. Integer ut ipsum. Duis facilisis mi non eros. Nulla sollicitudin orci at turpis luctus pharetra. Proin lobortis purus nec tortor. Quisque non metus. Nunc enim est, placerat nec, tristique sed, aliquam in, lectus. Aliquam viverra. Cum sociis natoque penatibus et magnis dis parturient montes, nascetur ridiculus mus. Proin vehicula venenatis odio. Donec viverra commodo lectus. Suspendisse potenti.

Figure 7-2. *Paragraphs within the normal (static) flow of a page*

Relative positioning: This means the positioning is very similar to static positioning, as the element will continue to follow the normal flow of the document until instructed to do otherwise. However, setting the top or left properties will cause the element to be shifted in relation to its original (static) position. An example of relative positioning is shown in Figure 7-3, with the CSS positioning of `position: relative; top: -50px; left: 50px;`.

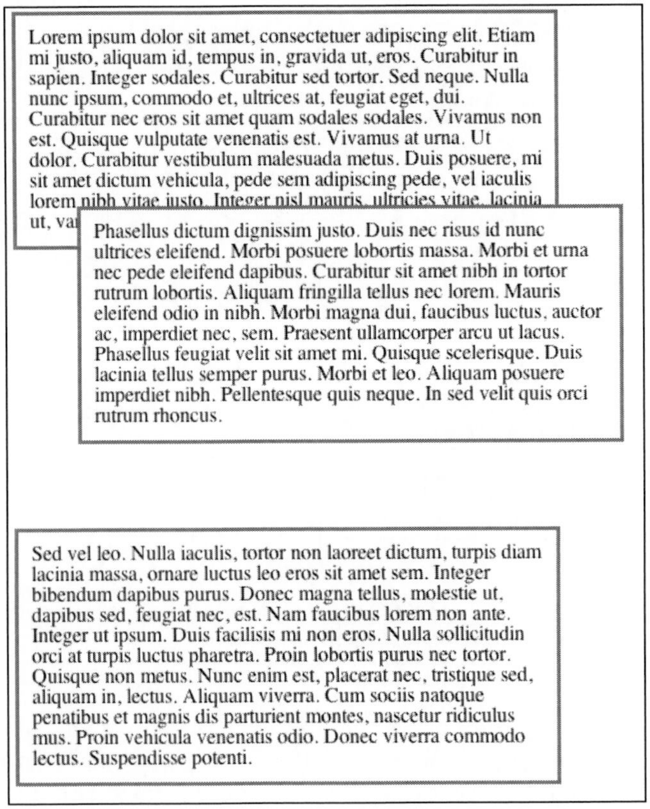

Lorem ipsum dolor sit amet, consectetuer adipiscing elit. Etiam mi justo, aliquam id, tempus in, gravida ut, eros. Curabitur in sapien. Integer sodales. Curabitur sed tortor. Sed neque. Nulla nunc ipsum, commodo et, ultrices at, feugiat eget, dui. Curabitur nec eros sit amet quam sodales sodales. Vivamus non est. Quisque vulputate venenatis est. Vivamus at urna. Ut dolor. Curabitur vestibulum malesuada metus. Duis posuere, mi sit amet dictum vehicula, pede sem adipiscing pede, vel iaculis lorem nibh vitae justo. Integer nisl mauris, ultricies vitae, lacinia ut, va

Phasellus dictum dignissim justo. Duis nec risus id nunc ultrices eleifend. Morbi posuere lobortis massa. Morbi et urna nec pede eleifend dapibus. Curabitur sit amet nibh in tortor rutrum lobortis. Aliquam fringilla tellus nec lorem. Mauris eleifend odio in nibh. Morbi magna dui, faucibus luctus, auctor ac, imperdiet nec, sem. Praesent ullamcorper arcu ut lacus. Phasellus feugiat velit sit amet mi. Quisque scelerisque. Duis lacinia tellus semper purus. Morbi et leo. Aliquam posuere imperdiet nibh. Pellentesque quis neque. In sed velit quis orci rutrum rhoncus.

Sed vel leo. Nulla iaculis, tortor non laoreet dictum, turpis diam lacinia massa, ornare luctus leo eros sit amet sem. Integer bibendum dapibus purus. Donec magna tellus, molestie ut, dapibus sed, feugiat nec, est. Nam faucibus lorem non ante. Integer ut ipsum. Duis facilisis mi non eros. Nulla sollicitudin orci at turpis luctus pharetra. Proin lobortis purus nec tortor. Quisque non metus. Nunc enim est, placerat nec, tristique sed, aliquam in, lectus. Aliquam viverra. Cum sociis natoque penatibus et magnis dis parturient montes, nascetur ridiculus mus. Proin vehicula venenatis odio. Donec viverra commodo lectus. Suspendisse potenti.

Figure 7-3. *Relative positioning, with the element shifted up and over the previous element, rather than following the normal flow of the document*

Absolute positioning: Positioning an element absolutely completely breaks it out of the normal flow of page layout. An element that's been positioned absolutely will be displayed in relation to the first parent element that has a nonstatic position. If no parent exists, it's positioned in relation to the entire document. An example of absolute positioning is shown in Figure 7-4, with the CSS positioning of `position: absolute; top: 20px; left: 0px;`.

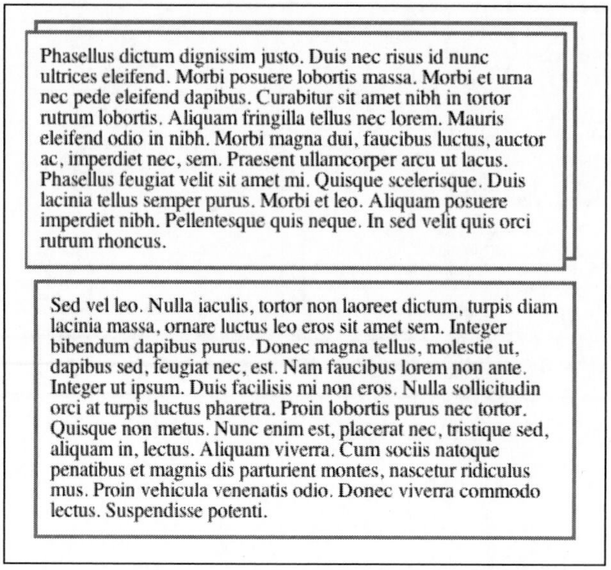

Phasellus dictum dignissim justo. Duis nec risus id nunc ultrices eleifend. Morbi posuere lobortis massa. Morbi et urna nec pede eleifend dapibus. Curabitur sit amet nibh in tortor rutrum lobortis. Aliquam fringilla tellus nec lorem. Mauris eleifend odio in nibh. Morbi magna dui, faucibus luctus, auctor ac, imperdiet nec, sem. Praesent ullamcorper arcu ut lacus. Phasellus feugiat velit sit amet mi. Quisque scelerisque. Duis lacinia tellus semper purus. Morbi et leo. Aliquam posuere imperdiet nibh. Pellentesque quis neque. In sed velit quis orci rutrum rhoncus.

Sed vel leo. Nulla iaculis, tortor non laoreet dictum, turpis diam lacinia massa, ornare luctus leo eros sit amet sem. Integer bibendum dapibus purus. Donec magna tellus, molestie ut, dapibus sed, feugiat nec, est. Nam faucibus lorem non ante. Integer ut ipsum. Duis facilisis mi non eros. Nulla sollicitudin orci at turpis luctus pharetra. Proin lobortis purus nec tortor. Quisque non metus. Nunc enim est, placerat nec, tristique sed, aliquam in, lectus. Aliquam viverra. Cum sociis natoque penatibus et magnis dis parturient montes, nascetur ridiculus mus. Proin vehicula venenatis odio. Donec viverra commodo lectus. Suspendisse potenti.

Figure 7-4. *Absolute positioning, with the element positioned toward the upper-left corner of the page, on top of the element already displayed there*

Fixed Positioning: Fixed positioning works by positioning an element relative to the browser window. Setting an element's top and left to 0 pixels will display that element in the top-left corner of the browser for as long as the user is on that page, completely ignoring any use of the browser's scrollbars. An example of fixed positioning is shown in Figure 7-5, with the CSS positioning of `position: fixed; top: 20px; right: 0px;`.

Knowing how an element can be positioned is important for knowing where an element should be located within a DOM structure, or what means of positioning you should use to achieve the best effect.

We will now look at how to extract and manipulate the exact position of an element, regardless of what layout is used or what CSS properties are set.

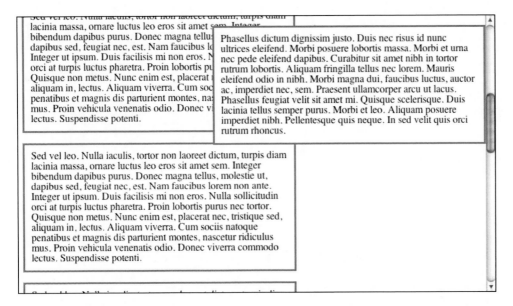

Figure 7-5. *Fixed positioning, with the element positioned in the upper-right corner of the page, even though the browser window has been scrolled down the page*

Getting the Position

Where an element is located varies depending on its CSS parameters and the content immediately adjacent to it. One thing that accessing CSS properties or their actual computed values does not afford you is the ability to know an element's exact position within the page or even within another element.

To start with, let's look at finding an element's position within a page. You have a couple element properties at your disposal that you can use to find this information. All modern browsers support the following three properties; how they handle them, however, is another matter:

offsetParent: Theoretically, this is the parent that an element is positioned within. However, in practice, the element that offsetParent refers to depends on the browser (for example, in Firefox it refers to the root node, and in Opera, the immediate parent).

offsetLeft and offsetTop: These parameters are the horizontal and vertical offsets of the element within the context of the offsetParent. Thankfully, this is always accurate in modern browsers.

The trick, now, is to find a way that you can determine a consistent cross-browser measure of an element's location. The most consistent way to do this is by using the methods presented in Listing 7-4, traversing up the DOM tree using the offsetParent property and adding up the offset values along the way.

Listing 7-4. *Two Helper Functions for Determining the x and y Locations of an Element Relative to the Entire Document*

```
// Find the X (Horizontal, Left) position of an element
function pageX(elem) {
    // See if we're at the root element, or not
    return elem.offsetParent ?

        // If we can still go up, add the current offset and recurse upwards
        elem.offsetLeft + pageX( elem.offsetParent ) :

        // Otherwise, just get the current offset
        elem.offsetLeft;
}

// Find the Y (Vertical, Top) position of an element
function pageY(elem) {
    // See if we're at the root element, or not
    return elem.offsetParent ?

        // If we can still go up, add the current offset and recurse upwards
        elem.offsetTop + pageY( elem.offsetParent ) :

        // Otherwise, just get the current offset
        elem.offsetTop;
}
```

The next piece of the positioning puzzle is figuring out the horizontal and vertical positioning of an element within its parent. It's important to note that it's not sufficient to simply use an element's style.left or style.top properties, as you may want to find an element's position that has not yet been styled using JavaScript or CSS.

Using the position of an element relative to its parent, you can add additional elements to the DOM, positioned relative to the parent. This value is perfect for building contextual tooltips, for example.

In order to find the positioning of an element relative to its parent element, you must again turn to the offsetParent property. Since that property is not guaranteed to return the actual parent of the specified element, you must use your pageX and pageY functions to find the difference between the parent element and the child element. In the two functions shown in Listing 7-5, I attempt to first use offsetParent, if it is the actual parent of the current element; otherwise, I continue to traverse up the DOM using the pageX and pageY methods to determine its actual positioning.

Listing 7-5. *Two Functions for Determining the Position of an Element Relative to Its Parent Element*

```
// Find the horizontal positioing of an element within its parent
function parentX(elem) {
    // If the offsetParent is the element's parent, break early
    return elem.parentNode == elem.offsetParent ?
        elem.offsetLeft :

        // Otherwise, we need to find the position relative to the entire
        // page for both elements, and find the difference
        pageX( elem ) - pageX( elem.parentNode );
}

// Find the vertical positioning of an element within its parent
function parentY(elem) {
    // If the offsetParent is the element's parent, break early
    return elem.parentNode == elem.offsetParent ?
        elem.offsetTop :

        // Otherwise, we need to find the position relative to the entire
        // page for both elements, and find the difference
        pageY( elem ) - pageY( elem.parentNode );
}
```

The final piece to working with an element's positioning is finding out the position of an element relative to its CSS container. As discussed previously, an element can actually be contained within one element but be positioned relative to another parent (with the use of relative and absolute positioning). With this in mind, you can turn back to the getStyle function to find the computed value of the CSS offsets, since that is what the positioning is equivalent to.

To handle this, there are two simple wrapper functions, shown in Listing 7-6, that you can use. They both simply call the getStyle function, but also remove any "extraneous" (unless you're using a non-pixel-based layout, then it's important) unit information (for example 100px would become 100).

Listing 7-6. *Helper Functions for Finding the CSS Positioning of an Element*

```
// Find the left position of an element
function posX(elem) {
    // Get the computed style and get the number out of the value
    return parseInt( getStyle( elem, "left" ) );
}
```

```
// Find the top position of an element
function posY(elem) {
    // Get the computed style and get the number out of the value
    return parseInt( getStyle( elem, "top" ) );
}
```

Setting the Position

Unlike with getting the position of an element, setting the position is much less flexible. But when used in combination with the various means of layout (absolute, relative, fixed) you can achieve comparable, and usable, results.

Currently, the only way to adjust the position of an element is through the modification of its CSS properties. To keep your methodology consistent, you will only modify the left and top properties, even though other properties exist (such as bottom and right). To begin with, you can easily create a pair of functions, as shown in Listing 7-7, that you can use to set the position of an element, regardless of its current location.

Listing 7-7. *A Pair of Functions for Setting the x and y Positions of an Element, Regardless of Its Current Position*

```
// A function for setting the horizontal position of an element
function setX(elem, pos) {
    // Set the 'left' CSS property, using pixel units
    elem.style.left = pos + "px";
}

// A function for setting the vertical position of an element
function setY(elem, pos) {
    // Set the 'left' CSS property, using pixel units
    elem.style.top = pos + "px";
}
```

Ultimately, however, you need to develop a second set of functions, such as those shown in Listing 7-8, that you can use to set the position of an element relative to its last position—for example, adjusting an element so that its left position is 5 pixels less than its current position. The use of these methods is directly tied to doing a variety of animations, which are a mainstay of DHTML development.

Listing 7-8. *A Pair of Functions for Adjusting the Position of an Element Relative to Its Current Position*

```
// A function for adding a number of pixels to the horizontal
// position of an element
function addX(elem,pos) {
    // Get the current horz. position and add the offset to it.
    setX( posX(elem) + pos );
}
```

```
// A function that can be used to add a number of pixels to the
// vertical position of an element
function addY(elem,pos) {
    // Get the current vertical position and add the offset to it
    setY( posY(elem) + pos );
}
```

I've now completely traversed the gamut of working with element positioning. Knowing how element positioning works and how to set and get accurate element positioning is a fundamental aspect of working with dynamic elements. The next aspect that you're going to look at is that of an element's exact size.

An Element's Size

Figuring out the height and width of an element can be both incredibly simple and painfully hard, depending on the situation and what you need it for. For a lot of cases, you'll only ever need to use a modified version of the getStyle function (as shown in Listing 7-9) to get the current height or width of an element.

Listing 7-9. *Two Functions for Retreiving the Current Height or Width of a DOM Element*

```
// Get the actual height (using the computed CSS) of an element
function getHeight( elem ) {
    // Gets the computed CSS value and parses out a usable number
    return parseInt( getStyle( elem, 'height' ) );
}

// Get the actual width (using the computed CSS) of an element
function getWidth( elem ) {
    // Gets the computed CSS value and parses out a usable number
    return parseInt( getStyle( elem, 'width' ) );
}
```

The trickiness arrives when you try to do two things: first, when you want to get the full height of an element that has a predefined height (for example, you start an animation at 0 pixels, but you need to know how tall or wide the element could be), and second, when an element has a display of none, you can't get that value. Both of these problems arise when you attempt to perform animations. You start the animation of an object at 0 pixels (and possibly already hidden with a display of none) and you need to expand the height of the element to its full potential.

The two functions presented in Listing 7-10 show how to find the full potential height and width of an element, regardless of its current height. This is done by accessing the clientWidth and clientHeight properties, which provide the total possible area that an element is capable of scrolling to.

Listing 7-10. *Two Functions for Finding the Full Potential Height or Width of an Element, Even If the Element Is Hidden*

```
// Find the full, possible, height of an element (not the actual,
// current, height)
function fullHeight( elem ) {
    // If the element is being displayed, then offsetHeight
    // should do the trick, barring that, getHeight() will work
    if ( getStyle( elem, 'display' ) != 'none' )
        return elem.offsetHeight || getHeight( elem );

    // Otherwise, we have to deal with an element with a display
    // of none, so we need to reset its CSS properties to get a more
    // accurate reading
    var old = resetCSS( elem, {
        display: '',
        visibility: 'hidden',
        position: 'absolute'
    });

    // Figure out what the full height of the element is, using clientHeight
    // and if that doesn't work, use getHeight
    var h = elem.clientHeight || getHeight( elem );

    // Finally, restore the CSS properties back to what they were
    restoreCSS( elem, old );

    // and return the full height of the element
    return h;
}

// Find the full, possible, width of an element (not the actual,
// current, width)
function fullWidth( elem ) {
    // If the element is being displayed, then offsetWidth
    // should do the trick, barring that, getWidth() will work
    if ( getStyle( elem, 'display' ) != 'none' )
        return elem.offsetWidth || getWidth( elem );

    // Otherwise, we have to deal with an element with a display
    // of none, so we need to reset its CSS properties to get a more
    // accurate reading
    var old = resetCSS( elem, {
        display: '',
        visibility: 'hidden',
        position: 'absolute'
    });
```

```
    // Figure out what the full width of the element is, using clientWidth
    // and if that doesn't work, use getWidth
    var w = elem.clientWidth || getWidth( elem );

    // Finally, restore the CSS properties back to what they were
    restoreCSS( elem, old );

    // and return the full width of the element
    return w;
}

// A function used for setting a set of CSS properties, which
// can then be restored back again later
function resetCSS( elem, prop ) {
    var old = {};

    // Go through each of the properties
    for ( var i in prop ) {
        // Remember the old property value
        old[ i ] = elem.style[ i ];

        // And set the new value
        elem.style[ i ] = prop[i];
    }

    // Retun the set of changed values, to be used by restoreCSS
    return old;
}

// A function for restoring the side effects of the resetCSS function
function restoreCSS( elem, prop ) {
    // Reset all the properties back to their original values
    for ( var i in prop )
        elem.style[ i ] = prop[ i ];
}
```

With the ability to get both the current and potential height and width of an element, you can explore some of the animations you can achieve by using these values. However, before I go into the details of animations, you need to look at how to modify the visibility of an element.

An Element's Visibility

The visibility of an element is a powerful tool that can be used in JavaScript to create everything from animations and effects to fast templating. More importantly, however, it can also be used to quickly hide an element from view, providing users with some basic user interaction capabilities.

Within CSS there are two different ways of effectively hiding an element from view; both have their benefits but can provide unintended consequences, depending on how you use them:

- The visibility property toggles whether an element is visible or not, while still leaving its normal flow properties intact. The visibility property has two values: visible (the default) and hidden (to make an element completely invisible). For example, if you had some text wrapped in a <b> tag, with its visibility set to hidden, the result would simply be a block of white space in the text, the same exact size as the original text. For example, compare the following two lines of text:

```
// Normal text:
Hello John, how are you today?

// 'John' has visibility: hidden applied to it
Hello       , how are you today?
```

- The display property provides more options to a developer for controlling the layout of an element. The options for it vary between inline (tags such as <b> and <span> are inline, in that they follow the normal flow of text), block (tags such as <p> and <div> are blocks, in that they break out of the normal flow of text), and none (which completely hides an element from a document). The result of setting a display property on an element looks exactly the same as if you had just removed the element from the document; however, that is not the case, as it can be quickly toggled back into view at a later time. The following lines show how the display property behaves:

```
// Normal text:
Hello John, how are you today?

// 'John' has display: none applied to it
Hello, how are you today?
```

While the visibility property has its specific uses, the importance of the display property cannot be overstated. The fact that an element still exists within the normal flow of a document when the visibility property is set to hidden discounts it as a viable option for most applications. In Listing 7-11 there are two methods that can be used to toggle the visibility of an element using the display property.

Listing 7-11. *A Set of Functions for Toggling the Visibility of an Element Using Its CSS Display Property*

```
// A function for hiding (using display) an element
function hide( elem ) {
    // Find out what its current display state is
    var curDisplay = getStyle( elem, 'display' );

    //  Remember its display state for later
    if ( curDisplay != 'none' )
        elem.$oldDisplay = curDisplay;
```

```
    // Set the display to none (hiding the element)
    elem.style.display = 'none';
}

// A function for showing (using display) an element
function show( elem ) {
    // Set the display property back to what it use to be, or use
    // 'block', if no previous display had been saved
    elem.style.display = elem.$oldDisplay || '';
}
```

The second aspect of visibility is that of an element's *opacity*. Adjusting the opacity of an element yields results that are very similar to adjusting the visibility of the element, but provides greater control over how visible something can be. This means that you can have an element that is 50% visible, making it so you can see elements that are beneath it. Once again, while all modern browsers support opacity to a degree, both Internet Explorer (as of IE 5.5) and W3C-compatible browsers differ in their implementation. To get around this, you can create a standard function for manipulating the opacity of an element, as shown in Listing 7-12. A level of 0 means that it's completely transparent, whereas a level of 100 means that the element is completely opaque.

Listing 7-12. *A Function for Adjusting the Opacity Level of an Element*

```
// Set an opacity level for an element
// (where level is a number 0-100)
function setOpacity( elem, level ) {
    // If filters exist, then this is IE, so set the Alpha filter
    if ( elem.filters )
        elem.style.filters = 'alpha(opacity=' + level + ')';

    // Otherwise use the W3C opacity property
    else
        elem.style.opacity = level / 100;
}
```

With ways to adjust the position, size, and visibility of an element, it's time to start exploring some of the fun things that you can build when you combine all of that power together.

Animations

Now that you have the basic skills necessary to perform basic DHTML operations, let's take a look at one of the most popular, and visible, effects of dynamic web applications: animations. When tactfully used, animations can provide a user with useful feedback, such as drawing attention to newly created elements on the screen.

We'll start by looking at two different popular animations and then revisit the topic again when we look at popular DHTML libraries.

Slide In

The first animation is where you take a hidden element (hidden using a display property of none) and instead of using the harsh show() function to reveal it, you gradually expose it by increasing its height over the course of a second. The function shown in Listing 7-13 can be used as a drop-in replacement to the show() function, providing a much smoother visual experience for the user.

Listing 7-13. *A Function for Slowly Revealing a Hidden Element by Increasing Its Height Over a Matter of One Second*

```
function slideDown( elem ) {
    // Start the slide down at  0
    elem.style.height = '0px';

    // Show the element (but you can see it, since the height is 0)
    show( elem );

    // Find the full, potential, height of the element
    var h = fullHeight( elem );

    // We're going to do a 20 'frame' animation that takes
    // place over one second
    for ( var i = 0; i <= 100; i += 5 ) {
        // A closure to make sure that we have the right 'i'
        (function(){
            var pos = i;

            // Set the timeout to occur at the specified time in the future
            setTimeout(function(){

                // Set the new height of the element
                elem,.style.height = ( pos / 100 ) * h ) + "px";

            }, ( pos + 1 ) * 10 );
        })();
    }
}
```

Fade In

The next animation that you're going to look at is very similar to the first, but utilizes the setOpacity() function that you built instead of modifying the height. This particular function (shown in Listing 7-14) reveals a hidden element and then fades its opacity in from 0 (totally transparent) to 100% (totally opaque). Much like the function shown in Listing 7-13, it provides a much smoother visual experience for the user.

Listing 7-14. *A Function for Slowly Revealing a Hidden Element by Increasing Its Opacity Over a Matter of One Second*

```
function fadeIn( elem ) {
    // Start the opacity at  0
    setOpacity( elem, 0 );

    // Show the element (but you can see it, since the opacity is 0)
    show( elem );

    // We're going to do a 20 'frame' animation that takes
    // place over one second
    for ( var i = 0; i <= 100; i += 5 ) {
        // A closure to make sure that we have the right 'i'
        (function(){
            var pos = i;

            // Set the timeout to occur at the specified time in the future
            setTimeout(function(){

                // Set the new opacity of the element
                setOpacity( elem, pos );

            }, ( pos + 1 ) * 10 );
        })();
    }
}
```

Examples of these animations, plus some others, can be seen in Chapter 9.

The Browser

After the manipulation of specific DOM elements, knowing how to modify or track the browser and its components can lend much to a user's interaction with the site. The two most important aspects of working with the browser are determining the positioning of the mouse cursor and determining how far along the page the user has scrolled.

Mouse Position

Locating the position of the mouse is an essential aspect of providing the user with drag-and-drop operations and contextual menus, both of which are only possible with the interaction between JavaScript and CSS.

The first two variables that you need to detect are the x and y positions of a cursor, relative to an entire web page (as shown in Listing 7-15). Since it's only possible to get the current mouse coordinates from a mouse event, you'll end up needing to use a common mouse event to capture them, such as MouseMove or MouseDown (more examples of this are in the section "Drag and Drop").

Listing 7-15. *Two Generic Functions for Finding the Current Position of the Mouse Cursor Within the Entire Web Page*

```
// Find the horizontal position of the cursor
function getX(e) {
    // Normalize the event object
    e = e || window.event;

    // Check for the non-IE position, then the IE position
    return e.pageX || e.clientX + document.body.scrollLeft;
}

// Find the vertical position of the cursor
function getY(e) {
    // Normalize the event object
    e = e || window.event;

    // Check for the non-IE position, then the IE position
    return e.pageY || e.clientY + document.body.scrollTop;
}
```

Finally, the second mouse-related variables that are good to know are the *x* and *y* positions of the mouse cursor relative to the element that's currently being interacted with. Examples of two possible functions that can be used to retrieve these values are shown in Listing 7-16.

Listing 7-16. *Two Functions for Retreiving the Position of the Mouse Relative to the Current Element*

```
// Get the X position of the mouse relative to the element target
// used in event object 'e'
function getElementX( e ) {
    // Find the appropriate element offset
    return ( e && e.layerX ) || window.event.offsetX;
}

// Get the Y position of the mouse relative to the element target
// used in event object 'e'
function getElementY( e ) {
    // Find the appropriate element offset
    return ( e && e.layerY ) || window.event.offsetY;
}
```

We'll be revisiting mouse interactions when we look at an implementation of drag-and-drop for the browser in the "Drag-and-Drop" section of this chapter. Additionally, for more examples of mouse events, look at Chapter 6 and Appendix B, which both have plenty more examples of working with the mouse.

The Viewport

The *viewport* of the browser can be thought of as everything inside the scrollbars of the browser. The viewport additionally contains a few components: the viewport window, the page, and the scrollbars. Figuring out the correct positioning and sizes of each of these is needed for developing clean interaction with long pieces of content (such as autoscrolling chat rooms, for example).

Page Size

The first set of properties that you need to look at are the height and width of the current web page. It's most likely that most of the actual page is cropped by the viewport (which can be determined by checking the viewport size and scrollbar position). The two functions shown in Listing 7-17 use the aforementioned scrollWidth and scrollHeight properties, which detail the total possible width and height of an item, not just what's currently shown.

Listing 7-17. *Two Functions for Determining the Length and Width of the Current Web Page*

```
// Returns the height of the web page
// (could change if new content is added to the page)
function pageHeight() {
    return document.body.scrollHeight;
}

// Returns the width of the web page
function pageWidth() {
    return document.body.scrollWidth;
}
```

Scrollbar Position

Next you're going to look at how to determine the position of the browser's scrollbar (or, in another sense, looking at how far down the page the viewport is currently located). Having these numbers (which can be retrieved using the functions shown in Listing 7-18) is necessary to provide dynamic scrolling within an application beyond what the browser provides by default.

Listing 7-18. *Two Functions for Determining Where the Viewport Is Positioned on Top of a Document*

```
// A function for determining how far horizontally the browser is scrolled
function scrollX() {
    // A shortcut, in case we're using Internet Explorer 6 in Strict Mode
    var de = document.documentElement;

    // If the pageXOffset of the browser is available, use that
    return self.pageXOffset ||
```

```
        // Otherwise, try to get the scroll left off of the root node
        ( de && de.scrollLeft ) ||

        // Finally, try to get the scroll left off of the body element
        document.body.scrollLeft;
}

// A function for determining how far vertically the browser is scrolled
function scrollY() {
    // A shortcut, in case we're using Internet Explorer 6 in Strict Mode
    var de = document.documentElement;

    // If the pageYOffset of the browser is available, use that
    return self.pageYOffset ||

        // Otherwise, try to get the scroll top off of the root node
        ( de && de.scrollTop ) ||

        // Finally, try to get the scroll top off of the body element
        document.body.scrollTop;
}
```

Moving the Scrollbar

Now that you have the current scrollbar offset into a page and the length of the page itself, you can look at the scrollTo method, provided by browsers, which can be used to adjust the current position of the viewport on the page.

The scrollTo method exists as a property of the window object (and any other element that contains scrollable content or an <iframe>) and takes two parameters, the x and y offset, to scroll the viewport (or element or <iframe>) to. Listing 7-19 shows two examples of using the scrollTo method.

Listing 7-19. *Examples of Using the scrollTo Method to Adjust the Position of the Browser Window*

```
// If you wanted to scroll the browser up to the top of the browser, you could do:
window.scrollTo(0,0);

// If you wanted to scroll to the position of a specific element, you could do:
window.scrollTo( 0, pageY( document.getElementById("body") ) );
```

Viewport Size

The final aspect of the viewport is perhaps the most obvious: the size of the viewport itself. Knowing the size of the viewport gives good insight into how much content the user can currently see, regardless of their screen's resolution or the size of their browser window. You can use two functions presented in Listing 7-20 to determine these values for yourself.

Listing 7-20. *Two Functions for Determining the Height and Width of the Browser Viewport*

```
// Find the height of the viewport
function windowHeight() {
    // A shortcut, in case we're using Internet Explorer 6 in Strict Mode
    var de = document.documentElement;

    // If the innerHeight of the browser is available, use that
    return self.innerHeight ||

        // Otherwise, try to get the height off of the root node
        ( de && de.clientHeight ) ||

        // Finally, try to get the height off of the body element
        document.body.clientHeight;
}

// Find the width of the viewport
function windowWidth() {
    // A shortcut, in case we're using Internet Explorer 6 in Strict Mode
    var de = document.documentElement;

    // If the innerWidth of the browser is available, use that
    return self.innerWidth ||

        // Otherwise, try to get the width off of the root node
        ( de && de.clientWidth ) ||

        // Finally, try to get the width off of the body element
        document.body.clientWidth;
}
```

The usefulness of working with the viewport cannot be overstated. You simply need to look at a modern web application, such as Gmail or Campfire, to see instances where manipulation of the viewport provides compelling results (with Gmail providing contextual overlays and Campfire providing autoscrolling chats). In Chapter 11 I discuss different ways that the viewport can be used to provide a better experience with highly interactive web applications.

Drag-and-Drop

One of the most popular user interactions available in a browser is that of being able to drag an element around a page. Using the skills that you've learned (the ability to determine an element's position, how to adjust its position, and the difference between the various types of positioning), you can now fully understand how a dragable-element system works.

To explore this technology, I've chosen to look at the DOM-Drag library created by Aaron Boodman (`http://boring.youngpup.net/2001/domdrag`). His library provides a lot of handy features, including the following:

Drag handles: You can have one parent element that is actually being moved and another subelement that is being dragged. This is great for creating windowlike elements for an interface.

Callback functions: You can watch for specific events, such as when the user begins dragging an element, is dragging an element, or has stopped dragging the element, along with information about the current location of the element.

Min/max drag area: You can restrict an element from being dragged outside of a certain area (such as outside of the screen). This is perfect for building scrollbars.

Custom coordinate systems: You can choose to work with any combination of *x*/*y* coordinate system mapping if you don't feel comfortable working with the CSS coordinate system.

Custom x and y coordinate system translation: You can cause your dragged element to move in nontraditional ways (such as fluctuating or waving around).

Using the DOM-Drag system is relatively straightforward. You begin by attaching a drag handler to an element (additionally specifying any extra options that you have) along with any extra watcher functions. Some examples of using DOM-Drag are shown in Listing 7-21.

Listing 7-21. *Using the DOM-Drag to Simulate In-Browser Draggable Windows*

```html
<html>
<head>
    <title>DOM-Drag - Draggable Window Demo</title>
    <script src="domdrag.js" type="text/javascript"></script>
    <script type="text/javascript">
    window.onload = function(){
        // Initalize the DOM-Drag function, making the element with
        // an ID of 'window' draggable
        Drag.init( document.getElementById("window") );
    };
    </script>
    <style>
    #window {
        border: 1px solid #DDD;
        border-top: 15px solid #DDD;
        width: 250px;
        height: 250px;
    }
    </style>
</head>
<body>
    <h1>Draggable Window Demo</h1>
```

```
    <div id="window">I am a draggable window, feel free to move me around!</div>
</body>
</html>
```

A fully documented copy of the DOM-Drag library is shown in Listing 7-22. The code exists as a single global object whose methods can be called on objects to initialize the draggable process.

Listing 7-22. *The Fully Documented DOM-Drag Library*

```
var Drag = {

    // The current element being dragged
    obj: null,

    // The initalization function for the drag object
    // o = The element to act as the drag handle
    // oRoot = The element to be dragged, if not specified,
    //           the handle will be the element dragged.
    // minX, maxX, minY, maxY = The min and max coordinates allowed for the element
    // bSwapHorzRef = Toggle the horizontal coordinate system
    // bSwapVertRef = Toggle the vertical coordinate system
    // fxMapper, fyMapper =  Functions for mapping x and y coordinates to others
    init: function(o, oRoot, minX, maxX, minY,
            maxY, bSwapHorzRef, bSwapVertRef, fXMapper, fYMapper) {

        // Watch for the drag event to start
        o.onmousedown = Drag.start;

        // Figure out which coordinate system is being used
        o.hmode = bSwapHorzRef ? false : true ;
        o.vmode = bSwapVertRef ? false : true ;

        // Figure out which element is acting as the draggable 'handle'
        o.root = oRoot && oRoot != null ? oRoot : o ;

        // Initalize the specified coordinate system
        if (o.hmode && isNaN(parseInt(o.root.style.left )))
            o.root.style.left   = "0px";
        if (o.vmode && isNaN(parseInt(o.root.style.top )))
            o.root.style.top    = "0px";
        if (!o.hmode && isNaN(parseInt(o.root.style.right )))
            o.root.style.right  = "0px";
        if (!o.vmode && isNaN(parseInt(o.root.style.bottom)))
            o.root.style.bottom = "0px";
```

```javascript
            // Look to see if the user provided min/max x/y coordinates
            o.minX = typeof minX != 'undefined' ? minX : null;
            o.minY = typeof minY != 'undefined' ? minY : null;
            o.maxX = typeof maxX != 'undefined' ? maxX : null;
            o.maxY = typeof maxY != 'undefined' ? maxY : null;

            // Check for any specified x and y coordinate mappers
            o.xMapper = fXMapper ? fXMapper : null;
            o.yMapper = fYMapper ? fYMapper : null;

            // Add shells for all the user-defined functions
            o.root.onDragStart = new Function();
            o.root.onDragEnd  = new Function();
            o.root.onDrag = new Function();

    },

    start: function(e) {
        // Figure out the object that's being dragged
        var o = Drag.obj = this;

        // Normalize the event object
        e = Drag.fixE(e);

        // Get the current x and y coordinates
        var y = parseInt(o.vmode ? o.root.style.top  : o.root.style.bottom);
        var x = parseInt(o.hmode ? o.root.style.left : o.root.style.right );

        // Call the user's function with the current x and y coordinates
        o.root.onDragStart(x, y);

        // Remember the starting mouse position
        o.lastMouseX = e.clientX;
        o.lastMouseY = e.clientY;

        // If we're using the CSS coordinate system
        if (o.hmode) {
            // set the min and max coordiantes, where applicable
            if (o.minX != null) o.minMouseX    = e.clientX - x + o.minX;
            if (o.maxX != null) o.maxMouseX    = o.minMouseX + o.maxX - o.minX;

        // Otherwise, we're using a traditional mathematical coordinate system
        } else {
            if (o.minX != null) o.maxMouseX = -o.minX + e.clientX + x;
            if (o.maxX != null) o.minMouseX = -o.maxX + e.clientX + x;
        }
```

```
    // If we're using the CSS coordinate system
    if (o.vmode) {
        // set the min and max coordiantes, where applicable
        if (o.minY != null) o.minMouseY   = e.clientY - y + o.minY;
        if (o.maxY != null) o.maxMouseY   = o.minMouseY + o.maxY - o.minY;

    // Otherwise, we're using a traditional mathematical coordinate system
    } else {
        if (o.minY != null) o.maxMouseY = -o.minY + e.clientY + y;
        if (o.maxY != null) o.minMouseY = -o.maxY + e.clientY + y;
    }

    // Watch for 'dragging' and 'drag end' events
    document.onmousemove = Drag.drag;
    document.onmouseup = Drag.end;

    return false;
},

// A function to watch for all movements of the mouse during the drag event
drag: function(e) {
    // Normalize the event object
    e = Drag.fixE(e);

    // Get our reference to the element being dragged
    var o = Drag.obj;

    // Get the position of the mouse within the window
    var ey = e.clientY;
    var ex = e.clientX;

    // Get the current x and y coordinates
    var y = parseInt(o.vmode ? o.root.style.top  : o.root.style.bottom);
    var x = parseInt(o.hmode ? o.root.style.left : o.root.style.right );
    var nx, ny;

    // If a minimum X position was set, make sure it doesn't go past that
    if (o.minX != null) ex = o.hmode ?
        Math.max(ex, o.minMouseX) : Math.min(ex, o.maxMouseX);

    // If a maximum X position was set, make sure it doesn't go past that
    if (o.maxX != null) ex = o.hmode ?
        Math.min(ex, o.maxMouseX) : Math.max(ex, o.minMouseX);

    // If a minimum Y position was set, make sure it doesn't go past that
    if (o.minY != null) ey = o.vmode ?
        Math.max(ey, o.minMouseY) : Math.min(ey, o.maxMouseY);
```

```javascript
    // If a maximum Y position was set, make sure it doesn't go past that
    if (o.maxY != null) ey = o.vmode ?
        Math.min(ey, o.maxMouseY) : Math.max(ey, o.minMouseY);

    // Figure out the newly translated x and y coordinates
    nx = x + ((ex - o.lastMouseX) * (o.hmode ? 1 : -1));
    ny = y + ((ey - o.lastMouseY) * (o.vmode ? 1 : -1));

    // and translate them using an x or y mapper function (if provided)
    if (o.xMapper) nx = o.xMapper(y)
    else if (o.yMapper) ny = o.yMapper(x)

    // Set the new x and y coordinates onto the element
    Drag.obj.root.style[o.hmode ? "left" : "right"] = nx + "px";
    Drag.obj.root.style[o.vmode ? "top" : "bottom"] = ny + "px";

    // and remember  the last position of the mouse
    Drag.obj.lastMouseX = ex;
    Drag.obj.lastMouseY = ey;

    // Call the user's onDrag  function with the current x and y coordinates
    Drag.obj.root.onDrag(nx, ny);

    return false;
},

// Function that handles the end of a drag event
end: function() {
    // No longer watch for mouse events (as the drag is done)
    document.onmousemove = null;
    document.onmouseup = null;

    // Call our special onDragEnd function with the x and y coordinates
    // of the element at the end of the drag event
    Drag.obj.root.onDragEnd(
        parseInt(Drag.obj.root.style[Drag.obj.hmode ? "left" : "right"]),
        parseInt(Drag.obj.root.style[Drag.obj.vmode ? "top" : "bottom"]));
    // No longer watch the object for drags
    Drag.obj = null;
},

// A function for normalizes the event object
fixE: function(e) {
    // If no event object exists, then this is IE, so provide IE's event object
    if (typeof e == 'undefined') e = window.event;
```

```
    // If the layer properties aren't set, get the values from the equivalent
    // offset properties
    if (typeof e.layerX == 'undefined') e.layerX = e.offsetX;
    if (typeof e.layerY == 'undefined') e.layerY = e.offsetY;

    return e;
  }
};
```

In all honesty, DOM-Drag is simply one of possibly hundreds of JavaScript drag-and-drop libraries. However, I have a particular fondness for it due to its clean object-oriented syntax and relative simplicity. In the next section I discuss the Scriptaculous library, which has an excellent and powerful drag-and-drop implementation that I highly recommend you check out.

Libraries

As with most tedious tasks in JavaScript, if there's effect or interaction that you want to develop, it's very possible that it's already been created. You're going to quickly look at three different libraries that provide various DHTML interactions so that you can get a feel for what's available to you as a developer.

moo.fx and jQuery

There exist two lightweight libraries that are very good at handling simple effects: moo.fx and jQuery. Both of these libraries provide basic effect combinations that can be combined to create effective but simple animations. More information about each library can be found on each of their associated web pages. Some basic examples of the two libraries can be found in Listing 7-23.

Listing 7-23. *Basic Examples of Animations Using Both moo.fx and jQuery*

```
// A simple animation where an element's hide is expanded, then
// when completed, contracted again

// moo.fx's implementation of that particular animation
new fx.Height( "side", {
    duration: 1000,
    onComplete: function() {
        new fx.Height( "side", { duration: 1000 } ).hide();
    }
}).show();

// jQuery's  implementation
$("#side").slideDown( 1000, function(){
    $(this).slideUp( 1000 );
});
```

```
// Another simple animation where the height, width, and opacity of
// an element are all shrunk (or diminished) together, resulting in a cool
// hiding effect

// moo.fx's implemention of this animation
new fx.Combo( "body", {
    height: true,
    width: true,
    opacity: true
}).hide();

// jQuery's implementation of the animation
$("#body").hide( "fast" );
```

As you can probably tell from the examples, both moo.fx and jQuery make it really easy to do some neat animations. Both projects provide plenty of examples of their code in use on their web sites, which is a great way to learn about how simple JavaScript animations work:

- *moo.fx home page*: http://moofx.mad4milk.net/

- *mootoolkit documentation examples*: http://moofx.mad4milk.net/documentation/

- *jQuery home page*: http://jquery.com/

- *jQuery effects documentation and examples*: http://jquery.com/docs/fx/

Scriptaculous

If one library had to be crowned king of all DHTML libraries, Scriptaculous would have to be it. Built on top of the popular Prototype library, Scriptaculous provides tons of different interactions, everything from animations and effects to interactions (such as drag and drop). A lot of information and samples can be found on the Scriptaculous web site:

- *Home page*: http://script.aculo.us/

- *Documentation*: http://wiki.script.aculo.us/scriptaculous/

- *Demos*: http://wiki.script.aculo.us/scriptaculous/show/Demos/

One of the areas that Scriptaculous provides the greatest level of power in, while still keeping the best level of simplicity, is its drag-and-drop implementation. I've provided a couple simple examples for you to take a look at.

Drag-and-Drop Reordering

One thing that Scriptaculous makes painfully simple is the reordering of lists. Considering how simple the code is (and how easy it is to hook in with Ajax functionality, as demonstrated on its web site), it's definitely a recommended solution for most web developers. The example shown in Listing 7-24 is a simple reorderable list, created using the Scriptaculous library.

Listing 7-24. *How to Create a List That's Able to Be Reordered Using the Drag-and-Drop Techniques Available in Scriptaculous*

```html
<html>
<head>
    <title>script.aculo.us - Drag and Drop Re-Ordering Demo</title>
    <script src="prototype.js" type="text/javascript"></script>
    <script src="scriptaculous.js" type="text/javascript"></script>
    <script src="effects.js" type="text/javascript"></script>
    <script src="dragdrop.js" type="text/javascript"></script>
    <script type="text/javascript">
    window.onload = function(){
        // Turn the element with an id of 'list' into a drag-and-drop
        // re-orderable list
        Sortable.create('list');
    };
    </script>
</head>
<body>
    <h1>Drag and Drop Re-Ordering</h1>

    <p>Drag and drop an item to re-order it.</p>

    <ul id="list">
        <li>Item number 1</li>
        <li>Item number 2</li>
        <li>Item number 3</li>
        <li>Item number 4</li>
        <li>Item number 5</li>
        <li>Item number 6</li>
    </ul>
</body>
</html>
```

I hope this convinces you of the power that's contained within this library, but if not, you can take a look at the next example, which is an example of creating a slider input control.

Slider Input

Scriptaculous provides a number of controls that you can use to solve common interface developments. A control that's fairly easy to implement with most drag-and-drop libraries is that of a slider input (sliding a bar to get a number input) and Scriptaculous is no exception, as shown by the code in Listing 7-25.

Listing 7-25. *Using the Slider Input Control from Scriptaculous to Create an Alternative Way to Input Your Age Into a Form*

```html
<html>
<head>
    <title>script.aculo.us - Slider Input Demo</title>
    <script src="prototype.js" type="text/javascript"></script>
    <script src="scriptaculous.js" type="text/javascript"></script>
    <script src="effects.js" type="text/javascript"></script>
    <script src="dragdrop.js" type="text/javascript"></script>
    <script src="controls.js" type="text/javascript"></script>
    <script type="text/javascript">
    window.onload = function(){
        // Turn the element with an ID of ageHandle into the draggable
        // slider handle and the element with an ID of ageBar into the
        // slider bar
        new Control.Slider( 'ageHandle', 'ageBar', {
            // When the slider is moved, or finished moving,
            // call the updateAge function
            onSlide: updateAge
        });

        // Handles any movements that occur within the slider
        function updateAge(v) {
            // When the slider updates, update the value of the age
            // element to represent the user's current age
            $('age').value = Math.floor( v * 100 );
        }
    };
    </script>
</head>
<body>
    <h1>Slider Input Demo</h1>

    <form action="" method="POST">
        <p>How old are you? <input type="text" name="age" id="age" /></p>

        <div id="ageBar" style="width:200px; background: #000; height:5px;">
            <div id="ageHandle" style="width:5px; height:10px;
                background: #000; cursor:move;"></div>
        </div>

        <input type="submit" value="Submit Age"/>
    </form>
</body>
</html>
```

I highly recommend that you check into some DHTML libraries before deciding to write your next piece of interaction, for the simple fact that the library authors most likely put a lot more time and effort into developing that one piece of interaction than you have for your whole application. Having the libraries at your disposal will obviously keep your development time down.

Summary

The power of using dynamic interactions within your web application is an incredible way to provide greater levels of speed and usability to your users. Additionally, if you use any of the popular libraries, you'll be able to easily keep your development time down while doing so. In the next chapter you will combine all of the interactive techniques that you learned in this chapter to build a fully usable, interactive application.

In this chapter you looked at all the different techniques needed to achieve a level of symbiosis between JavaScript and CSS. The result, however, is the ability to create impressive animations and dynamic user interactions.

You should remember that adding any form of dynamic interaction to a web page has the potential to alienate part of your audience. You should always be careful that your application is still usable, even with JavaScript or CSS disabled. Building a web application that's capable of degrading gracefully should be the ideal situation for any JavaScript developer.

■ ■ ■

## CHAPTER 8

Improving Forms

Forms exist as a means through which structured data can be received from a user, and therefore are immensely useful to a web developer. Inherently, however, there exist very few restrictions upon what a user can do with a form, what data he can enter, or how usable the form is.

It is at this stage of the development, after you've already constructed a semantically designed form, that it comes time to add some JavaScript to provide additional feedback to the user. With the knowledge of how or why something may happen within a form, the user will be able to move through it faster, and subsequently will have a better user experience.

In this chapter you're going to look at performing basic client-side form validation and presenting the result of that validation back to the user in a manner that makes sense and is unobtrusive. Next you're going to look at a number of ways that the overall usability of forms can be improved. Combined, these two techniques can be used to provide a significantly improved form that users may even enjoy filling out.

Form Validation

Adding client-side form validation to a web page can provide users with a faster experience, but not without a catch: client-side form validation should never replace server-side validation, only enhance it. This means that adding client-side form validation to a web page is a perfect example of the unobtrusive scripting techniques that you've learned.

Before you begin any form scripting of any sort, you should build your form and make sure that it works completely as intended (e.g., validating the user's input, giving appropriate error messages, etc.). For this chapter, you're going to use a semantically written XHTML form. Within it, all <input> elements are nicely classed (e.g., elements with a type of text also have a class of text), and are contained within appropriate fieldsets with accurate labels. All of this is shown in Listing 8-1.

Listing 8-1. *A Simple XHTML Form That You'll Enhance with JavaScript*

```
<html>
<head>
    <title>Simple Form</title>
</head>
```

```
<body>
<form action="" method="POST">
    <fieldset class="login">
       <legend>Login Information</legend>
       <label for="username" class="hover">Username</label>
       <input type="text" id="username" class="required text"/>

       <label for="password" class="hover">Password</label>
       <input type="password" id="password" class="required text"/>
    </fieldset>
    <fieldset>
        <legend>Personal Information</legend>

        <label for="name">Name</label>
        <input type="text" id="name" class="required text"/><br/>

        <label for="email">Email</label>
        <input type="text" id="email" class="required email text"/><br/>

        <label for="date">Date</label>
        <input type="text" id="date" class="required date text"/><br/>

        <label for="url">Website</label>
        <input type="text" id="url" class="url text" value="http://"/><br/>

        <label for="phone">Phone</label>
        <input type="text" id="phone" class="phone text"/><br/>

        <label for="age">Over 13?</label>
        <input type="checkbox" id="age" name="age" value="yes"/><br/>

        <input type="submit" value="Submit Form" class="submit"/>
    </fieldset>
</form>
</body>
</html>
```

The next step is to apply some basic CSS styling to your form to make it look more presentable. This will help you, in the upcoming sections of this chapter, to display error messages and feedback in a presentable manner. The CSS used on the form is shown in Listing 8-2.

Listing 8-2. *The CSS Styles Used to Improve the Visual Quality of Your Form*

```css
form {
    font-family: Arial;
    font-size: 14px;
    width: 300px;
}

fieldset {
    border: 1px solid #CCC;
    margin-bottom: 10px;
}

fieldset.login input {
    width: 125px;
}

legend {
    font-weight: bold;
    font-size: 1.1em;
}

label {
    display: block;
    width: 60px;
    text-align: right;
    float: left;
    padding-right: 10px;
    margin: 5px 0;
}

input {
    margin: 5px 0;
}

input.text {
    padding: 0 0 0 3px;
    width: 172px;
}

input.submit {
    margin: 15px 0 0 70px;
}
```

The screenshot in Figure 8-1 will give you a sense of what your form (ready for layers of JavaScript behavior) looks like.

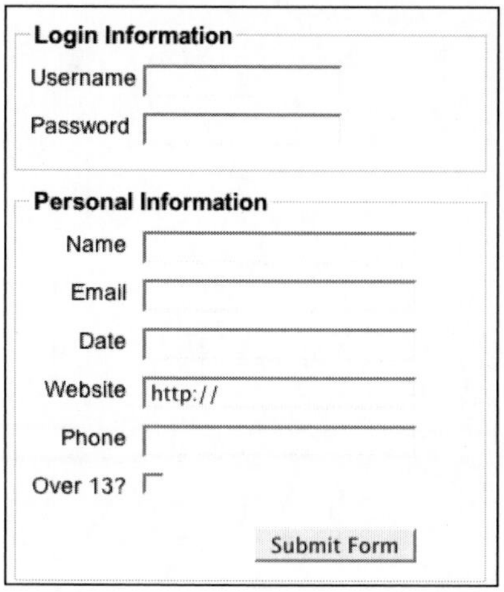

Figure 8-1. *A screenshot of the styled form that you'll be adding JavaScript behavior to*

Now that you have a nicely styled form, you should begin looking at the issue of client-side form validation more in depth. There are a number of different validation techniques that are often employed on forms. All of the techniques revolve around making sure that the data entered into the form by the user is what the server-side software is expecting.

The primary advantage of providing client-side validation is that users will have virtually instantaneous feedback concerning their input, which can only help to improve the overall experience of entering information into the form. It should be clearly stated that just because you choose to implement client-side form validation, it doesn't mean that you should remove or ignore server-side validation. You should continue to test all of your forms with JavaScript turned off, making sure that users who don't have JavaScript enabled continue to have a usable experience.

In this section you're going to look at the specific code needed to validate a number of different input elements, making sure that they contain the specific data that is required by the form. Each of these validation routines may not mean much individually, but when combined they can provide a full validation and testing suite, which you'll see in the next section.

Required Fields

Possibly the most important field validation that can be performed is that of a field being *required* (meaning that an entry must be made by the user). Generally, this requirement can be reduced to a check that verifies that a field is not blank. Sometimes, however, a field may have a default value entered into it; this means that you also need to have a check that is aware of that possibility and make sure that the user at least changes any default data provided by the field. These two checks cover the majority of form fields, including <input type="text">, <select>, and <textarea>s.

However, a problem occurs when you attempt to see whether the user has modified required check boxes or radio buttons. To circumvent this issue you need to find all fields that have the same name (which is how field elements are clustered together), then check to see whether the user has checked any of them.

An example of checking for required fields is shown in Listing 8-3.

Listing 8-3. *Checking Whether a Required Field Has Been Modified (Including Check Boxes and Radio Buttons)*

```
// A generic function for checking to see if an input element has
// had information entered into it
function checkRequired( elem ) {
    if ( elem.type == "checkbox" || elem.type == "radio" )
        return getInputsByName( elem.name ).numChecked;
    else
        return elem.value.length > 0 && elem.value != elem.defaultValue;
}


// Find all input elements that have a specified name (good for finding
// and dealing with checkboxes or radio buttons)
function getInputsByName( name ) {
    // The array of input elements that will be matched
    var results = [];
    // Keep track of how many of them were checked
    results.numChecked = 0;

    // Find all the input elements in the document
    var input = document.getElementsByTagName("input");
    for ( var i = 0; i < input.length; i++ ) {
        // Find all the fields that have the specified name
        if ( input[i].name == name ) {
            // Save the result, to be returned later
            results.push( input[i] );

            // Remember how many of the fields were checked
            if ( input[i].checked )
                results.numChecked++;
        }
    }

    // Return the set of matched fields
    return results;
}
```

```
// Wait for the document to finish loading
window.onload = function()
    // Get the form and watch for a submit attempt.
    document.getElementsByTagName("form")[0].onsubmit = function(){

        // Get an input element to check
        var elem = document.getElementById("age");

        // Make sure that the required age field has been checked
        if ( ! checkRequired( elem ) ) {
            // Display an error and keep the form from submitting.
            alert( "Required field is empty - " +
                "you must be over 13 to use this site." );
            return false;
        }

        // Get an input element to check
        var elem = document.getElementById("name");

        // Make sure that some text has been entered into the name field
        if ( ! checkRequired( elem ) ) {
          // Otherwise display an error and keep the form from submitting
          alert( "Required field is empty - please provide your  name." );
          return false;
        }

    };
};
```

With required field checking handled, you need to make sure that the contents of the fields contain the values that you expect them to have. In the next section, you're going to see how to verify the contents of fields.

Pattern Matching

The secondary component to validating most input elements (especially those that are text fields) is that of *pattern matching*, verifying that the contents of the fields are what they're supposed to be.

An important point to realize when using the following techniques is that your field requirements should be explicitly and clearly defined; otherwise, you might end up with a number of confused users who are baffled by what it is that you're requiring. A good example of this requirement is asking for dates in a specific format, as date formats change from culture to culture and even from specification to specification.

In this section you're going to see a number of different techniques that can be used to verify the contents of fields, including e-mail addresses, URLs, phone numbers, and dates.

E-mail

Asking for an e-mail address is an incredibly common field to have in a web form, as it's a near ubiquitous form of identification and communication. But doing a true check for the validity of an e-mail address (according to the specification that it's based upon) is incredibly complicated. You can instead provide a simple check that will work for all instances that you could encounter. Listing 8-4 shows an example of checking an input field to see whether it contains an e-mail address.

Listing 8-4. *Checking Whether a Specific Input Element Has an E-mail Address in It*

```
// A generic function for checking to see if an input element
// looks like an email address
function checkEmail( elem ) {
    // Make sure that something was entered and that it looks like
    // a valid email address
    return elem.value == '' ||
        /^[a-z0-9_+.-]+\@([a-z0-9-]+\.)+[a-z0-9]{2,4}$/i.test( elem.value );
}

// Get an input element to check
var elem = document.getElementById("email");

// Check to see if the field is valid, or not
if ( ! checkEmail( elem ) ) {
    alert( "Field is not an email address." );
}
```

URL

A common request on most comment entry forms (and other networking areas) is to ask for a user's web site in the form of a URL. URLs are another example (along with e-mail addresses) of where it's quite difficult to fully implement the specification that defines them. However, this is another case where what you need is actually a small subset of the full specification. In reality, you only need http or https-based web addresses (if you need something different, it's easy enough to change). Additionally, it's rather common for a URL field to start with the string http://, so you need to be sure to take that into account when checking the form. An example of checking the validity of URLs in forms is shown in Listing 8-5.

Listing 8-5. *Checking Whether an Input Element Has a URL in It*

```
// A generic function for checking to see if an input element has
// a  URL contained in it
function checkURL( elem ) {
```

```
    // Make sure that some text was entered, and that it's
    // not the default http:// text
    return elem.value == '' || !elem.value == 'http://' ||
        // Make sure that it looks like a valid URL
        /^https?:\/\/([a-z0-9-]+\.)+[a-z0-9]{2,4}.*$/.test( elem.value );
}

// Get an input element to check
var elem = document.getElementById("url");

// Check to see if the field is a valid URL
if ( ! checkURL( elem ) ) {
    alert( "Field does not contain a URL." );
}
```

Phone Number

You're now going to take a look at two different fields that differ based on your locale: phone numbers and dates. For simplicity, I'll use U.S.-centric phone numbers (and dates); changing them to be applicable to another country isn't entirely difficult.

With that in mind, you're going to try something different with the phone number field. Phone numbers can be written in a number of different ways, so you'll want to allow for these (e.g., 123-456-7890, or (123) 456-7890).

You're going to not only validate the phone number but you're going to force it into a specific format. You do this with an incredibly generic search against the value of the phone number field to simply see if it has two clusters of three numbers and one cluster of four numbers, ignoring any additional formatting that the user wraps around it.

The code to perform this validation and forced-value check is shown in Listing 8-6.

Listing 8-6. *Checking Whether a Field Contains a Phone Number*

```
// A generic function for checking to see if an input element has
// a Phone Number entered in it
function checkPhone( elem ) {
    // Check to see if we have something that looks like
    // a valid phone number
    var m = /(\d{3}).*(\d{3}).*(\d{4})/.exec( elem.value );

    // If it is, seemingly, valid - force it into the specific
    // format that we desire: (123) 456-7890
    if ( m !== null )
        elem.value = "(" + m[1] + ") " + m[2] + "-" + m[3];

    return elem.value == '' || m !== null;
}
```

```
// Get an input element to check
var elem = document.getElementById("phone");

// Check to see if the field contains a valid phone number
if ( ! checkPhone( elem ) ) {
    alert( "Field does not contain a phone number." );
}
```

Date

The final piece that you're going to look at is the validation of dates. Again, you're going to look at a U.S.-centric style of writing dates (MM/DD/YYYY). As with phone numbers or other internationally different fields, the validation regular expression can be easily tweaked to fit your nationality, if need be. With the particular validation function, shown in Listing 8-7, you perform a simple check to verify the contents of the date field.

Listing 8-7. *Checking Whether a Field Has a Date in It*

```
// A generic function for checking to see if an input element has
// a date entered into it
function checkDate( elem ) {
    // Make sure that something is entered, and that it
    // looks like a valid MM/DD/YYYY date
    return !elem.value || /^\d{2}\/\d{2}\/\d{2,4}$/.test(elem.value);
}

// Get an input element to check
var elem = document.getElementById("date");

// Check to see if the field contains a valid date
if ( ! checkDate( elem ) ) {
    alert( "Field is not a date." );
}
```

Rule Set

Using the different validation functions from the previous section, you can now build a generic structure for dealing with all the different validation techniques. It's important that all the tests be handled identically with common names and semantic error messages. The complete rule set data structure can be found in Listing 8-8.

Listing 8-8. *A Standard Set of Rules and Descriptive Error Messages for Building a Basic Validation Engine*

```
var errMsg = {
    // Checks for when a specified field is required
    required: {
        msg: "This field is required.",
        test: function(obj,load) {
            // Make sure that there is no text was entered in the field and that
            // we aren't checking on page load (showing 'field required' messages
            // would be annoying on page load)
            return obj.value.length > 0 || load || obj.value == obj.defaultValue;
        }
    },

    // Makes sure that the field s a valid email address
    email: {
        msg: "Not a valid email address.",
        test: function(obj) {
            // Make sure that something was entered and that it looks like
            // an email address
            return !obj.value ||
                /^[a-z0-9_+.-]+\@([a-z0-9-]+\.)+[a-z0-9]{2,4}$/i.test( obj.value );
        }
    },

    // Makes sure the field is a phone number and
    // auto-formats the number if it is one
    phone: {
        msg: "Not a valid phone number.",
        test: function(obj) {
            // Check to see if we have something that looks like
            // a valid phone number
            var m = /(\d{3}).*(\d{3}).*(\d{4})/.exec( obj.value );

            // If it is, seemingly, valid - force it into the specific
            // format that we desire: (123) 456-7890
            if ( m ) obj.value = "(" + m[1] + ") " + m[2] + "-" + m[3];

            return !obj.value || m;
        }
    },
```

```
    // Makes sure that the field is a valid MM/DD/YYYY date
    date: {
        msg: "Not a valid date.",
        test: function(obj) {
            // Make sure that something is entered, and that it
            // looks like a valid MM/DD/YYYY date
            return !obj.value || /^\d{2}\/\d{2}\/\d{2,4}$/.test(obj.value);
        }
    },

    // Makes sure that the field is a valid URL
    url: {
        msg: "Not a valid URL.",
        test: function(obj) {
            // Make sure that some text was entered, and that it's
            // not the default http:// text
                return !obj.value || obj.value == 'http://' ||
                    // Make sure that it looks like a valid URL
                    /^https?:\/\/([a-z0-9-]+\.)+[a-z0-9]{2,4}.*$/.test( obj.value );
        }
    }
};
```

Using this new rule set data structure you can now write a common, consistent means of form validation and a display of error messages, which I discuss in the next section.

Displaying Error Messages

While the process of form validation isn't *too* difficult to achieve, displaying contextual error messages that can help the user better complete the form is often challenging. You're going to use what you built in the previous section to create a full system of validation and message display. You're going to look at how form validation and message displaying take place and when they should occur so that they are most understandable to the user.

Validation

With the new data structure you can build a consistent, extensible pair of functions that can be used to validate a form or a single field and display a contextual error message based upon it.

To achieve the goal of dynamic form validation there are a couple of techniques. The first one that's provided by browsers is part of the HTML DOM specification. All <form> elements (in the DOM) have an additional property called *elements*. This property contains an array of all the fields within the form, which makes it incredibly easy to traverse through all the possible fields to check for input errors.

The second important aspect is to include additional classes on all of the fields to trigger the different validation rules. For example, having a class of *required* will make the input field require some form of input. Each of the classes should match those provided by the rule set shown in Listing 8-8.

Using these two techniques you can now build two generic functions for validating entire forms and individual fields (both of which you'll need for a fully functional validation scenario). These two functions are shown in Listing 8-9.

Listing 8-9. *Functions for Performing Form Validation and Triggering the Display of Error Messages*

```
// A function for validating all fields within a form.
// The form argument should be a reference to a form element
// The load argument should be a boolean referring to the fact that
// the validation function is being run on page load, versus dynamically
function validateForm( form, load ) {
    var valid = true;

    // Go through all the field elements in form
    // form.elements is an array of all fields in a form
    for ( var i = 0; i < form.elements.length; i++ ) {

        // Hide any error messages, if they're being shown
        hideErrors( form.elements[i] );

        // Check to see if the field contains valid contents, or not
        if ( ! validateField( form.elements[i], load ) )
            valid = false;

    }

    // Return false if a field does not have valid contents
    // true if all fields are valid
    return valid;
}

// Validate a single field's contents
function validateField( elem, load ) {
    var errors = [];

    // Go through all the possible validation techniques
    for ( var name in errMsg ) {
        // See if the field has the class specified by the error type
        var re = new RegExp("(^|\\s)" + name + "(\\s|$)");
```

```
    // Check to see if  the element has the class and that it passes the
    // validation test
    if ( re.test( elem.className ) && !errMsg[name].test( elem, load ) )
        // If it fails the validation, add the error message to list
        errors.push( errMsg[name].msg );
}

// Show the error messages, if they exist
if ( errors.length )
    showErrors( elem, errors );

// Return false if the field fails any of the validation routines
return errors.length > 0;
}
```

As you probably noticed in the previous code there are two missing functions, both of which relate to the hiding and showing of validation error messages. Depending on how you want to display error messages you'll probably want to customize these functions some. For this particular form I decided to display the error messages inside the form itself, just after each of the fields. The two functions needed to handle this are shown in Listing 8-10.

Listing 8-10. *Functions for Showing and Hiding Validation Error Messages Against a Specific Form Field*

```
// Hide any validation error messages that are currently shown
function hideErrors( elem ) {
    // Find the next element after the current field
    var next = elem.nextSibling;

    // If the next element is a ul and has a class of errors
    if ( next && next.nodeName == "UL" && next.className == "errors" )
        // Remove it (which is our means of  'hiding')
        elem.parenttNode.removeChild( next );
}

// Show a set of errors messages for a specific field within a form
function showErrors( elem, errors ) {
    // Find the next element after the field
    var next = elem.nextSibling;

    // If the field isn't one of our special error-holders.
    if ( next && ( next.nodeName != "UL" || next.className != "errors" ) ) {
        // We need to make one instead
        next = document.createElement( "ul" );
        next.className = "errors";
```

```
    // and then insert into the correct place in the DOM
    elem.paretNode.insertBefore( next, elem.nextSibling );
}

// Now that we have a reference to the error holder UL
// We then loop through all the error messages
for ( var i = 0; i < errors.length; i++ ) {
    // Create a new li wrapper for each
    var li = document.createElement( "li" );
    li.innerHTML = errors[i];

    // and insert it into the DOM
    next.appendChild( li );
}
}
```

Now that you have all the JavaScript code out of the way, the only step left is to add some additional styling to the error messages to make it look nice. The CSS code to do this is shown in Listing 8-11.

Listing 8-11. *The Extra CSS Used to Make the Validation Error Messages Look Reasonable*

```
ul.errors {
    list-style: none;
    background: #FFCECE;
    padding: 3px;
    margin: 3px 0 3px 70px;
    font-size: 0.9em;
    width: 165px;
}
```

Finally, now that all the pieces have come together, you can see in Figure 8-2 the final result of your JavaScript and styling (once you hook in with the event watchers explained in the next section).

Now that you know exactly how to validate a form (and the fields that are contained within it) and display error messages based upon any failed validations, you need to determine when you should run your validation routines. It is not always best that all fields are validated simultaneously; it is often better that they are done incrementally. I discuss the benefits of all the different times at which validation is appropriate in the next section.

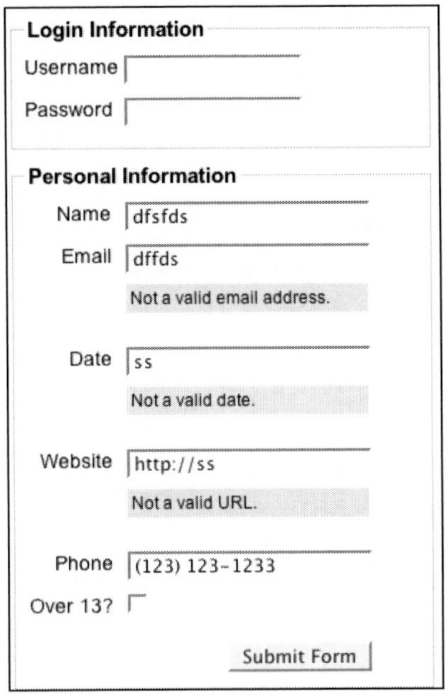

Figure 8-2. *An example of valid and invalid input in your newly styled and scripted form*

When to Validate

One of the most troublesome aspects of form validation is determining when it's appropriate to show error messages. There are three different times that a form (or a field) can be validated: on form submission, on field change, and on page load. Each has its own unique advantages and disadvantages, which I'll discuss individually. Using the functions developed in the previous section, this process is made simple and easy to understand.

Validating Upon Form Submission

Validating upon form submission is the most common technique, simply due to the fact that it's what's most similar to normal form validation techniques. In order to watch for a form submission you must bind an event handler that waits until the user has finished the form and has clicked the Submit button (or hit the Enter key). It is not a prerequisite that all fields have something entered into them by the user; however, once the form is submitted it is checked against all the rules specified by the rule set. If any field fails any rule, the form will not be submitted, and the user will be forced to deal with each of the error messages presented to him or her (this is done by preventing the default action with the submit event handler). The code necessary to implement this technique is shown in Listing 8-12.

Listing 8-12. *Waiting Until a Form Is Submitted to Run the Form Validation Function*

```
function watchForm( form ) {
    // Watch the form for submission
    addEvent( form, 'submit', function(){

        // make sure that the form's contents validate correctly
        return validateForm( form );

    });
}

// Find the first form on the page
var form = document.getElementsByTagName( "form" )[0];

// and watch for when its submitted, to validate it
watchForm( form );
```

Validating Upon Field Changes

Another technique that can be used for form validation is watching for changes within individual form fields. This could be accomplished using a keypress event; however, this leads to undesired results. Having error-checking occur every time a key is pressed within a field can be very confusing for users. They may begin to enter their e-mail address (for example) and see an error stating that their address is incorrect. However, this may not be the case, as they're still typing it in to the field. In general, this practice is discouraged, as it provides a bad user experience.

The second way of watching for field changes is to wait until the user has left the field (hopefully after having entered all their information). Doing validation in this manner provides a much smoother user experience, as the user is given ample opportunity to enter all the information that he or she desires, while still being provided with faster validation error messages.

An example of an implementation of this technique is shown in Listing 8-13.

Listing 8-13. *Watching Fields for a Change Before Running Any Field Validation Functions*

```
function watchFields( form ) {
    // Go through all the field elements in form
    for ( var i = 0; i < form.elements.length; i++ ) {

        // and attach a 'change' event handler (which watches for a user
        // to lose focus of an input element)
        addEvent( form.elements[i], 'change', function(){
            // Once the focus has been lost, re-validate the field
            return validateField( this );
        });
```

```
    }
}

// Locate the first form on the page
var form = document.getElementsByTagName( "form" )[0];

// Watch all the fields in the form for changes
watchFields( form );
```

Validating Upon Page Load

Validating forms on page load isn't as necessary as the previous two techniques but is important to include if you wish to catch an important fringe case. If a user enters information into
a form and reloads the browser window (or if user information is prepopulated into a form by
the browser or the application itself), it is possible that errors can occur within this prepopulated information. This particular technique is designed to run a validation upon the form
whenever the page loads, to validate the quality of data that's already been entered into it.
This gives the user the opportunity to deal with the errors immediately, rather than waiting
for the final form submission check of the data.

An example of the code required to enable page load form validation is shown in
Listing 8-14.

Listing 8-14. *Performing Form Validation Upon Page Load*

```
addEvent( window, "load", function() {
    // Find all the forms on the page
    var forms = document.getElementsByTagName("form");

    // Go through all the forms on the page
    for ( var i = 0; i < forms.length; i++ ) {

        // Validate each of the forms, being sure to set the 'load' argument to
        // true, which stops certain, unnecessary, errors from appearing
        validateForm( forms[i], true );

    }
});
```

Having gone through all the different forms of validation, the ways of displaying error
messages, and even looking at when to properly validate a form, you've reached a noble goal:
completing client-side form validation. With this out of the way, you can now explore a couple
additional techniques that can be used to improve the usability of forms and specific field
types in general.

Usability Improvements

With forms being one of the most commonly used elements of web pages, improving their usability can only benefit the user. In this section I'm going to walk you through two different common techniques that are frequently used to improve the overall usability of forms.

Additionally, this is another opportunity for you to try using a JavaScript library to simplify the tedious DOM traversing and modification necessary to add the usability improvements. For both of these particular techniques I chose to use the jQuery JavaScript library (http://jquery.com/), which is particularly good at both DOM traversing and modification.

Hover Labels

The first usability improvement that I'm going to discuss is that of positioning (*hovering*) labels on top of their associated field and hiding them when their field is focused upon. The purpose of this particular technique is twofold. It is expressed clearly to the user what it is that's supposed to be entered into the specific field (since what's supposed to be entered into it is written right on top of it). Secondly, it helps to decrease the total amount of space required by a field and its associated label.

In your original form, you're going to add these new hover labels to both the username and password fields, creating a result that looks like Figure 8-3.

Figure 8-3. *Using hover labels on the username and password fields*

The JavaScript code needed to achieve this particular effect is (comparatively) complex. There are a lot of little details that go into it to make it work seamlessly. Let's look at a couple of the details necessary to achieve the final result.

First, in order to position the label on top of the input element itself, you must first wrap both the label and the input element in a wrapper div. This div is used so that you can position the label absolutely on top of the field.

Second, you must make it so that every time the field receives or loses focus that you hide (or show) the label appropriately. Additionally, when the user moves away from the field you need to check to see if the field has a value in it; if so, you must not reveal the label again.

Finally, you need to be sure not to reveal the label if a value is in the field by default (otherwise, you'll have something of a jumbled text mess).

With all of these aspects in mind, let's look at the code needed to achieve the result of hover labels within a form, as shown in Listing 8-15.

Listing 8-15. *Hover Labels Appearing Over Fields Using the jQuery JavaScript Library*

```
// Find all input elements that are after labels that have a class of hover
$("label.hover+input")

    // Wrap a div (with a class of hover-wrap) around the input element,
    // resulting in HTML that looks like:
    // <div class='hover-wrap'><input type="text" …/></div>
    .wrap("<div class='hover-wrap'></div>")

    // Whenever the input element is focused upon (either through a click
    // or by keyboard), hide the label
    .focus(function(){
        $(this).prev().hide();
    })

    // Whenever the user has left the input element (and no text has been
    //  entered into it) reveal the label again.
    .blur(function(){
        if ( !this.value ) $(this).prev().show()
    })

    // Go through each of the input elements individually
    .each(function(){
        // Move the label to go inside of the <div class='hover-wrap'></div>
        $(this).before( $(this).parent().prev() );

        // Make sure that if a value is already in the form, that the label is
        //  automatically hidden
        if ( this.value ) $(this).prev().hide();
    });
```

The JavaScript alone is not enough to achieve the desired result, however. You still need to be sure to include the additional CSS styling necessary to place the labels and fields in their correct positions. This code is shown in Listing 8-16.

Listing 8-16. *CSS Styling to Make Labels Display on Top of Their Associated Fields*

```
div.hover-wrap {
    position: relative;
    display: inline;
}
```

```
div.hover-wrap input.invalid {
    border: 2px solid red;
}

div.hover-wrap ul.errors {
    display: none;
}

div.hover-wrap label.hover {
    position: absolute;
    top: -0.7em;
    left: 5px;
    color: #666;
}
```

Without too much fuss, you've created a very useful field usability improvement. Using this particular technique you can save space on the screen while still giving the user appropriate direction—a win-win situation.

Marking Required Fields

The second technique that you're going to look at is that of marking required fields with a visual cue. Marking required fields with a red star is a common technique that most web developers have adopted on their web sites. However, the additional markup necessary to include these stars is rather unsemantic and should be discouraged. Instead, this is a perfect opportunity to use JavaScript to add in these visual cues. An example of this technique is shown in Figure 8-4.

Figure 8-4. *The result of adding contextual stars to required form fields*

One aspect of adding these cues to the required field labels is the addition of specific helper text to guide the user. Using the title attribute you could provide users with a message explaining exactly what the red star means (in case they are unfamiliar with it). All told, the implementation of this improvement is rather simple and is shown in Listing 8-17.

Listing 8-17. *Adding Contextual Stars (*) and Help Messages to Required Form Field Labels Using the jQuery JavaScript Library*

```
// Find all input fields that have been marked as required
$("input.required")
    // then locate the previous label
    .prev("label")

    // Change the cursor, over the label, to being more helpful
    .css("cursor", "help")

    // Make it so that when the user hovers their mouse over, a description
    // of the * is explained
    .title( errMsg.required )

    // Finally, add a * at the end of the label, to signify
    // the field as being required
    .append(" <span class='required'>*</span>");
```

To get the styling just right you need to add the additional red coloring to the new cue, which is shown in Listing 8-18.

Listing 8-18. *Additional CSS for Styling the **

```
label span.required {
    color: red;
}
```

Together the addition of visual cues and the use of hover labels are a powerful usability improvement that can be achieved using JavaScript in an unobtrusive but useful sense. Within your specific applications, I'm sure you'll find a number of instances where the usability of forms and fields can be improved using simple JavaScript.

Summary

Having shown you a number of aspects that bog down the use of forms in web applications, I hope you feel better knowing that with some simple JavaScript additions to your site the overall usability of your forms will generally be improved. An example of what you achieved in this chapter is shown in Figure 8-5.

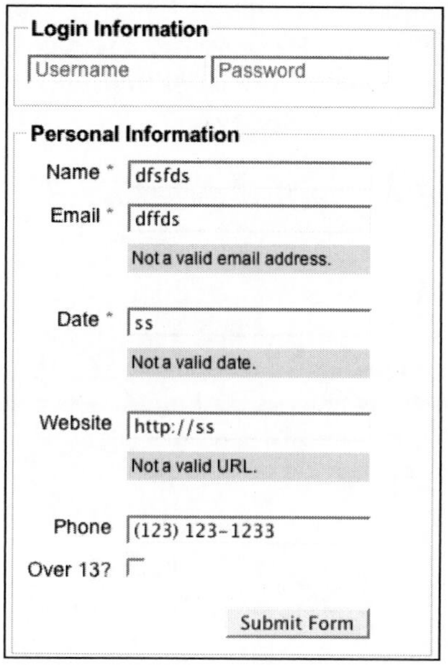

Figure 8-5. *The final JavaScript-improved form*

In this chapter you first saw how the most accurate client-side validation can be achieved while providing the best experience to the user. This is done by building a set of validation rules, validating the form fields at appropriate times, and displaying helpful error messages to the user. You also saw a couple techniques for improving the usability of forms by hovering labels and marking required fields.

I hope all the techniques presented, taken together, can be of much use to you in the upcoming forms that you develop.

CHAPTER 9

■ ■ ■

Building an Image Gallery

Acommon use of DOM manipulation, traversing, and dynamic CSS manipulation is to create a more responsive experience for the web site end user. One application that benefits from this particular advantage is that of an image gallery (for viewing and browsing images). As browsers have improved in quality, so have dynamic scripts and utilities. Recently, these improvements have lead to a number of high-quality image galleries being released.

In this chapter you will take a look at a couple of these image galleries and see what makes them particularly unique, and then build your own image gallery using dynamic, unobtrusive JavaScript. There are a number of issues that you'll look at, surrounding the design and implementation of the gallery in detail. The final result will be a powerful image gallery script that can be easily dropped into any web site. Additionally, this is a great time to utilize all the functions that you developed in Chapters 5 and 7 on the DOM and JavaScript and CSS, working together to make a seamless and understandable piece of code.

Example Galleries

There have been a number of excellent, modern image gallery scripts released that are visually impressive, easy to use, and completely unobtrusive. The two scripts that we're going to look at in particular both create very similar visual effects while using different libraries as code bases.

The following summarizes how the two example galleries behave:

- When an image in the image gallery is clicked, an image gallery overlay is displayed instead of directing the user to the actual image.

- When the image gallery overlay is displayed, a transparent gray overlay is placed on top of the page (dimming everything beneath it).

- The image gallery overlay has some form of a caption for the currently displayed image.

- There is some way to navigate from image to image within the gallery.

The specific galleries that you're going to see in this section are Lightbox and ThickBox, two very popular libraries.

Lightbox

Lightbox is the first of the "new style" DOM image galleries. Its release has spurred the development of a number of other similar-style image galleries, creating the basis for this chapter.

This particular gallery was developed from scratch (using no particular base JavaScript library). However, it has since been adapted to use a number of different libraries instead (cutting down on its overall code size). More information about the script can be found at `http://www.huddletogether.com/projects/lightbox/` and `http://particletree.com/features/lightbox-gone-wild/`, which provides information about Lightbox using the Prototype JavaScript library.

Figure 9-1 shows a sample screenshot of the Lightbox gallery in action, with its unique transparent overlay and centralized image.

Figure 9-1. *Lightbox displaying a single image within a gallery of images*

Lightbox operates in a completely unobtrusive manner. In order to use it, you simply include the script in the head of your HTML file, modify the HTML of the images that you wish to display using Lightbox, and the code does the rest:

```
<a href="images/image-1.jpg" rel="lightbox" title="my caption">image #1</a>
```

Unfortunately, the unobtrusive nature of the code isn't as perfect as it could be (it waits until all the images on the page are loaded, as opposed to when the DOM is ready). However, the DOM scripting used by it (as shown in Listing 9-1) is perfectly applicable and reasonable.

Listing 9-1. *Locating All Lightbox Anchor Elements and Converting Them to Display Correctly*

```
// Locate all anchor tags on the page
var anchors = document.getElementsByTagName("a");

// Loop through all anchor tags
for ( var i=0; i < anchors.length; i++ ) {
    var anchor = anchors[i];

    // Make sure that the link is a "lightbox" link
    if ( anchor.href && anchor.rel == "lightbox" ) {

        // Make it so that a Lightbox is shown on click
        anchor.onclick = function () {
            showLightbox(this);
            return false;
        };

    }
}
```

Lightbox has evolved gradually as new users have given feedback, adding features, such as keyboard navigation and animations. However, at its simplest core, Lightbox provides plenty of inspiration for building your own similar image gallery.

ThickBox

The second image gallery that I'd like to show you is ThickBox, created by Cody Lindley using the jQuery JavaScript library. This particular implementation is very similar to Lightbox but is much smaller in size and supports the loading of external HTML files using Ajax. More information about the library can be found on its web site (http://codylindley.com/Javascript/ 257/thickbox-one-box-to-rule-them-all), along with a demo of it in action (http:// jquery.com/demo/thickbox/).

As you can see from the screenshot in Figure 9-2, the result of displaying images with ThickBox is very similar to that of Lightbox.

As with Lightbox, ThickBox uses an unobtrusive means of loading and executing itself. Simply by including the script inside the head of a web page, it will go through the DOM and find all the links that have a class of "thickbox," as shown in the following code:

```
<a href="ajaxLogin.htm?height=100&width=250" class="thickbox">ThickBox login</a>
```

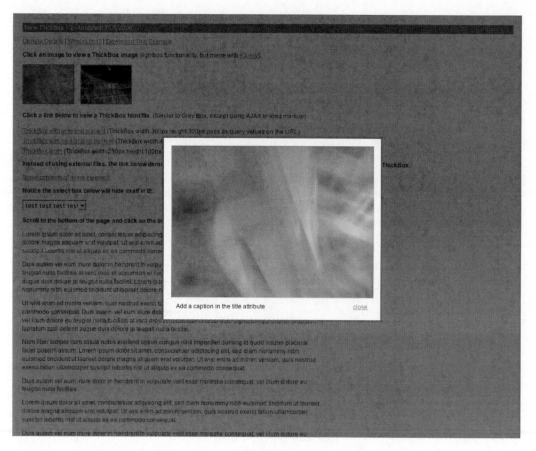

Figure 9-2. *ThickBox displaying a single image on top of the rest of the page*

Listing 9-2 shows the code that ThickBox uses to dynamically and unobtrusively apply its functionality whenever the DOM is ready (which will be before all the images on the page have loaded, allowing for a better user experience).

Listing 9-2. *Applying Functionality to All Anchor Elements That Have a Class of "thickbox"*

```
// Look for thickboxes when the DOM is ready
$(document).ready(function(){

    // add thickbox to href elements that have a class of .thickbox
    $("a.thickbox").click(function(){
        // Figure out the caption for the thickbox
        var t = this.title || this.name || this.href || null;

        // Display the thickbox
        TB_show(t,this.href);
```

```
        // Remove the focus from the link
        this.blur();

        // Make sure that the link doesn't work as normal
        return false;
    });

});
```

Due to the amount of extra features that ThickBox includes, along with its reduced code base, it is certainly a desirable alternative to Lightbox.

Next you're going to see how to build your own gallery clone, taking into account many of the intricacies necessary to build one correctly.

Building the Gallery

The first step to building an image gallery is to have a set of images through which you can traverse. I'm going to assume that there can be any number of galleries on a page and that every gallery can have any number of images within it. Additionally, it is very important that the images be displayed in a semantic and understandable manner before your JavaScript is ever executed. This helps to ensure that users who don't have JavaScript enabled (or who are lacking CSS support) still receive an acceptable user experience.

The basic HTML that you're going to use for your gallery is shown in Listing 9-3.

Listing 9-3. *The Basic HTML of a Page That Will Hold Your Gallery of Images*

```
<!DOCTYPE html PUBLIC "-//W3C//DTD XHTML 1.0 Transitional//EN"
        "http://www.w3.org/TR/xhtml1/DTD/xhtml1-transitional.dtd">
<html>
<head>
    <title>Random Cat Pictures</title>
</head>
<body>
    <h1>Random Cat Pictures</h1>

    <p>Lorem ipsum dolor . . . </p>

    <!--
        Our Gallery, it must be a <ul> with a class of
        "gallery" - and should have a title associated with it.
    --->
    <ul class="gallery" title="Random Cat Pictures">
```

```
<!--
    Each image of the gallery should be contained within an <li>
    and have a link pointing to the images actual location. If an image
    is tall, be sure to include the class "tall" with it too.
-->

<li><a href="image1.jpg"><img src="image1.jpg"
    alt="Fat Cat Sleeping"/></a></li>
<li><a href="image2.jpg"><img src="image2.jpg"
    alt="Sharing the Bed"/></a></li>
<li class="tall"><a href="image3.jpg"><img src="image3.jpg"
    alt="Out the Window"/></a></li>
<li class="tall"><a href="image4.jpg"><img src="image4.jpg"
    alt="In the Sun"/></a></li>
<li><a href="image5.jpg"><img src="image5.jpg"
    alt="Very Comfortable"/></a></li>

</ul>

<p>Lorem ipsum dolor . . . </p>
</body>
</html>
```

Second, you need to provide some additional styling to the image to create something that looks more presentable and navigable. The CSS to do so is shown in Listing 9-4.

Listing 9-4. *The CSS for Styling the Page Appropriately*

```
body {
    font-family: Arial;
    font-siz: 14px;
}

/* Include a nice box around the gallery of image. */
ul.gallery {
    list-style: none;
    padding: 5px;
    background: #EEE;
    overflow: auto;
    border: 1px solid #AAA;
    margin-top: 0px;
}
```

```
/* Create a standard-width and height box around all of the individual images. */
ul.gallery li {
    float: left;
    margin: 6px;
    width: 110px;
    height: 110px;
    background: #FFF;
    border: 2px solid #AAA;
}

/* Horizontal images are 100px wide */
ul.gallery img {
    width: 100px;
    margin: 5px;
    border: 0px;
    margin-top: 17px;
}

/* Vertical images are 100px tall */
ul.gallery li.tall img {
    height: 100px;
    width: auto;
    margin-top: 5px;
    margin-left: 17px;
}
```

Finally, the results of the basic HTML and CSS are shown in Figure 9-3.

With a basic HTML page setup, you're now ready to begin putting together the components that you need to make your beautiful JavaScript-powered image gallery.

luctus, massa vitae placerat rhoncus, neque mauris lobortis enim, id ullamcorper dui nunc et enim. Integer faucibus rhoncus elit. Vestibulum ut ante. Morbi a sem. Vivamus accumsan.

Maecenas bibendum tellus at ante. Maecenas pharetra volutpat mauris. Vivamus vulputate. Pellentesque nec pede. Pellentesque aliquet, tellus nec placerat bibendum, lacus augue mattis tellus, id iaculis enim augue ac sapien. Maecenas commodo ante quis tellus. Phasellus tempor, massa non malesuada cursus, tortor justo mollis diam, eget sagittis dolor ipsum at velit. Curabitur at pede eu magna sollicitudin accumsan. Duis quis velit nec justo condimentum aliquet. Mauris dignissim mi. Phasellus non mauris. Aliquam sagittis blandit magna.

Etiam quam. Sed nisi. Maecenas viverra pellentesque ante. Fusce vulputate porta metus. Maecenas turpis urna, porta vitae, tempor vel, dapibus vestibulum, felis. Pellentesque sit amet nisl. Curabitur blandit. Sed in nisl et neque condimentum lacinia. Morbi arcu dui, dignissim in, consectetuer quis, gravida ac, felis. Proin lacinia aliquet augue. Mauris nec odio. Vestibulum eu orci nec ligula consequat rhoncus. Phasellus nunc nunc, vulputate posuere, semper in, cursus nec, orci. Curabitur sem justo, ullamcorper vitae, adipiscing in, malesuada vel, elit. Maecenas eleifend, justo sed ornare consequat, sem ipsum pellentesque turpis, in rutrum orci neque sed massa. Vestibulum laoreet dui eget arcu. Quisque in lorem. Morbi quis lacus. Maecenas nonummy metus auctor nunc.

Lorem ipsum dolor sit amet, consectetuer adipiscing elit. Nullam at sem. Ut ultrices, dolor sit amet pharetra pretium, leo metus accumsan urna, eu ultrices purus augue at ligula. Nam gravida. Mauris neque lacus, vehicula et, hendrerit nec, semper quis, nibh. Nulla facilisi. Curabitur id ante. Proin felis ipsum, commodo non, hendrerit et, ultrices in, eros. Nulla tincidunt vulputate felis. Morbi convallis libero sed erat. Etiam lectus pede, dictum et, rutrum id, commodo nec, augue. Vestibulum massa. Fusce nec felis. Vivamus consectetuer elementum elit.

Etiam mattis egestas felis. Proin sed magna at orci aliquet mattis. Vivamus ligula metus, interdum quis, viverra nec, vehicula vitae, mauris. Pellentesque venenatis pede vel augue. Aliquam fringilla nunc eget eros. Pellentesque eget ipsum. Morbi augue. Praesent sit amet ipsum. Ut vitae sem et diam mattis imperdiet. Phasellus a pede. Suspendisse potenti. Maecenas in sapien sit amet urna ultrices dignissim. Duis aliquet faucibus odio. Nunc a turpis vitae sem porta viverra. Vestibulum convallis dignissim nisl. Fusce enim. Morbi quam. Praesent tortor. Suspendisse eu dolor. Ut tempus tortor in dui.

Aenean justo. Integer egestas pharetra quam. Nulla faucibus, mi vel mollis tempus, tortor libero fringilla odio, ac iaculis eros quam eget lorem. Pellentesque nec enim. Cras porta. Duis ornare libero vel risus. In hac habitasse platea dictumst. Quisque luctus, massa vitae placerat rhoncus, neque mauris lobortis enim, id ullamcorper dui nunc et enim. Integer faucibus rhoncus elit. Vestibulum ut ante. Morbi a sem. Vivamus accumsan.

Maecenas bibendum tellus at ante. Maecenas pharetra volutpat mauris. Vivamus vulputate. Pellentesque nec pede. Pellentesque aliquet, tellus nec placerat bibendum, lacus augue mattis tellus, id iaculis enim augue ac sapien. Maecenas commodo ante quis tellus. Phasellus tempor, massa non malesuada cursus, tortor justo mollis diam, eget sagittis dolor ipsum at velit. Curabitur at pede eu magna sollicitudin accumsan. Duis quis velit nec justo condimentum aliquet. Mauris dignissim mi. Phasellus non mauris. Aliquam sagittis blandit magna.

Figure 9-3. *A simply styled web page with images*

Loading Unobtrusively

One aspect that you should want your image gallery to embody is that of unobtrusive scripting. You don't want the users of the script to have to include any unnecessary (and unsemantic) HTML in their web pages simply for the sake of adding some additional eye candy. So you're going to start by injecting a number of HTML elements into the page's DOM once the page has finished loading. The code to do this is shown in Listing 9-5.

Listing 9-5. *Injecting the Initial HTML Into the DOM and Binding All the Required Event Handlers to Each of the Elements*

```
// Keep track of which image we're current looking at
var curImage = null;

// Wait for the document to finish loading before modifying
// or traversing the DOM
window.onload = function() {
    /*
     * Create the following DOM structure:
     * <div id="overlay"></div>
     * <div id="gallery">
     *     <div id="gallery_image"></div>
     *     <div id="gallery_prev"><a href="">&laquo; Prev</a></div>
     *     <div id="gallery_next"><a href="">Next &raquo;</a></div>
     *     <div id="gallery_title"></div>
     * </div>
     */

    // Create the overall gallery holder
    var gallery = document.createElement("div");
    gallery.id = "gallery";

    // And add in all the organization divs
    gallery.innerHTML = '<div id="gallery_image"></div>' +
        '<div id="gallery_prev"><a href="">&laquo; Prev</a></div>' +
        '<div id="gallery_next"><a href="">Next &raquo;</a></div>' +
        '<div id="gallery_title"></div>';

    // Add the gallery into the DOM
    document.body.appendChild( gallery );

    // Handle support for which the next and previous links
    // are clicked within the gallery
    id("gallery_next").onclick = nextImage;
    id("gallery_prev").onclick = prevImage;

    // Locate all the galleries on the page
    var g = byClass( "gallery", "ul" );

    // Go through all of the galleries
    for ( var i = 0; i < g.length; i++ ) {
        // And locate all the links to the slideshow images
        var link = tag( "a", g[i] );
```

```
        // Go through each of the image links
        for ( var j = 0; j < link.length; j++ ) {
            // Make it such that, when clicked, they display the
            // image gallery instead of going to the imagae
            link[j].onclick = function(){
                // Show the gray background
                showOverlay();

                // Show the image, in the gallery
                showImage( this.parentNode );

                // Make sure that the browser doesn't go the
                // image, like it normally would
                return false;
            };
        }

        // Add the slideshow navigation to the gallery
        addSlideShow( g[i] );
    }
};
```

With that important step taken care of, you can begin building the various components of the image gallery itself.

Transparent Overlay

The first item that you're going to build is the dark transparent overlay that is used in both Lightbox and ThickBox. You're going to find that for the most part this is a simple task, with only one tricky aspect: making the transparent overlay match the height and width of the current page. Luckily, you developed the functions that you need to achieve this back in Chapter 7: pageWidth() and pageHeight().

You're going to begin by creating a simple div element with an ID attribute (so that you can access it later) and adding it to the DOM. This is shown in Listing 9-6.

Listing 9-6. *Creating a Simple div Element and Adding It to the DOM*

```
// Create the transparent, gray, overlay
var overlay = document.createElement("div");
overlay.id = "overlay";

// Make it so that when the gray background is clicked,
// the gallery and background are hidden
overlay.onclick = hideOverlay;

// Add the overlay into the DOM
document.body.appendChild( overlay );
```

Next, you need to create the two functions necessary for hiding and revealing the overlay. This is where the tricky part comes in. The hiding and showing process is rather trivial, but finding the correct width and height of the overlay is not. Normally, it would be OK to only size the overlay with a height and width of 100%, but this is not possible, as the user may scroll down the page while the gallery is shown (causing the overlay to slip away). The fix for this is to make the overlay the exact height and width as the page itself. You can use the pageHeight() and pageWidth() functions that you made in Chapter 7 to find those numbers.

The complete code for hiding and showing the overlay is shown in Listing 9-7.

Listing 9-7. *Two Functions Necessary for Hiding and Showing the Image Gallery Transparent Overlay*

```
// Hide the gray overlay and the current gallery
function hideOverlay() {
    // Make sure that we reset the current image
    curImage = null;

    // and hide the overlay and gallery
    hide( id("overlay") );
    hide( id("gallery") );
}

// Show the gray overlay
function showOverlay() {
    // Find the overlay
    var over = id("overlay");

    // Make it as tall and wide as the entire page
    // (this helps with scrolling)
    over.style.height = pageHeight() + "px";
    over.style.width = pageWidth() + "px";

    // And fade it in
    fadeIn( over, 50, 10 );
}
```

Finally, let's pull together the CSS necessary to display the transparent overlay correctly. The code to do so is shown in Listing 9-8.

Listing 9-8. *The CSS Necessary to Display the Transparent Overlay Correctly*

```
#overlay {
    background: #000;
    opacity: 0.5;
    display: none;
    position: absolute;
```

```
        top: 0px;
        left: 0px;
        width: 100%;
        height: 100%;
        z-index: 100;
        cursor: pointer;
        cursor: hand;
    }
```

Together, the injected HTML and CSS will look something like what's shown in Figure 9-4.

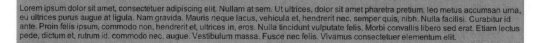

Figure 9-4. *The result of displaying a transparent overlay on top of a page*

With the overlay constructed and injected into the page, you're ready to begin working to display the image on top of it.

Positioned Box

The component of the image gallery that you need to build is the container that will be floated above the transparent overlay, holding the current image. Unfortunately, due to poor CSS 2 support in some modern browsers, this step is inappropriately difficult to complete. With proper CSS support, the image would simply have a fixed position (thus creating the illusion of being positioned on top of everything, regardless of where on the page you're currently scrolled).

You're going to start out by assuming that you have a DOM structure, like the one shown in Listing 9-9, already in the page (you added this into the page in Listing 9-5).

Listing 9-9. *HTML for Displaying a Positioned Image Gallery Above a Transparent Overlay*

```
<div id="gallery">
    <div id="gallery_image"></div>
    <div id="gallery_prev"><a href="">&laquo; Prev</a></div>
    <div id="gallery_next"><a href="">Next &raquo;</a></div>
    <div id="gallery_title"></div>
 </div>
```

With your basic HTML structure, you'll need to create an appropriate function for revealing the gallery div and adding the image to it. There are a couple ways in which this particular function could be triggered, but the most obvious way would be whenever the user clicks one of the images in your gallery (shown on the main HTML page), revealing the larger version of itself on top of everything else. The function to do this display is shown in Listing 9-10.

Listing 9-10. *Showing the Image Gallery Based Upon the Selected Image*

```
// Show the current gallery image
function showImage(cur) {
    // Remember which image we're currently dealing with
    curImage = cur;

    // Find the gallery image
    var img = id("gallery_image");

    // Remove the image, if there's one already there
    if ( img.firstChild )
        img.removeChild( img.firstChild );

    // And add our new image in, instead
    img.appendChild( cur.firstChild.cloneNode( true ) );

    // We're setting the caption of the gallery image to
    // the 'alt' contents of the regular image
    id("gallery_title").innerHTML = cur.firstChild.firstChild.alt;
```

```
// Locate the main gallery
var gallery = id("gallery");

// Set the correct class (so that it's the correct size)
gallery.className = cur.className;

// Then fade it in smoothly
fadeIn( gallery, 100, 10 );

// Make sure that the gallery is positioned in the right place
// on the screen
adjust();
}
```

In the showImage function, the last step is a call to the adjust function. The adjust function is responsible for repositioning the image gallery at the exact center of the user's window (even if the user has scrolled the mouse or resized the window). This is an important step, shown in Listing 9-11, which allows the gallery to behave and look very natural.

Listing 9-11. *Repositioning the Gallery Based on Height and Width of the Image and Where the User Scrolls*

```
// Reposition the gallery to be at the center of the page
// even when the page has been scrolled
function adjust(){
    // Locate the gallery
    var obj = id("gallery");

    // Make sure that the gallery exists
    if ( !obj ) return;

    // Find its current height and width
    var w = getWidth( obj );
    var h = getHeight( obj );

    // Position the box, vertically, in the middle of the window
    var t = scrollY() + ( windowHeight() / 2 ) - ( h / 2 );

    // But no heigher than the top of the page
    if ( t < 0 ) t = 0;

    // Position the box, horizontally, in the middle of the window
    var l = scrollX() + ( windowWidth() / 2 ) - ( w / 2 );

    // But no less than the left of the page
    if ( l < 0 ) l = 0;
```

```
    // Set the adjusted position of the element
    setY( obj, t );
    setX( obj, l );
};

// Readjust the position of the gallery every time
// the user scrolls the page or resizes the browser
window.onresize = document.onscroll = adjust;
```

Finally, Listing 9-12 shows the CSS that is necessary to keep the gallery positioned correctly. As you'll note, it's really nothing more than an absolutely positioned div with a large z-index style property that places it above everything else on the page.

Listing 9-12. *The CSS for Positioning the Gallery in Its Correct Location*

```
#gallery {
    position: absolute;
    width: 650px;
    height: 510px;
    background: #FFF;
    z-index: 110;
    display: none;
}


#gallery_title {
    position: absolute;
    bottom: 5px;
    left: 5px;
    width: 100%;
    font-size: 16px;
    text-align: center;
}

#gallery img {
    position: absolute;
    top: 5px;
    left: 5px;
    width: 640px;
    height: 480px;
    border: 0px;
    z-index: 115;
}
```

```
#gallery.tall {
    width: 430px;
    height: 590px;
}

#gallery.tall img {
    width: 420px;
    height: 560px;
}
```

With the CSS, HTML, and JavaScript working together you now have a positioned image gallery that looks rather sharp, as you can see in Figure 9-5.

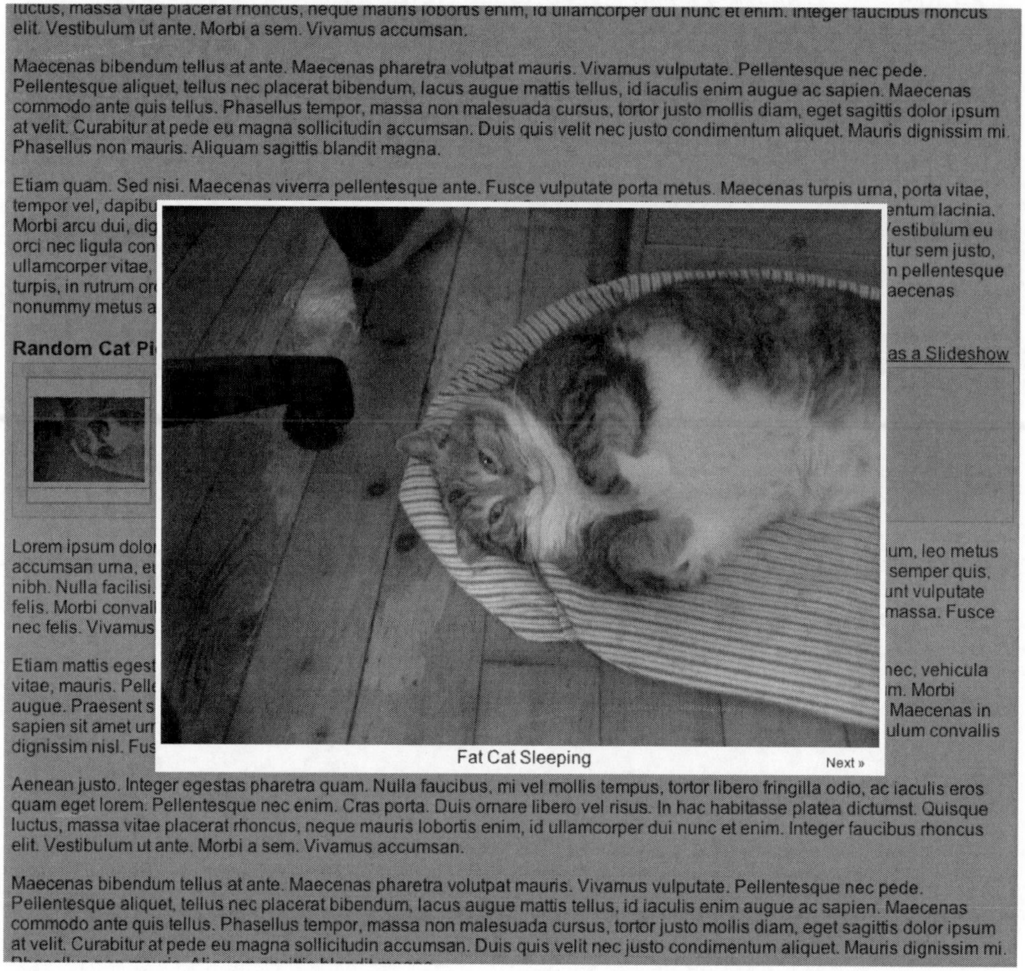

Figure 9-5. *The positioned image gallery displayed on top of the transparent overlay*

Now that you have the important step of creating a nice-looking image gallery out of the way, you need to begin concentrating on making it easier for the user to navigate through the various images of the gallery.

Navigation

With your image displaying above the rest of the page (and an overlay between it and the page itself), you need to add in a better means of navigation between the different images of the gallery. Earlier, when you specified the HTML for the gallery overlay, you included links that you could use as navigation. Using these links makes it possible for a user to move forward and backward through a gallery completely from the revealed overlay.

You're able to add this functionality to your image gallery by keeping track of which image is currently being viewed (in this case, a reference to the image stored in the curImage variable). Using this state, you can easily determine where a user is in the gallery and direct them to their desired location, as shown in Listing 9-13.

Listing 9-13. *Two Functions Necessary to Direct Users to Their Desired Position in the Gallery*

```
// Find the previous image and show it
function prevImage() {
    // Locate the previous gallery image and show it
    showImage( prev( curImage ) );

    // Prevent the link from operating as normal
    return false;
}

// Find the next image and show it
function nextImage() {
    // Locate the next gallery image and show it
    showImage( next( curImage ) );

    // Prevent the link from operating as normal
     return false;
}
```

The trick to the navigational links is that you need to determine when it's appropriate to display them. You want to make sure that the links are only shown when there's an image before or after the current image (in the gallery) to navigate to. Contextually hiding or showing the image gallery links will be used from your showImage() function to show the navigational links where appropriate. The code to handle this navigational state is shown in Listing 9-14.

Listing 9-14. *Figuring Out When the Next and Previous Navigational Links Should Be Hidden or Revealed*

```
// Hide the next link if we're at the end of the slideshow
if ( !next(cur) )
    hide( id("gallery_next") );

// Otherwise, make sure that it's visible
else
    show( id("gallery_next") );

// Hide the previous link if we're at the start of the slideshow
if ( !prev(cur) )
    hide( id("gallery_prev") );

// Otherwise, we need to be sure that it's visible
else
    show( id("gallery_prev") );
```

Finally, Listing 9-15 shows the CSS styling necessary to position the navigational links in their correct positions.

Listing 9-15. *The CSS for Positioning the Navigational Links*

```
#gallery_prev, #gallery_next {
    position: absolute;
    bottom: 0px;
    right: 0px;
    z-index: 120;
    width: 60px;
    text-align: center;
    font-size: 12px;
    padding: 4px;
}

#gallery_prev {
    left: 0px;
}

#gallery_prev a, #gallery_next a {
    color: #000;
    text-decoration: none;
}
```

An example of the navigation in use is shown in Figure 9-5. Notice that at the bottom of the image gallery there is a link directing the user to visit the next image in the gallery. The link is hidden and shown appropriately, based on where the user currently is in the gallery.

Slideshow

The final piece of your image gallery is a nice touch that many users will enjoy: a dynamic, graceful slideshow of all the images in the gallery. This particular addition is fairly simple to add in, considering the amount of previous navigational work. Quite simply, the process of creating a slideshow is broken down into two steps:

1. Create an additional link in the document for the user to click to start the slideshow.

2. Build the slideshow process itself (which controls which images to display and when to switch between them).

The first step is shown in Listing 9-16.

Listing 9-16. *Adding Additional Navigation to the DOM for the User to Initalize the Slideshow*

```
function addSlideshow( elem ) {
    // We're going to create some extra contextual information
    // surrounding the slideshow

    // Create the slideshow header, wrapper
    var div = document.createElement("div");
    div.className = "slideshow";

    // Show the name of the slideshow, based upon the
    // title of the gallery
    var span = document.createElement("span");
    span.innerHTML = g[i].title;
    div.appendChild( span );

     // Create a link so that we can view all the
     // gallery images as a slideshow
     var a = document.createElement("a");
     a.href = "";
     a.innerHTML = "&raquo; View as a Slideshow";

    // Make it so that it starts the slideshow
    // whenever it's clicked
    a.onclick = function(){
        startShow( this.parentNode.nextSibling );
        return false;
    };

    // Add the new navigation and header to the page
    div.appendChild( a );
    elem.parentNode.insertBefore( div, elem );
}
```

You must now build the control that manages the entire slideshow series of animations. This entire control is managed with a series of time-outs, which are all initialized simultaneously (even though they are all set to go off at staggered times). The final result is a smooth, graceful show that appears to be very seamless. The slideshow trigger code is shown in Listing 9-17.

Listing 9-17. *The Code That Initalizes a Slideshow Over a Particular Gallery*

```
// Start a slideshow of all the images within a particular gallery
function startShow(obj) {
    // Locate all the individual images of the gallery
    var elem = tag( "li", obj );

    // Locate the overall display gallery
    var gallery = id("gallery");

    // Go through each of the matched gallery images
    for ( var i = 0; i < elem.length; i++ )  new function() {
        // Remember which current element is being referenced
        var cur = elem[i];

        // We're going to show a new image every 5 seconds
        setTimeout(function(){
            // Show the specific image
            showImage( cur );

            // And start fading it out after 3.5 seconds
            // (for a 1 second fade)
            setTimeout(function(){
                fadeOut( gallery, 0, 10 );
            }, 3500 );
        }, i * 5000 );

    };

    // And then hide the overlay when it's all over
    setTimeout( hideOverlay, 5000 * elem.length );

    // But show the overlay, as the slideshow is just starting
    showOverlay();
}
```

Finally, you need to remember the extra, necessary CSS to style the slideshow initiation link. That code is shown in Listing 9-18.

Listing 9-18. *Additional CSS for Displaying the Slideshow Link Navigation*

```
div.slideshow {
    text-align: right;
    padding: 4px;
    margin-top: 10px;
    position: relative;
}

div.slideshow span {
    position: absolute;
    bottom: 3px;
    left: 0px;
    font-size: 18px;
    font-weight: bold;
}

div.slideshow a {
    color: #000;
}
```

While it's particularly hard to take a screenshot of the slideshow in action, you can at least look at the navigational link that you added to the page, as shown in Figure 9-6.

With the slideshow and the navigation presented previously, it really begins to show the possibilities of building your own dynamic web applications (such as a piece of presentation software). To get a better sense for how the slideshow behaves, I recommend that you set up the code presented in this chapter and see its simple but convincing results.

luctus, massa vitae placerat rhoncus, neque mauris lobortis enim, id ullamcorper dui nunc et enim. Integer faucibus rhoncus elit. Vestibulum ut ante. Morbi a sem. Vivamus accumsan.

Maecenas bibendum tellus at ante. Maecenas pharetra volutpat mauris. Vivamus vulputate. Pellentesque nec pede. Pellentesque aliquet, tellus nec placerat bibendum, lacus augue mattis tellus, id iaculis enim augue ac sapien. Maecenas commodo ante quis tellus. Phasellus tempor, massa non malesuada cursus, tortor justo mollis diam, eget sagittis dolor ipsum at velit. Curabitur at pede eu magna sollicitudin accumsan. Duis quis velit nec justo condimentum aliquet. Mauris dignissim mi. Phasellus non mauris. Aliquam sagittis blandit magna.

Etiam quam. Sed nisi. Maecenas viverra pellentesque ante. Fusce vulputate porta metus. Maecenas turpis urna, porta vitae, tempor vel, dapibus vestibulum, felis. Pellentesque sit amet nisl. Curabitur blandit. Sed in nisl et neque condimentum lacinia. Morbi arcu dui, dignissim in, consectetuer quis, gravida ac, felis. Proin lacinia aliquet augue. Mauris nec odio. Vestibulum eu orci nec ligula consequat rhoncus. Phasellus nunc nunc, vulputate posuere, semper in, cursus nec, orci. Curabitur sem justo, ullamcorper vitae, adipiscing in, malesuada vel, elit. Maecenas eleifend, justo sed ornare consequat, sem ipsum pellentesque turpis, in rutrum orci neque sed massa. Vestibulum laoreet dui eget arcu. Quisque in lorem. Morbi quis lacus. Maecenas nonummy metus auctor nunc.

Random Cat Pictures   » View as a Slideshow

Lorem ipsum dolor sit amet, consectetuer adipiscing elit. Nullam at sem. Ut ultrices, dolor sit amet pharetra pretium, leo metus accumsan urna, eu ultrices purus augue at ligula. Nam gravida. Mauris neque lacus, vehicula et, hendrerit nec, semper quis, nibh. Nulla facilisi. Curabitur id ante. Proin felis ipsum, commodo non, hendrerit et, ultrices in, eros. Nulla tincidunt vulputate felis. Morbi convallis libero sed erat. Etiam lectus pede, dictum et, rutrum id, commodo nec, augue. Vestibulum massa. Fusce nec felis. Vivamus consectetuer elementum elit.

Etiam mattis egestas felis. Proin sed magna at orci aliquet mattis. Vivamus ligula metus, interdum quis, viverra nec, vehicula vitae, mauris. Pellentesque venenatis pede vel augue. Aliquam fringilla nunc eget eros. Pellentesque eget ipsum. Morbi augue. Praesent sit amet ipsum. Ut vitae sem et diam mattis imperdiet. Phasellus a pede. Suspendisse potenti. Maecenas in sapien sit amet urna ultrices dignissim. Duis aliquet faucibus odio. Nunc a turpis vitae sem porta viverra. Vestibulum convallis dignissim nisl. Fusce enim. Morbi quam. Praesent tortor. Suspendisse eu dolor. Ut tempus tortor in dui.

Aenean justo. Integer egestas pharetra quam. Nulla faucibus, mi vel mollis tempus, tortor libero fringilla odio, ac iaculis eros quam eget lorem. Pellentesque nec enim. Cras porta. Duis ornare libero vel risus. In hac habitasse platea dictumst. Quisque luctus, massa vitae placerat rhoncus, neque mauris lobortis enim, id ullamcorper dui nunc et enim. Integer faucibus rhoncus elit. Vestibulum ut ante. Morbi a sem. Vivamus accumsan.

Maecenas bibendum tellus at ante. Maecenas pharetra volutpat mauris. Vivamus vulputate. Pellentesque nec pede. Pellentesque aliquet, tellus nec placerat bibendum, lacus augue mattis tellus, id iaculis enim augue ac sapien. Maecenas commodo ante quis tellus. Phasellus tempor, massa non malesuada cursus, tortor justo mollis diam, eget sagittis dolor ipsum at velit. Curabitur at pede eu magna sollicitudin accumsan. Duis quis velit nec justo condimentum aliquet. Mauris dignissim mi. Phasellus non mauris. Aliquam sagittis blandit magna.

Figure 9-6. *The extra slideshow navigation added to the page*

Summary

The image gallery, navigation, and slideshow presented in this chapter really show the usefulness of DOM scripting in creating additional functionality within a page, without too much hassle or confusion. Building upon what you've learned already, it should be apparent that there isn't much that you can't accomplish with dynamic, unobtrusive DOM scripting.

In this chapter you looked at a couple of other image galleries from which to draw inspiration for building our own. You then defined a standard HTML syntax and display for the gallery and set about building its fundamental units of display (including an overlay, a positioned box, and navigation). As a finishing touch, you added an animated slideshow that can be started by the user. You have created a powerful piece of dynamic DOM scripting with a minimal amount of code and fuss.

PART 4

■ ■ ■

Ajax

CHAPTER 10

■ ■ ■

Introduction to Ajax

A*jax* is a term coined by Jesse James Garrett of Adaptive Path to explain the asynchronous client-to-server communication that's made possible using the XMLHttpRequest object, provided by all modern browsers. Standing for *Asynchronous JavaScript and XML*, Ajax is simply a term used to encapsulate the techniques necessary to create a dynamic web application. Additionally, the individual components of the Ajax technique are completely interchangeable—using HTML instead of XML (for example) is perfectly valid.

In this chapter you're going to see the details that make up the full Ajax process (which is itself centered on making a request to a server from a browser). I discuss everything from the physical request itself, to the JavaScript interaction, and the data manipulation necessary to get the job done. This includes the following:

- Examining the different types of HTTP requests and determining how to best send data objects to a server.

- Looking at the entire HTTP response and attempting to handle all the errors that can occur with it, including server time-outs.

- Reading, traversing, and manipulating the data result that comes from the server in its response.

Through this full understanding of how the Ajax process works and how it can be implemented, you'll see how it can be used in everything from common situations to full applications. In Chapters 11, 12, and 13, you will also explore a series of case studies that utilize Ajax techniques.

Using Ajax

Much code isn't required to create a simple Ajax implementation, however, what the implementation affords you is great. For example, instead of having to force the user to request an entirely new web page after a form submission, the submission process can be handled asynchronously, and then a small portion of desired results can be loaded upon completion. For example, the process of searching for available domain names (to purchase) can be slow and laborious. Every time you want to search for a new name you have to type your request into a form, submit it, and watch the page reload. By using Ajax, you can get an instantaneous result, such as with the online application site Instant Domain Search (`http://instantdomainsearch.com/`), for example, which is shown in Figure 10-1.

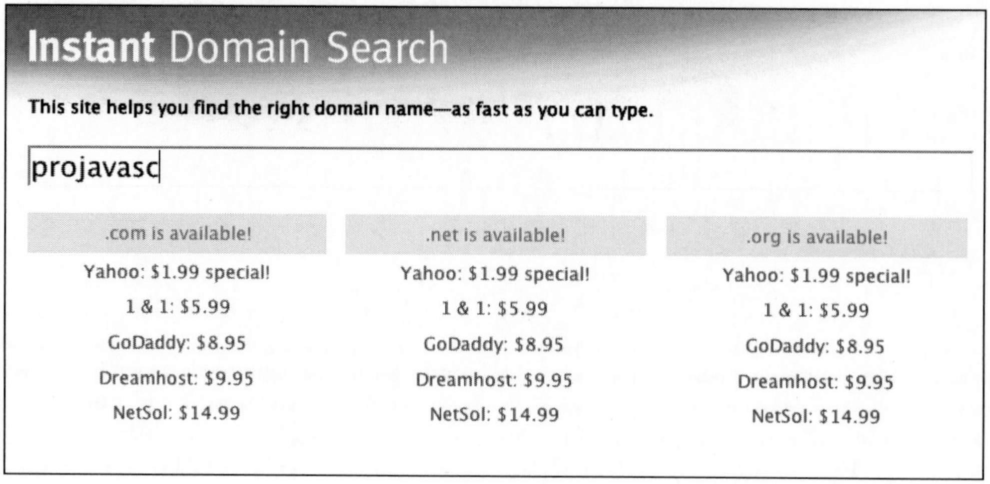

Figure 10-1. *An example of Instant Domain Search looking for domain names as you type*

HTTP Requests

The most important and probably most consistent aspect of Ajax is the HTTP request portion of the process. The Hypertext Transfer Protocol (HTTP) was designed to simply transfer HTML documents and similar files. Thankfully, all modern browsers support a means of establishing HTTP connections dynamically, using JavaScript. This proves to be incredibly useful in developing more responsive web applications.

Asynchronously sending data to the server and receiving additional data back is the ultimate purpose of Ajax. How the data is formatted ultimately depends on your specific requirements, which I discuss in detail in the "Handling Response Data" section of this chapter.

In the following sections you're going see how to format data to be transferred to a server using the different HTTP requests. You're then going to look at how to establish basic connections with the server, and you'll see the necessary details to make this happen in a cross-browser environment.

Establishing a Connection

The primary aspect of the Ajax process is the opening of a connection to the server. There are a number of different ways to achieve this goal, but we'll be looking at a specific means through which you can both send and receive data easily. This technique is generally called "using the XMLHttpRequest object."

The communication of data is conducted in two different ways using the XMLHttpRequest object, depending on the user's browser:

1. Internet Explorer, which pioneered this means of browser-based communication, establishes all of its connections using an ActiveXObject (the exact version of which changes depending on the version of Internet Explorer). Thankfully, Internet Explorer 7 has native support for the XMLHttpRequest object.

2. All other modern browsers have localized the capabilities of the XMLHttpRequest object into an object of the same name. This includes Firefox, Opera, and Safari.

Thankfully, even though Internet Explorer's method of creating an XMLHttpRequest object is different from all other modern browsers, it still has the same set of useful functionalities. The XMLHttpRequest object has a number of methods that are used to establish a connection and read data from the server. Listing 10-1 shows how to establish a basic GET request with the server.

Listing 10-1. *A Cross-Browser Means of Establishing an HTTP GET Request with the Server*

```
// If IE is used, create a wrapper for the XMLHttpRequest object
if ( typeof XMLHttpRequest == "undefined" )
        XMLHttpRequest = function(){
                // Internet Explorer uses an ActiveXObject to create a new
                // XMLHttpRequest object
                return new ActiveXObject(
                        // IE 5 uses a different XMLHTTP object from IE 6
                        navigator.userAgent.indexOf("MSIE 5") >= 0 ?
                        "Microsoft.XMLHTTP" : "Msxml2.XMLHTTP"
                );
        };

// Create the request object
var xml = new XMLHttpRequest();

// Open the socket
xml.open("GET", "/some/url.cgi", true);

// Establish the connection to the server and send any additional data
xml.send();
```

The code needed to establish a connection with a server, as you can see, is quite simple; there really isn't much to it. The difficulty arises when you want advanced features (such as checking for time-outs or modified data); however, I get to those details in the "HTTP Response" section of this chapter.

The most important feature of the whole Ajax methodology is the transmission of data on the client (e.g., the web browser) to the server. With that in mind, let's take a look at the details needed to package up the data and send it to a server.

Serializing Data

The first step of sending a set of data to a server is to format it so that the server can easily read it; this process is called *serialization*. There are two serialization cases of data that can give you the greatest range of transmission possibilities:

1. The transmission of a regular JavaScript object, which can be used to hold pairs of keys/values (where the values are either numbers or strings).

2. The submission of the values from a number of form input elements (this case is different from the first, in that the order of the submitted elements matters, whereas the order of the values submitted in the first case can be in any order).

Let's take a look at some examples of the type of data that you can send to the server, along with their resulting server-friendly, serialized output, shown in Listing 10-2.

Listing 10-2. *Examples of Raw JavaScript Objects Converted to Their Serialized Form*

```
// A simple object holding key/value pairs
{
    name: "John",
    last: "Resig",
    city: "Cambridge",
    zip: 02140
}

// Serialized form
name=John&last=Resig&city=Cambridge&zip=02140

// Another set of data, with multiple values
[
    { name: "name", value: "John" },
    { name: "last", value: "Resig" },
    { name: "lang", value: "JavaScript" },
    { name: "lang", value: "Perl" },
    { name: "lang", value: "Java" }
]

// And the serialized form of that data
name=John&last=Resig&lang=JavaScript&lang=Perl&lang=Java

// Finally, lets find some input elements (using the id() method that
// we made in the DOM chapter)
[
    id( "name" ),
    id( "last" ),
    id( "username" ),
    id( "password" )
]

// And serialize them into a data string
name=John&last=Resig&username=jeresig&password=test
```

The format that you're using to serialize the data is the standard format for passing additional parameters in an HTTP request. You're likely to have seen them in a standard HTTP GET request looking like this:

```
http://someurl.com/?name=John&last=Resig
```

This data can also be passed in to a POST request (and in a much greater quantity than a simple post). You'll be looking at those differences in the upcoming section.

For now, let's build a standard means of serializing the data structures presented in Listing 10-2. A function to do just that can be found in Listing 10-3. This particular function is capable of serializing most form input elements, with the exception of multiple-select inputs.

Listing 10-3. *A Standard Function for Serializing Data Structures to an HTTP-Compatible Parameter Scheme*

```
// Serialize a set of data. It can take two different types of objects:
//  - An array of input elements.
//  - A hash of key/value pairs
// The function returns a serialized string
function serialize(a) {
    // The set of serialize results
    var s = [];

    // If an array was passed in, assume that it is an array
    // of form elements
    if ( a.constructor == Array ) {

        // Serialize the form elements
        for ( var i = 0; i < a.length; i++ )
            s.push( a[i].name + "=" + encodeURIComponent( a[i].value ) );

    // Otherwise, assume that it's an object of key/value pairs
    } else {

        // Serialize the key/values
        for ( var j in a )
            s.push( j + "=" + encodeURIComponent( a[j] ) );

    }

    // Return the resulting serialization
    return s.join("&");
}
```

Now that there is a serialized form of your data (in a simple string), you can look at how to send that data to the server using a GET or a POST request.

Establishing a GET Request

Let's revisit establishing an HTTP GET request with a server, using XMLHttpRequest, but this time sending along additional serialized data. A simple example of this is shown in Listing 10-4.

Listing 10-4. *A Cross-Browser Means of Establishing an HTTP GET Request with the Server (and Not Reading Any Resulting Data)*

```
// Create the request object
var xml = new XMLHttpRequest();

// Open the asynchronous GET request
xml.open("GET", "/some/url.cgi?" + serialize( data ), true);

// Establish the connection to the server
xml.send();
```

The important part to note is that the serialized data is appended to the server URL (separated by a ? character). All web servers and application frameworks know to interpret the data included after the ? as a serialized set of key/value pairs. I discuss how to handle the response that the server returns (based upon the submitted data) in the "Handling Response Data" section.

Establishing a POST Request

The other form of establishing an HTTP request with a server, using XMLHttpRequest, is by doing a POST, which involves a fundamentally different way of sending data to the server. Primarily, a POST request is capable of sending data of any format and of any length (not just limited to your serialized string of data).

The serialization format that you've been using for your data is generally given the content type of application/x-www-form-urlencoded when passed to the server. This means that you could also send pure XML to the server (with a content type of text/xml or application/xml) or even a JavaScript object (using the content type application/json).

A simple example of establishing the request and sending additional serialized data is shown in Listing 10-5.

Listing 10-5. *A Cross-Browser Means of Establishing an HTTP POST Request with the Server (and Not Reading Any Resulting Data)*

```
// Create the request object
var xml = new XMLHttpRequest();

// Open the asynchronous POST request
xml.open("POST", "/some/url.cgi", true);

// Set the content-type header, so that the server
// knows how to interpret the data that we're sending
xml.setRequestHeader(
    "Content-Type", "application/x-www-form-urlencoded");
```

```
// Make sure the browser sends the right content length of the serialized data -
// Mozilla-based browsers sometimes have trouble with this
if ( xml.overrideMimeType )
    xml.setRequestHeader("Connection", "close");

// Establish the connection to the server and send the serialized data
xml.send( serialize( data ) );
```

To expand on the previous point, let's look at a case were you send data to the server that is not in your "serialized" format. You can see an example of this in Listing 10-6.

Listing 10-6. *An Example of POSTing XML Data to a Server*

```
// Create the request object
var xml = new XMLHttpRequest();

// Open the asynchronous POST request
xml.open("POST", "/some/url.cgi", true);

// Set the content-type header, so that the server
// knows how to interpret the XML data that we're sending
xml.setRequestHeader( "Content-Type", "text/xml");

// Make sure the browser sends the right content length of the serialized data -
// Mozilla-based browsers sometimes have trouble with this
if ( xml.overrideMimeType )
    xml.setRequestHeader("Connection", "close");

// Establish the connection to the server and send the serialized data
xml.send( "<items><item id='one'/><item id='two'/></items>" );
```

The ability to send bulk amounts of data (there is no limit on the amount of data that you can send, as opposed to with a GET request, which maxes out at just a couple KB of data, depending on the browser) is extremely important. With it you can create implementations of different communication protocols, such as XML-RPC or SOAP.

However, for the sake of simplicity, you're going to limit yourself to some of the most common and useful data formats that can be made available as an HTTP response.

HTTP Response

The aspect of creating and using an XMLHttpRequest that elevates it above other simplistic forms of one-way communication is its ability to read different textual data formats from a server. This includes one of the cornerstones of Ajax: XML (although it's not explicitly stated that only XML should be used when creating an Ajax application. The "Handling Response Data" section shows different alternative data formats in that respect).

To start, let's look at a very naïve example of processing the data from a server response, as shown in Listing 10-7.

Listing 10-7. *Establishing a Connection with a Server and Reading the Resulting Data*

```
// Create the request object
var xml = new XMLHttpRequest();

// Open the asynchronous POST request
xml.open("GET", "/some/url.cgi", true);

// Watch for when the state of the document gets updated
xml.onreadystatechange = function(){
    // Wait until the data is fully loaded
    if ( xml.readyState == 4 ) {

        // xml.responseXML contains the XML Document (if one was returned)
        // xml.responseText contains the response text
        // (if no XML document was provided)

        // Clean up after ourselves, to avoid memory leaks
        xml = null;
    }
};

// Establish the connection to the server
xml.send();
```

In this example you can see how you would access different blocks of data from an HTTP response. The two properties, responseXML and responseText, will each contain their appropriately formatted data. For example, if an XML document is returned from the server, a DOM document will exist in responseXML; any other response and the results will exist in responseText.

Before you get into actually handling, traversing, and manipulating the response data, let's work to create a more robust version of the onreadystatechange function (from Listing 10-7) to handle server errors and connection time-outs.

Handling Errors

It's unfortunate that the XMLHttpRequest object doesn't have any built-in mechanism for handling server errors; it would be a great time-saver if it did. However, with a little bit of work you can create your own. There are a number of request cases that you need to look for to determine whether the server has had troubles with your request:

- *Successful response codes*: The way one would expect to check for errors would be by looking at the HTTP response status code. This is included in the HTTP specification as a way for the client to know what the server is doing. A successful request is classi- fied as one where the status code of the request is within the 200 range.

- *Not modified response*: A document returned from the server could be labeled as "Not Modified" (status code 304). This means that the data from the server has not been modified and is instead loaded from the browser's personal cache. It is important to not classify this as an error, as data is still available to be read by the client.

- *Locally hosted files*: If you're running an Ajax application on your local computer (but not through a web server) there will be no status code returned—even if the request is successful. This means that you need to make sure that if no status code is provided, and you're looking at a local file, you classify it as a successful response.

- *Not modified and Safari*: Safari returns a status code of "undefined" if the document has not been modified since the last request (and if you explicitly send an IF-MODIFIED-SINCE header to the server). This is a rather strange case, and a frustrating one to debug later.

With all of these cases in mind, let's look at the code in Listing 10-8, which presents an implementation of the response checks that I previously outlined.

Listing 10-8. *A Function That Can Be Used to Check the Success State of an HTTP Response From a Server*

```
// Check to see if an XMLHttpRequest object has a 'Success' state, or not.
// The function takes one argument, the XMLHttpRequest object
function httpSuccess(r) {
    try {
        // If no server status is provided, and we're actually
        // requesting a local file, then it was successful
        return !r.status && location.protocol == "file:" ||

            // Any status in the 200 range is good
            ( r.status >= 200 && r.status < 300 ) ||

            // Successful if the document has not been modified
            r.status == 304 ||

            // Safari returns an empty status if the file has not been modified
            navigator.userAgent.indexOf("Safari") >= 0 &&
                typeof r.status == "undefined";
    } catch(e){}

    // If checking the status failed, then assume that the request failed too
    return false;
}
```

Checking the success state of an HTTP response is an essential step; not doing so can lead to some terribly unpredictable results (for example, a server returning an HTML error page instead of an XML document).

You'll be integrating the function into a complete Ajax solution in the section "The Complete Ajax Package."

Checking for Time-Outs

Another useful technique that is not included in the default XMLHttpRequest implementation is determining when a request to the server has timed out and is no longer usable.

Implementing this feature isn't as cut-and-dry, but determining the success state of the request (as you did in the previous section) is possible with a little bit of work.

Listing 10-9 shows how you would go about checking for a request time-out in an application of your own.

Listing 10-9. *An Example of Checking for a Request Time-Out*

```
// Create the request object
var xml = new XMLHttpRequest();

// Open the asynchronous POST request
xml.open("GET", "/some/url.cgi", true);

// We're going to wait for a request for 5 seconds, before giving up
var timeoutLength = 5000;

// Keep track of when the request has been succesfully completed
var requestDone = false;

// Initalize a callback which will fire 5 seconds from now, cancelling
// the request (if it has not already occurred).
setTimeout(function(){
    requestDone = true;
}, timeoutLength);

// Watch for when the state of the document gets updated
xml.onreadystatechange = function(){
    // Wait until the data is fully loaded,
    // and make sure that the request hasn't already timed out
    if ( xml.readyState == 4 && !requestDone ) {

        // xml.responseXML contains the XML Document (if one was returned)
        // xml.responseText contains the response text
        // (if no XML document was provided)

        // Clean up after ourselves, to avoid memory leaks
        xml = null;
    }
};

// Establish the connection to the server
xml.send();
```

With all the details of communicating with the server taken care of, including many of the possible errors that can occur, it's time to get into the details of handling the response data returned from the server.

Handling Response Data

In all the examples up to this point you've simply used a placeholder for the response data coming from a server, and for a simple reason: there's virtually an infinite number of possible data formats that can be returned by a server. In reality, however, the XMLHttpRequest only deals with text-based data formats. And even then, it deals with some (XML) better than others (JSON). In this chapter you're going to look at three different data formats that can be returned by the server, then read and manipulated by the client:

- *XML*: Thankfully, all modern browsers provide hooks to handle XML documents natively, automatically transforming them into useful DOM documents.

- *HTML*: This is different from an XML document in that it usually only exists as a plain text string, holding only an HTML snippet.

- *JavaScript/JSON*: This encompasses two data formats—raw, executable JavaScript code, and the JSON (JavaScript Object Notation) data format.

Each of these data formats has different cases in which they would be particularly useful. There are plenty of instances where it would make more sense to return an HTML snippet instead of an XML document, for example.

The important aspect of retrieving the data from the HTTP response lies in two properties of the XMLHttpRequest object:

- *responseXML*: This property will contain a reference to a precomputed DOM document (which represents an XML document) if an XML document has been returned from the server. This will only be the case if the server has explicitly specified its content headers as "Content-type: text/xml," or a similar XML data type.

- *responseText*: This property contains a reference to the raw text string of data returned by the server. Both the HTML and JavaScript data types rely on this method for accessing their data.

With these two properties, you can easily develop a generic function for deterministically retrieving data from an HTTP response (and even figure out if you're dealing with an XML-based response or a plain text one). Listing 10-10 shows the function that you can use to do just that.

Listing 10-10. *A Function for Extracting the Correct Data From an HTTP Server Response*

```
// A function for extracting data from an HTTP reponse
// It takes two arguments, the XMLHttpRequest object and
// An optional argument - the type of data that you're expecting from the server
// Correct values include: xml, script, text, or html - the default is "", which
// determines what the data type is based upon the content-type header
function httpData(r, type) {
    // Get the content-type header
    var ct = r.getResponseHeader("content-type");
```

```
    // If no default type was provided, determine if some
    // form of XML was returned from the server
    var data = !type && ct && ct.indexOf("xml") >= 0;

    // Get the XML Document object if XML was returned from
    // the server, otherwise return the text contents returned by the server
    data = type == "xml" || data ? r.responseXML : r.responseText;

    // If the specified type is "script", execute the returned text
    // response as if it was JavaScript
    if ( type == "script" )
        eval.call( window, data );

    // Return the response data (either an XML Document or a text string)
    return data;
}
```

With this data extraction function you now have all the components that you need to build a complete function for doing common Ajax calls to a server. You will find a complete implementation of the function in the next section.

The Complete Ajax Package

Using all the concepts that you've learned up to this point, you can build a generic function to handle all of your Ajax requests and their associated responses. Fundamentally, this function will become the cornerstone of all your Ajax-based development in future chapters, allowing you to quickly query servers for additional information.

The complete Ajax function can be found in Listing 10-11.

Listing 10-11. *A Complete Function Capable of Performing the Necessary Ajax-Related Tasks*

```
// A generic function for performming Ajax requests
// It takes one argument, which is an object that contains a set of options
// All of which are outline in the comments, below
function ajax( options ) {

    // Load the options object with defaults, if no
    // values were provided by the user
    options = {
        // The type of HTTP Request
        type: options.type || "POST",

        // The URL the request will be made to
        url: options.url || "",

        // How long to wait before considering the request to be a timeout
        timeout: options.timeout || 5000,
```

```
    // Functions to call when the request fails, succeeds,
    // or completes (either fail or succeed)
    onComplete: options.onComplete || function(){},
    onError: options.onError || function(){},
    onSuccess: options.onSuccess || function(){},

    // The data type that'll be returned from the server
    // the default is simply to determine what data was returned from the
    // and act accordingly.
    data: options.data || ""
};

// Create the request object
var xml = new XMLHttpRequest();

// Open the asynchronous request
xml.open(options.type, options.url, true);

// We're going to wait for a request for 5 seconds, before giving up
var timeoutLength = options.timeout;

// Keep track of when the request has been succesfully completed
var requestDone = false;

// Initalize a callback which will fire 5 seconds from now, cancelling
// the request (if it has not already occurred).
setTimeout(function(){
    requestDone = true;
}, timeoutLength);

// Watch for when the state of the document gets updated
xml.onreadystatechange = function(){
    // Wait until the data is fully loaded,
    // and make sure that the request hasn't already timed out
    if ( xml.readyState == 4 && !requestDone ) {

        // Check to see if the request was successful
        if ( httpSuccess( xml ) ) {

            // Execute the success callback with the
            // data returned from the server
            options.onSuccess( httpData( xml, options.type ) );

        // Otherwise, an error occurred, so execute the error callback
        } else {
            options.onError();
        }
```

```javascript
            // Call the completion callback
            options.onComplete();

            // Clean up after ourselves, to avoid memory leaks
            xml = null;
        }
};

// Establish the connection to the server
xml.send();

// Determine the success of the HTTP response
function httpSuccess(r) {
    try {
        // If no server status is provided, and we're actually
        // requesting a local file, then it was successful
        return !r.status && location.protocol == "file:" ||

            // Any status in the 200 range is good
            ( r.status >= 200 && r.status < 300 ) ||

            // Successful if the document has not been modified
            r.status == 304 ||

            // Safari returns an empty status if the file has not been modified
            navigator.userAgent.indexOf("Safari") >= 0
                && typeof r.status == "undefined";
    } catch(e){}

    // If checking the status failed, then assume that the request failed too
    return false;
}

// Extract the correct data from the HTTP response
function httpData(r,type) {
    // Get the content-type header
    var ct = r.getResponseHeader("content-type");

    // If no default type was provided, determine if some
    // form of XML was returned from the server
    var data = !type && ct && ct.indexOf("xml") >= 0;

    // Get the XML Document object if XML was returned from
    // the server, otherwise return the text contents returned by the server
    data = type == "xml" || data ? r.responseXML : r.responseText;
```

```
        // If the specified type is "script", execute the returned text
        // response as if it was JavaScript
        if ( type == "script" )
            eval.call( window, data );

        // Return the response data (either an XML Document or a text string)
        return data;
    }

}
```

It's important to note that it's not possible to request pages that aren't on the same domain as the page itself. This is due to security restrictions in place in all modern browsers (in an attempt to stop people from stealing your personal information). With this powerful function in hand, it is time to work through some examples of what is possible with your newfound Ajax power.

Examples of Different Data Usage

Fundamentally, doing a simple Ajax request isn't much different from one situation to another, however, what really changes is the data that a server responds with. Depending on the goal that you're trying to achieve, having different data formats can be highly beneficial. It is for that reason that I'm going to show you how to perform some common tasks with a number of different data formats.

An XML-Based RSS Feed

By far the most popular format for server-returned data is that of XML, and for good reason. Modern browsers all have native support for XML documents, converting them into DOM representations on the fly. Since the browser does all the hard work of parsing, all you have left to do is traverse it like any other DOM document. It's important to note, however, that it's generally not possible to traverse remotely retrieved XML documents using the getElementById function. Simply, it's because regular non-HTML XML documents have no unique ID attribute selector preprogrammed into them. However, with that said, it's still possible to efficiently traverse XML documents.

Listing 10-12 shows a simple example of using some returned XML to create a dynamic RSS feed widget inside your web site.

Listing 10-12. *Loading the Titles of Items Contained Within a Remote XML-Based RSS Feed*

```html
<html>
<head>
    <title>Dynamic RSS Feed Widget</title>
    <!--Load in our generic Ajax function -->
    <script src="ajax.js"></script>
```

```html
<script>
    // Wait for the document to be fully loaded
    window.onload = function(){
        // Then load the RSS feed using Ajax
        ajax({
            // The URL of the RSS feed
            url: "rss.xml",

            // It's an XML document
            type: "xml",

            // This function will be executed whenever the request is complete
            onSuccess: function( rss ) {
                // We're going to be inserting all the item titles into the
                // <ol> that has an id of "feed"
                var feed = document.getElementById("feed");

                // Grab all the titles out of the RSS XML document
                var titles = rss.getElementsByTagName("title");

                // Go through each of the matched item titles
                for ( var i = 0; i < titles.length; i++ ) {
                    // Create an <li> element to house the item title
                    var li = document.createElement("li");

                    // Set its contents to the title of the item
                    li.innerHTML = titles[i].firstChild.nodeValue;

                    // and add it into the DOM, in the <ol> element
                    feed.appendChild( li );
                }
            }
        });
    };
</script>
</head>
<body>
    <h1>Dynamic RSS Feed Widget</h1>
    <p>Check out my RSS feed:</p>
    <!--This is where the RSS feed is going to be inserted -->
    <ol id="feed"></ol>
</body>
</html>
```

As you can see, there really isn't much to it, once you remove the complexities of the Ajax request/response process. Additionally, because browsers make XML document traversal so simple, it really does become a great way to quickly transfer data from a server to a client.

An HTML Injector

Another useful technique that can be executed using Ajax is the dynamic loading of HTML snippets into a document. This technique is different from the previously discussed XML document method in that you don't intend to parse or traverse the data that you receive from the server; you'll only use it to insert it into the document. Using this method is a really quick and dirty way of getting your page to update quickly and easily. An example of this method is shown in Listing 10-13.

Listing 10-13. *Loading an HTML Snippet From a Remote File and Injecting It Into the Current Web Page*

```html
<html>
<head>
    <title>HTML Sports Scores Loaded via Ajax</title>
    <!--Load in our generic Ajax function -->
    <script src="ajax.js"></script>
    <script>
        // Wait for the document to be fully loaded
        window.onload = function(){
            // Then load the RSS feed using Ajax
            ajax({
                // The URL of the HTML sports scores
                url: "scores.html",

                // It's an HTML document
                type: "html",

                // This function will be executed whenever the request is complete
                onSuccess: function( html ) {
                    // We're going to be inserting into the div
                    // that has an id of 'scores'
                    var scores = document.getElementById("scores");

                    // Inject the new HTML into the document
                    scores.innerHTML = html;
                }
            });
        };
    </script>
</head>
<body>
    <h1> HTML Sports Scores Loaded via Ajax </h1>
    <!--This is where the Sports Scores to be inserted -->
    <div id="scores"></div>
</body>
</html>
```

The most important aspect of the dynamic HTML technique is that you can continue to leave all application-level templating to the server-side code, allowing you to keep your templating code base centralized and easier to maintain.

However, the simplicity of loading a simple HTML file cannot be understated, making it the easiest way to make a web application more responsive to a user's interactions.

JSON and JavaScript: Remote Execution

The final data format that I'm going to discuss (and one that we'll be revisiting in the wiki case study in Chapter 13) is the transfer of JSON data strings and raw JavaScript code. The transfer of JSON-serialized data can serve as a lightweight alternative to transferring XML documents from a server to a client. Additionally, serving up raw JavaScript code from a server is a great way to build dynamic multiuser web applications. To keep things simple, let's take a look at loading a remote JavaScript file into your application, as shown in Listing 10-14.

Listing 10-14. *Dynamically Loading and Executing a Remote JavaScript File*

```
<html>
<head>
    <!--Load in our generic Ajax function -->
    <script src="ajax.js"></script>
    <script>
        // Load a remote Javascript file
        ajax({
            // The URL of the JavaScript file
            url: "myscript.js",

            // Force it to execute as JavaScript
            type: "script"
        });
    </script>
</head>
<body></body>
</html>
```

Summary

While deceptively simple, the concept of Ajax web applications is a powerful one. By dynamically loading extra pieces of information into a JavaScript-based application while it's still running, you're able to build a more responsive interface that your users can enjoy.

In this chapter you learned how the fundamental concepts of Ajax work, including the specifics of the HTTP request and response, error handling, data formatting, and data parsing. The result is a generic function that you can reuse to easily make any web-based application more dynamic. You'll be using this function in the next three chapters to build a number of dynamic Ajax-based interactions.

CHAPTER 11

■ ■ ■

Enhancing Blogs with Ajax

One thing that Ajax technology affords us is the ability to provide additional levels of interaction for users, within static web pages. This means that you can begin to change how a static web page actually operates while still providing a seamless user experience.

One area that could stand to use some improvement is that of *web logs* (or blogs). From a pure data perspective, a web log is nothing more than a listing of entries consisting of the text entry, a title, and a link to the full entry. However, the means of browsing old entries and checking for new entries is rather crippled.

In this chapter you'll see two different ways that a typical web log can be improved by using some JavaScript code that uses Ajax techniques. One is a means to easily scroll down a large list of blog entries without ever leaving the current page, and the other is a way to watch for new blog entries without reloading the web page continually.

Never-Ending Blog

The first enhancement that you're going to add to a blog is the ability to scroll back through the archives without having to ever click a navigational link. A common feature of a blog, or any other time-based content site, is the ability to navigate to older entries. Often there is a Next and/or a Previous link at the bottom of the page that lets the user navigate through the archives.

You're going to explore a way that this whole process can be circumvented using Ajax. In order to build up the utility that can do this, you need to make a few assumptions:

- You have a web page with a series of chronologically ordered posts.

- When a user gets near the bottom of the page, the user will want to read more previous posts.

- You have a data source that you can pull posts from. In this case, you're going to be using the WordPress blogging software (http://wordpress.org/) that supports this quite well.

The premise for your script, then, is that whenever a user scrolls near the bottom of a page, additional posts will be automatically loaded in to allow the user to continue to scroll and navigate through the archives, creating the illusion of a never-ending web page. This script will be built to use the functionality of the WordPress blogging software. You will be able to easily drop it in to your own WordPress-powered blog, adding in additional functionality.

The Blog Template

You're going to start with a basic template that's provided with a default WordPress installation. The template is commonly called Kubrik and is quite popular. Figure 11-1 shows an example of a basic Kubrik-themed page.

Figure 11-1. *An example of a default Kubrik theme in WordPress*

You can see that the page has a main column, a header, and a sidebar. The header is the most important area; it is where you will be looking at posts and adding new information. Let's look at a simplified version of the HTML used to structure this blog, shown in Listing 11-1.

Listing 11-1. *Simplified Version of HTML Produced by the Kubrik Theme and WordPress*

```
<html>
<head>
    <title>Never-ending Wordpress</title>
    <script>
        <!-- Our Script Goes Here -->
    </script>
</head>
```

```
<body>
    <div id="page">
        <div id="header">
            <!-- Header Contents -->
        </div>
        <div id="content">

            <!-- The First Post -->
            <div class="post">
                <!-- The Post's header -->
                <h2><a href=" /test/?p=1">Test Post</a></h2>
                <small>October 24th, 2006</small>

                <div class="entry">
                    <!-- The Post's Contents -->
                </div>

                <p class="postmetadata">
                    <a href="/test/?p=1#comments">Comments</a></p>
            </div>

            <!-- More Posts . . .  -->

        </div>
    </div>
</body>
</html>
```

You'll notice that all of the web log entries are contained within the <div> that has an ID of "content." Additionally, each of the posts has a specific format under which it is structured. With this in mind, you'll need to build a simple set of DOM functions that you can execute to take some data and push it into this web log page. Listing 11-2 shows the DOM operations needed to complete the page.

Listing 11-2. *The DOM Operations for Adding the HTML Necessary to Complete the Page*

```
// We're loading the new posts into the <div> that has an ID of "content"
var content = document.getElementById("content");

// We're going to iterate through each of the posts in the RSS feed
var items = rss.getElementsByTagName("item");
for ( var i = 0; i < items.length; i++ ) {

    // Let's extract the Link, Title, and Description data from each feed post
    var data = getData( items[i] );
```

```
// Creating a new wrapper <div> to hold the post
var div = document.createElement("div");
div.className = "post";

// Create the post header
var h2 = document.createElement("h2");

// This holds the title of the feed and has a link that points back to the post.
h2.innerHTML = "<a href='" + data.link + "'>" + data.title + "</a>";

// Add it in to the post wrapper <div>
div.appendChild( h2 );

// Now let's create a <div> to hold the long post contents
var entry = document.createElement("div");
entry.className = "entry";

// Add the contents to the inside of the <div>
entry.innerHTML = data.desc;
div.appendChild( entry );

// Finally, let's add a footer that links back
var meta = document.createElement("p");
meta.className = "postmetadata";

var a = document.createElement("a");
a.href = data.link + "#comments";
a.innerHTML = "Comment";
meta.appendChild( a );

div.appendChild( meta );

// Place the new entry into the document
content.appendChild( div );
}
```

However, all of these DOM operations don't mean a whole lot if you don't know what the data is you're dealing with. In the next section you're going to look at the data that is being passed to you from the server, and how you can inject it into the document using the DOM operations.

The Data Source

WordPress provides an easy means of accessing post data. All WordPress blogs include a default RSS feed that you can use to see the ten most recent posts. However, that alone is not sufficient enough; you need access to all posts, going back to the very beginning of the site. Luckily, there's a hidden feature that you can use to achieve just that.

In WordPress, the URL for the RSS feed typically looks something like this: `/blog/?feed=rss`; however, if you add an additional parameter, `/blog/?feed=rss&paged=N`, you can go farther back into the history of the blog (with an *N* of 1 showing the ten most recent posts, 2 showing the ten previous posts, etc.). Listing 11-3 shows an example of what the RSS feed looks like that contains the post data.

Listing 11-3. *The XML RSS Feed Returned by WordPress, Containing Ten Posts in a Nicely Formatted Structure*

```xml
<?xml version="1.0" encoding="UTF-8"?>
<rss version="2.0">

<channel>
    <title>Test Wordpress Web log</title>
    <link>http://someurl.com/test/</link>
    <description>Test Web log.</description>
    <pubDate>Fri, 08 Oct 2006 02:50:23 +0000</pubDate>
    <generator>http://wordpress.org/?v=2.0</generator>
    <language>en</language>

    <item>
        <title>Test Post</title>
        <link>http://someurl.com/?p=9</link>
        <pubDate>Thu, 07 Sep 2006 09:58:07 +0000</pubDate>
        <dc:creator>John Resig</dc:creator>
        <category>Uncategorized</category>
        <description><![CDATA[ Post content goes here . . . ]]></description>
    </item>

    <!-- A lot more items -->
</channel>
</rss>
```

By tapping into the RSS feed, you're given a nicely formatted XML file to work with (and that JavaScript is very good at traversing). Listing 11-4 shows the code necessary to traverse the RSS XML document and extract all the relevant information from it.

Listing 11-4. *Extracting Post Information From an XML RSS Feed*

```javascript
// We're going to iterate through each of the posts in the RSS feed
var items = rss.getElementsByTagName("item");

for ( var i = 0; i < items.length; i++ ) {
```

```
    // Extract the title, description, and link from the rss feed <item> elements
    var title = elem.getElementsByTagName("title")[0].firstChild.nodeValue;
    var desc = elem.getElementsByTagName("description")[0].firstChild.nodeValue;
    var link = elem.getElementsByTagName("link")[0].firstChild.nodeValue;

}
```

With your data source intact, and with a solid structure for inserting the results into the HTML document, it's time to glue everything together with an Ajax request and some basic event detection.

Event Detection

The primary interaction that the user is going to undertake in order to activate your script is simply scrolling near the bottom of the page. Whenever the browser viewport moves, you need to verify whether it's near the bottom of the screen.

The script to handle this is relatively simple; you simply need to bind a single event handler to the window's scroll event. This will let you know every time the user moves the viewport on the page (and possibly near the bottom of the page). All you have to do is use a couple methods defined in Chapter 7 to determine where exactly the user's viewport is positioned on the page: pageHeight (to determine how tall the entire page is), scrollY (to know where the top of the viewport is currently scrolled to), and windowHeight (to know how tall the viewport is). This is shown in Listing 11-5.

Listing 11-5. *Determining the Position of the User's Viewport*

```
// We're going to see if we should load some more content based upon where
// the user is currently located on the page
window.onscroll = function(){
    // Check the position of the viewport within the page
    if ( curPage >= 1 && !loading &&
        pageHeight() - scrollY() - windowHeight() < windowHeight() ) {
        // Request the RSS XML feed using an Ajax request
    }
};
```

You now have all the components that you need; the final aspect is to add in the Ajax request to retrieve the data that you need to make everything work smoothly.

The Request

The core of this whole application ties back to using Ajax requests to dynamically load in new blocks of posts that you can then insert into the page. The request that you need to make is simple: establish an HTTP GET to a specific URL (one that points to the next batch of posts) and retrieve the XML document that's there. The code in Listing 11-6, which uses the complete Ajax function (from Chapter 10), does just this.

Listing 11-6. *The Ajax Request for Loading in a New Block of Posts*

```
// Load the posts using our handy ajax() function
ajax({

    // We're just requesting a simple web page, so just use GET
    type: "GET",

    // We're expecting an RSS feed, which is just an XML file
    data: "xml",

    // Get the RSS feed of the Nth page. When we first load this page
    // we're on page '1', so we start at 2 and work our way back in time
    url: "./?feed=rss&paged=" + ( ++curPage ),

    // Watch for when the RSS feed has been successfully retrieved
    onSuccess: function( rss ){
        // Traverse the RSS XML document through its DOM
    }

});
```

After you've constructed the mechanism to make a page request, you can tie everything together into a cohesive package that you can easily drop right into your WordPress blog.

The Result

Taking the DOM construction code and combining it with the RSS XML traversing is perhaps the simplest part of this application, but when combined with the scroll-event detection and the Ajax request, you have the makings for a compelling addition to a blog—the ability to continuously scroll through all blog posts without leaving the page. Listing 11-7 shows the full code required to enhance a WordPress blog with this functionality.

Listing 11-7. *JavaScript Code Required for Never-Ending Page Abilities in a WordPress Blog*

```
// Keep track of what "page" of the contents that we're currently on
var curPage = 1;

// Make sure that we don't load a page twice, at the same time
var loading = false;

// We're going to see if we should load some more content based upon where
// the user is currently located on the page
```

```
window.onscroll = function(){
    // We need to verify a couple things before we try and load some more contents
    // 1) We need to make sure that we're not at the last page of contents.
    // 2) We need to make sure that we're not already loading some new posts.
    // 3) We're only going to load new posts if we're
    //       scrolled near the bottom of the page
    if ( curPage >= 1 && !loading
        && pageHeight() - scrollY() - windowHeight() < windowHeight() ) {

        // Remember that we've started to load the new posts.
        loading = true;

        // Load the posts using our handy ajax() function
        ajax({

            // We're just requesting a simple web page, so just use GET
            type: "GET",

            // We're expecting an RSS feed, which is just an XML file
            data: "xml",

            // Get the RSS feed of the Nth page. When we first load this page
            // we're on page '1', so we start at 2 and work our way back in time
            url: "./?feed=rss&paged=" + ( ++curPage ),

            // Watch for when the RSS feed has been successfully retrieved
            onSuccess: function( rss ){

                // We're loading the new posts into the <div>
                // that has an ID of "content"
                var content = document.getElementById("content");

                // We're going to iterate through each of the posts in the RSS feed
                var items = rss.getElementsByTagName("item");
                for ( var i = 0; i < items.length; i++ ) {

                    // Place the new entry into the document
                    content.appendChild( makePost( items[i] ) );

                }

                // If there are no items to retrieve from the XML document,
                // we must be back as far as we can go
                if ( items.length == 0 ) {
                    curPage = 0;
                }
            },
```

```
            // Whenever the request has completed, we can try
            // to load new items again
            onComplete: function(){
                loading = false;
            }
        });
    }
};

// A function for creating the complex DOM structure of a single post
function makePost( elem ) {
    // Let's extract the Link, Title, and Description data from each feed post
    var data = getData( elem );

    // Creating a new wrapper <div> to hold the post
    var div = document.createElement("div");
    div.className = "post";

    // Create the post header
    var h2 = document.createElement("h2");

    // This holds the title of the feed and has a link that points back to the post.
    h2.innerHTML = "<a href='" + data.link + "'>" + data.title + "</a>";

    // Add it in to the post wrapper <div>
    div.appendChild( h2 );

    // Now let's create a <div> to hold the long post contents
    var entry = document.createElement("div");
    entry.className = "entry";

    // Add the contents to the inside of the <div>
    entry.innerHTML = data.desc;
    div.appendChild( entry );

    // Finally, let's add a footer that links back
    var meta = document.createElement("p");
    meta.className = "postmetadata";
    meta.innerHTML = "<a href='" + data.link + "#comments'>Comment</a>";
    div.appendChild( meta );

    return div;
}
```

```
// A simple function for extracting data from a DOM element
function getData( elem ) {
    // We're going to return the data as a nicely formatted object
    return {
        // Extract the title, description, and link from the rss feed <item> element
        title: elem.getElementsByTagName("title")[0].firstChild.nodeValue,
        desc: elem.getElementsByTagName("description")[0].firstChild.nodeValue,
        link: elem.getElementsByTagName("link")[0].firstChild.nodeValue
    };
}
```

Adding that code to the top of your WordPress header template file would be sufficient enough to create a result similar to that in Figure 11-2. Notice that the scrollbar is rather small (signifying that extra posts have been dynamically loaded in).

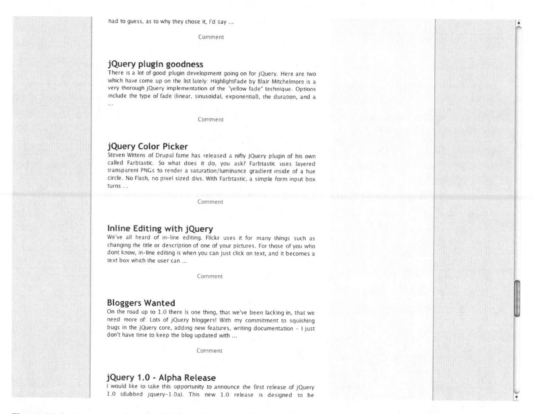

Figure 11-2. *An example of additional content loaded into view while scrolling farther down the page*

Dynamic content loading is a common use case of Ajax. Almost entirely, it makes the page-browsing process easier for the user and "lightweight" for the server. The number of applications for pulling in additional content is not limited to web logs in any respect. Web-based applications can benefit from this technology dramatically, and you'll be looking at that aspect more in the next chapter.

In the next section you'll see another example of loading dynamic content using the same Ajax techniques, but you will create a real-time blogging experience for your viewers.

Live Blogging

Now that you've done all the hard work of building dynamic posts, retrieving post data, and parsing the data, you can explore another application that's directly useful for a WordPress web log.

One aspect that typical web logs miss is the immediacy of news and updates. Users are presented with a static page that lists the most recent posts of the blog, and if they want additional updates, they must refresh the page in their browser. However, there are plenty of instances where the blogger would want to communicate an immediate piece of information to the user while the user is still viewing the page. Theoretically, a user should be able to load a page, leave it open, return to it later, and new posts will be shown.

Once again, this is a perfect application of Ajax technology. You can use the same techniques that you used in the previous section to load in new content from your RSS XML feed. The following is a list of the actions that need to be performed in order to create the experience of live blogging within a normal web log:

- Retrieving a list of the most recently published posts on the web log at a standard interval (such as once a minute).

- Finding the posts that have not yet been displayed.

- Adding the posts to the top of the page.

This flow of operations is quite simple, as is the implementation, shown in Listing 11-8.

Listing 11-8. *Implementation of a Blog That Updates on the Fly From an XML-Based RSS Feed*

```
// We're going to load new page contents repeatedly, at a certain interval
setInterval(function(){

    // Load the posts using our handy ajax() function
    ajax({

        // We're just requesting a simple web page, so just use GET
        type: "GET",

        // We're expecting an RSS feed, which is just an XML file
        data: "xml",
```

```
            // Get the current RSS feed (with the latest posts in it)
            url: "./?feed=rss&paged=1",

            // Watch for when the RSS feed has been successfully retrieved
            onSuccess: function( rss ){

                // We're loading the new posts into the <div>
                // that has an ID of "content"
                var content = document.getElementById("content");

                // Get the URL of the most recent post (to make sure that
                // we don't do any duplicate posts)
                var recentURL = content.getElementsByTagName("h2")[0].firstChild.href;

                // We're going to iterate through each of the posts in the RSS feed
                var items = rss.getElementsByTagName("item");

                // We're going to be putting all the new items in a separate array
                var newItems = [];

                // Go through each of the items
                for ( var i = 0; i < items.length; i++ ) {

                    // Forcefully stop the loop if an "old" post was found
                    if ( getData( items[i] ).link == recentURL )
                        break;

                    // Add the new item to the temporary array
                    newItems.push( items[i] );

                }

                // Go through all of the new items, in reverse order, to make
                // sure that they're in the right order when they go into the site
                for ( var i = newItems.length - 1; i >= 0; i-- ) {
                    // Place the new entry into the document
                    content.insertBefore( makePost( newItems[i] ), content.firstChild );
                }

            }
        });

    // Load the new page contents once a minute
}, 60000 );
```

When you add this script into your WordPress template (along with the code that you built in the first section to create a never-ending page) you get a result similar to what's shown in Figure 11-3.

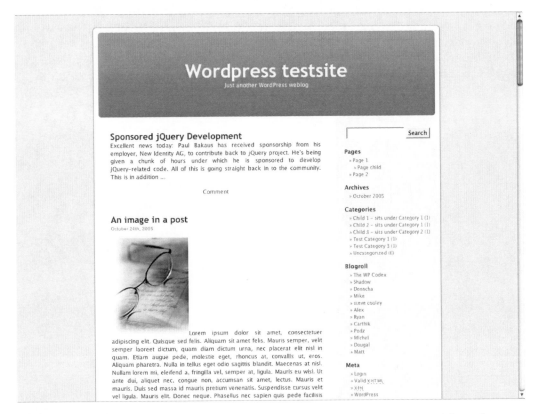

Figure 11-3. *WordPress pulling in a single new post in front of other older posts without the user refreshing the page*

With this last enhancement, you can effectively turn a simple blog into a live blogging platform. The next time you want to write live updates when you're at a conference, just add this script into your site and your readers will get your updates as soon as they are posted, without having to refresh pages.

Summary

The most important concept discussed in this chapter, and the one that you should take away with you, is that Ajax-related technology lets you imagine new ways of how typical, static applications work. Since processing XML documents and converting them into usable HTML snippets is so easy it's entirely possible to implement this in applications of your own.

In this chapter you built two add-ons to a typical WordPress-based blogging platform. Specifically, you removed the need for navigating old posts with antiquated links and pagination. Instead, you are loading blocks of posts dynamically while the user is browsing the page. Additionally, if a new post is posted while the user is looking at the page, the post will be added, allowing the user to continue reading without ever leaving the page. Both of these additions allow for the browsing experience to become much more dynamic and fluid, without posts being broken up between multiple pages.

In the next chapter you will build up an advanced piece of Ajax functionality: an autocomplete search.

CHAPTER 12

∎∎∎

Autocomplete Search

The most important functionality that Ajax technology affords is the ability to create highly inter-active user interfaces, many of which weren't previously possible. An example of one of these new user interface elements is what's known as the *autocomplete search* field. The autocomplete search field is much like a normal text field, but it automatically completes search terms as you begin to type them in. This means that as you're typing a search query, the client is sending requests to the server (in the background) in an attempt to give you faster and more accurate results.

In this chapter I go through each of the components that are needed to build a full auto-complete search. First you'll see how to construct and lay out the page, followed by how to watch for user input in the text entry field. All of this will hook into a simple Ajax request that will go to a simple server-side database.

Examples of Autocomplete Search

An autocomplete search field can manifest in a couple different ways. For example, Google has an autocomplete version of its search box called Google Suggest (http://www.google.com/webhp?complete=1). When you begin typing your search query into the field, it shows you other searches that other users have frequently made, beginning with the same characters that you've already typed. An example of an autocomplete search is shown in Figure 12-1.

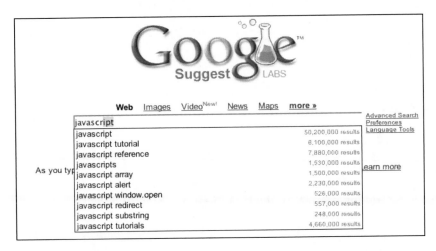

Figure 12-1. *An example of what typical autocomplete results look like*

Another popular example is called Instant Domain Search (`http://instantdomainsearch.com/`). This particular application lets you know whether a domain name is available to be purchased as you type the name. This is different from the Google implementation in that it automatically completes the search, as opposed to completing the query itself. This means that as you type a domain name to search for, the server automatically completes your queries in the background, giving you relevant results as you type. An example is shown in Figure 12-2.

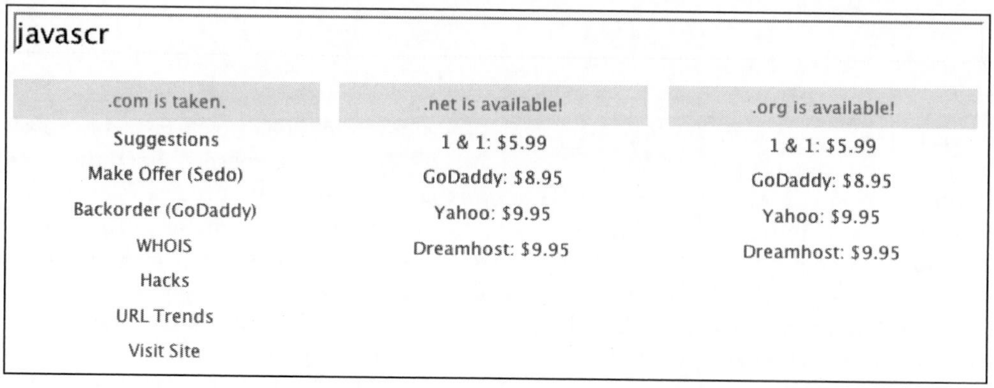

Figure 12-2. *An example of an autocompleted Instant Domain Search*

The final example, and the one that's most similar to the one that you'll be building, is the autocomplete mechanism provided by the online bookmarking service del.icio.us (`http://del.icio.us/`). It provides a means through which you can tag links with specific words by allowing you to autocomplete multiple words within a single text entry field. An example of this is shown in Figure 12-3.

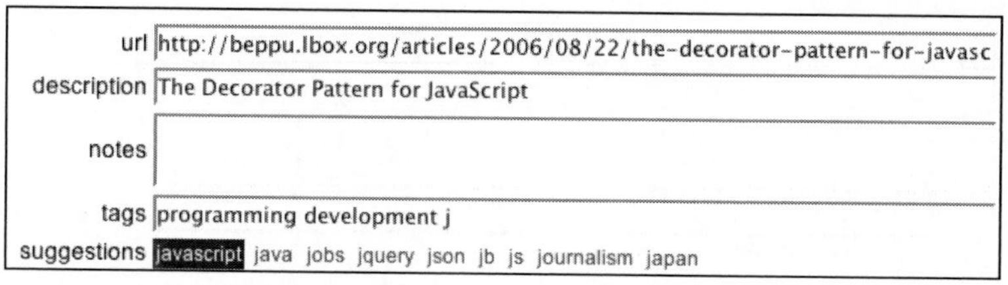

Figure 12-3. *An example of del.icio.us autocomplete in action, completing a new tag*

You're about to build your own autocomplete search. It'll be a simple form for sending a message to a group of friends on a web site. The autocomplete field will behave very similarly to del.icio.us, in that there will be a field for entering usernames, which can then be autocompleted in the background using Ajax. You'll be able to autocomplete each of your friends' usernames, based on what's stored in the central database, into a comma-delimited list of usernames to send messages to. An example of the effect that you're going to achieve is shown in Figure 12-4.

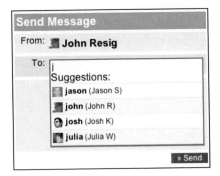

Figure 12-4. *An example of a username autocomplete, based on entering a single letter*

Building the Page

The first step of building your autocomplete search field is to construct a simple form that will house the complete setup. This page is structured like a simple form for sending a message to a group of users on a web site. There are three important aspects that you need to include on the page, in addition to the normal message-sending form (which consists of a To field and an area for the message that's being sent):

The text entry field: You need to make sure that it has the autocomplete property set to off. This will disable the browser's default autocomplete mechanism (which autocompletes entries that you've previously entered into an input area):

```
<input type="text" id="to" name="to" autocomplete="off"/>
```

The loading image: This is a small spinning image laid on top of the text input field to denote when new data is being loaded from the server:

```
<img src="indicator.gif" id="qloading"/>
```

The results area: All results coming back from the server will be put into a results area and be displayed on demand. The physical results will be returned as a set of <li> elements, each containing information about an individual user:

```
<div id="results"><div class="suggest">Suggestions:</div><ul></ul></div>
```

Both the loading indicator and the results area will be included via JavaScript. The full HTML for the page is shown in Listing 12-1.

Listing 12-1. *The Full HTML of the Autocomplete Form for Sending Messages to Users*

```
<html>
<head>
    <script src="dom.js"></script>
    <script src="delay.js"></script>
    <script src="script.js"></script>
    <link rel="stylesheet" href="style.css"/>
</head>
```

```
<body>
    <form action="" method="POST" id="auto">
        <div id="top">
            <div id="mhead"><strong>Send Message</strong></div>
            <div class="light">
                <label>From:</label>
                <div class="rest from">
                    <img src="icons/john_icon.jpg"/>
                    <strong>John Resig</strong>
                </div>
            </div>
            <div class="query dark">
                <label>To:</label>
                <div class="rest">
                    <input type="text" id="to" name="to" autocomplete="off"/>
                </div>
            </div>
            <div class="light"><textarea></textarea></div>
            <div class="submit"><input type="submit" value="&raquo; Send"/></div>
        </div>
    </form>
</body>
</html>
```

Figure 12-5 shows a screenshot of how the page looks fully styled.

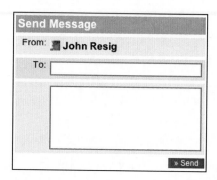

Figure 12-5. *The result of your form mockup with some simple styling*

The next step, now that you have your form set up and ready for user input, is to watch for the user entering information into the username text entry field and to react appropriately.

Watching for Key Input

One important aspect of an autocomplete search is creating a natural-feeling interface through which a user can enter input and have it be expanded into a full entry. For most search inputs, most of the actual search interface revolves around a single text entry field. You will continue to use this interface for your application, too.

When constructing this input mechanism you need to take a couple things into account to make sure that the level of interaction is ideal:

- Make sure autocomplete searches are triggered at appropriate intervals, where the response happens quickly enough for the user to react to it.

- Make sure searches against the server happen as slowly as can be allowed. The faster the searches occur, the greater the strain placed on the server.

- Make sure you know when it's appropriate to do a new autocomplete search and open the results; not do a search, but open the old results; and hide the results.

With these points laid out, you can now define a more exact user interaction that you want to implement:

- Autocomplete results should be displayed based on what the user has entered in the text input field. Additionally, a minimum number of characters should be provided by the user in order to trigger the search (to avoid overly ambiguous searches).

- Result searches should be triggered at regular intervals (as to avoid server overload from fast-typing users), but only when the text input contents have changed.

- The result set should be revealed, or hidden, based on the focus that the user is currently giving the input element (e.g., if the user focuses away from the input element, the result set should be hidden).

With all of these points in mind, you can develop a single function for attaching the interaction that you need on a single text input field. Listing 12-2 shows a function that can be used to achieve your desired results. This function only handles a case where a search should occur or where the results should be shown or hidden, not the actual searching or visual results (you'll be adding that later).

Listing 12-2. *A Function for Binding Autocomplete Searching Abilities to a Text Input Field*

```
function delayedInput(opt) {
    // The amount of time to wait before looking for new user input
    opt.time = opt.time || 400;

    // The minimum number of characters to wait for, before firing a request
    opt.chars = opt.chars != null ? opt.chars : 3;

    // The callback to fire when the results popup should be opened,
    // and possibly when a new request should be made
    opt.open = opt.open || function(){};
```

```
// The callback to execute when the results popup should be closed
opt.close = opt.close || function(){};

// Should the focus of the field be taken into account, for
// opening/closing the results popup
opt.focus = opt.focus !== null ? opt.focus : false;

// Remember the original value that we're starting with
var old = opt.elem.value;

// And the current open/close state of the results popup
var open = false;

// Check to see if there's been a change in the input,
// at a given interval
setInterval(function(){
    // The new input value
    var newValue = opt.elem.value;

    // The number of characters that've been entered
    var len = s.length;

    // Quickly check to see if the value has changed since the last
    // time that we checked the input
    if ( old != newValue ) {

        // If not enough characters have been entered, and the 'popup'
        // is currently open
        if ( v < opt.chars && open ) {

            // Close the display
            opt.close();

            // And remember that it's closed
            open = false;

        // Otherwise, if the minimum number of characters have been entered
        // as long as its more than one character
        } else if ( v >= opt.chars && v > 0 ) {

            // Open the results popup with the current value
            opt.open( newValue, open );

            // Remember that the popup is current open
            open = true;

        }
```

```
                // Save the current value for later
                old = newValue;
            }
    }, opt.time );

    // Watch for a key press
    opt.elem.onkeyup = function(){
        // If the keypress resulted in their being no more characters left,
        // close the results popup
        if ( this.value.length == 0 ) {
            // Close the popup
            opt.close();

            // Remember that it's closed
            open = false;
        }
    };

    // If we're also checking for user focus (to handle opening/closing)
    // the results popup
    if ( opt.focus ) {
        // Watch for when the user moves away from the input
        opt.elem.onblur = function(){
            // If its currently open
            if ( open ) {
                // Close the popup
                opt.close();

                // And remember that its closed
                open = false;
            }
        }

        // Watch for when the user focus' back on the popup
        opt.elem.focus = function(){
            // If it has a value, and its currently closed
            if ( this.value.length != 0 && !open ) {
                // Re-open the popup - but with a blank value
                // (this lets the 'open' function know not to re-retreive
                // new results from the server, just re-open the popup).
                opt.open( '', open );

                // And remembr that the popup is open
                open = true;
            }
        };
    }
}
```

Listing 12-3 shows how to use the simple delayedInput function within your autocomplete implementation for watching user input.

Listing 12-3. *Using the Generic delayedInput() Function Within Your Autocomplete Implementation*

```
// Initialize the delayed input checks on our input
delayedInput({
    // We're attaching to the input text field
    elem: id("to"),

    // We're going to start searching after only 1 character of input
    chars: 1,

    // When the text field loses focus, close the results popup
    focus: true,

    // Handle when the result popup should be opened up
    open: function(q,open){
        // Get the last word out of the comma-separated list of words
        var w = trim( q.substr( q.lastIndexOf(',')+1, q.length ) );

        // Make sure that we're dealing with a word, at least
        if ( w ) {
            // Show the loading spinner animation
            show( id("qloading") );

            // Load and process the results from the server
        }
    },

    // When the popup needs to be closed
    close: function(){
        // Hide the result set
        hide( id("results") );
    }
});
```

With a generic function for watching user input, you now have the task of tying this to the server-side script, which will serve up the user data that you can load into your site.

Retrieving the Results

The next fundamental aspect of building an autocomplete search is the loading of data to be shown to the user. It's not a requirement that this data be loaded via Ajax (which you'll be doing in this particular implementation); it could instead be written as a data structure and loaded into the page at run time.

Your autocomplete implementation requires one thing to be complete: users. These user-names will be displayed with more contextual information (including the user's full name and a user icon). With this in mind, it's far easier to simply return a chunk of HTML from the server (in the form of a number of <li> elements), containing the information that you need about all of the matched users.

Listing 12-4 shows the simple Ajax call required to load the HTML snippet from the server into the results pop-up.

Listing 12-4. *The AJAX Request for Loading an HTML Snippet (Containing User Information) Into Your Autocomplete Result Set*

```
// Do a request for new data
ajax({
    // Do a simple GET request to the CGI script which
    // returns an HTML block of LI elements
    type: "GET",
    url: "auto.cgi?to=" + w,

    // Watch for when the HTML comes back
    onSuccess: function(html){
        // Insert it in to the results UL
        results.innerHTML = html;

        // And hide the loading animation
        hide( id("qloading") );

        // Process the results...
    }
});
```

You should notice that in Listing 12-4 you're loading your HTML results from a server-side application named auto.cgi, which takes one argument, which is the current text that you're searching for (most likely a partial username). The auto.cgi script, which is written using Perl, is shown in Listing 12-5. It searches across a small dataset looking for a match, returning all matched users as a long HTML snippet.

Listing 12-5. *A Simple Perl Script That Searches for Matched Users*

```
#!/usr/bin/perl

use CGI;

# Get the 'q' parameter out of the incoming Query String
my $cgi = new CGI();
my $q = $cgi->param('to');
```

```perl
# Our limited "database" contains five users
# with their username and full name.
my @data = (
    {
        user => "bradley",
        name => "Bradley S"
    },
    {
        user => "jason",
        name => "Jason S"
    },
    {
        user => "john",
        name => "John R"
    },
    {
        user => "josh",
        name => "Josh K"
    },
    {
        user => "julia",
        name => "Julia W"
    }
);


# Make sure that we print out the correct HTML header
print "Content-type: text/html\n\n";

# Now we "search" through the data
foreach my $row (@data) {

    # Looking for users that match our auto-complete search
    if ( $row->{user} =~ /$q/i || $row->{name} =~ /$q/i ) {

        # If the user matches, print out the necessary HTML
        print qq~<li id="$row->{user}">
            <img src="icons/$row->{user}_icon.jpg"/>
            <div>
                <strong>$row->{user}</strong> ($row->{name})
            </div>
        </li>~;

    }

}
```

The result returned from the CGI script is nothing more than an HTML snippet containing <li> elements corresponding to each user matched. Listing 12-6 shows the results of a search for the letter *j*.

Listing 12-6. *An HTML Snippet Returned From the Server, Representing a Number of Different Users*

```
<li id="jason">
    <img src="icons/jason_icon.jpg"/>
    <div>
        <strong>jason</strong> (Jason S)
    </div>
</li><li id="john">
    <img src="icons/john_icon.jpg"/>
    <div>
        <strong>john</strong> (John R)
    </div>
</li><li id="josh">
    <img src="icons/josh_icon.jpg"/>
    <div>
        <strong>josh</strong> (Josh K)
    </div>
</li><li id="julia">
    <img src="icons/julia_icon.jpg"/>
    <div>
        <strong>julia</strong> (Julia W)
    </div>
</li>
```

With the server searching through a small dataset, returning an HTML snippet, and the HTML being injected into the site, the next logical step is to add on ways for the user to navigate the results.

Navigating the Result List

Finally, now that the user has entered some text into the text entry field, and some results have been loaded from the server, it's time to add on a way for the user to navigate the returned result set. In your implementation of the autocomplete search, you're going to offer two different ways to navigate the results: via keyboard and mouse.

Keyboard Navigation

Navigating the results via keyboard is in all likelihood the most important aspect to implement. Since a user is already in the process of typing out a username, giving him the ability to keep his hands on the keyboard to finish the autocomplete is necessary.

You need to support the use of the Tab key to complete the currently selected user, and the up and down arrows to select different users in the returned result set. Listing 12-7 shows how to achieve this.

Listing 12-7. *The Event Handler for Navigational Keypresses*

```
// Watch for input in the entry field
id("to").onkeypress = function(e){
    // Get all of the users in the result set
    var li = id("results").getElementsByTagName("li");

    // If the [TAB] or [Enter] keys are pressed
    if ( e.keyCode == 9 || e.keyCode == 13 ) {
        // Add the user to the text entry field

    // If the up key is presssed
    } else if ( e.keyCode == 38 )
        // Select the previous user, or the last user (if we're at the beginning)
        return updatePos( curPos.previousSibling || li[ li.length - 1 ] );

    // If the down key is pressed
    else if ( e.keyCode == 40 )
        // Select the next user, or the first user (if we're at the end)
        return updatePos( curPos.nextSibling || li[0] );
};
```

Mouse Navigation

Unlike with keyboard navigation, all mouse navigation must be bound dynamically every time a new set of results comes in from the server. The premise for the mouse navigation is that every time you move your mouse over one of the user <li> elements, it becomes the currently "selected" element; and if you were to click it, the <li>'s associated username would be appended to the text entry field. An example of the code required to handle this is shown in Listing 12-8.

Listing 12-8. *Binding Mouse Navigation Events to a User <li> Element*

```
// Whenever the user mouses over the li,
// set it to be the currently highlighted user
li[i].onmouseover = function(){
    updatePos( this );
};

// When the user is clicked
li[i].onclick = function(){
    // Add the user to the input
    addUser( this );
```

```
    // And focus back on the input again
    id("to").focus();
};
```

With all the navigation in place, you've now finished the main components of your auto-complete search. The final result of your work is shown in the next section.

The Final Result

All the necessary components of the autocomplete search have been completed: watching for user input, communication with the server, and result navigation. It's now time to tie it all together and put it in the page. Listing 12-9 shows the final JavaScript code to make your full autocomplete search.

Listing 12-9. *The Full JavaScript Code of Your Autocomplete Search*

```
domReady(function(){
    // Make sure that the results popup is closed, to begin with
    hide( id("results") );

    // Keep track of which users have already been entered
    var doneUsers = {};

    // Keep track of which user is currently selected
    var curPos;

    // Create the loading image
    var img = document.createElement("img");
    img.src = "indicator.gif";
    img.id = "qloading";

    // And add it to the document, next to the input box
    id("to").parentNode.insertBefore( img, id("to") );

    // Create the results area
    var div = document.createElement("div");
    div.id = "results";
    div.innerHTML = "<div class='suggest'>Suggestions:</div><ul></ul>";

    // And add it in after the input box
    id("to").parentNode.appendChild( div );

    // Watch for input in the entry field
    id("to").onkeypress = function(e){
        // Get all of the users in the result set
        var li = id("results").getElementsByTagName("li");
```

```
            // If the [TAB] or [Enter] keys are pressed
            if ( e.keyCode == 9 || e.keyCode == 13 ) {
                // Reset the list of current users
                loadDone();

                // If the currently selected user is not in the list of selected
                // users, add it on to the input
                if ( !doneUsers[ curPos.id ] )
                    addUser( curPos );

                // Stop the key from doing its normal action
                e.preventDefault();
                return false;

            // If the up key is pressed
            } else if ( e.keyCode == 38 )
                // Select the previous user, or the last user
                // (if we're at the beginning)
                return updatePos( curPos.previousSibling || li[ li.length - 1 ] );

            // If the down key is pressed
            else if ( e.keyCode == 40 )
                // Select the next user, or the first user (if we're at the end)
                return updatePos( curPos.nextSibling || li[0] );
    };

    // Initialize the delayed input checks on our input
    delayedInput({
        // We're attaching to the input text field
        elem: id("to"),

        // We're going to start searching after only 1 character of input
        chars: 1,

        // When the text field loses focus, close the results popup
        focus: true,

        // Handle when the result popup should be opened up
        open: function(q,open){
            // Get the last word out of the comma-separated list of words
            var w = trim( q.substr( q.lastIndexOf(',')+1, q.length ) );

            // Make sure that we're dealing with a word, at least
            if ( w ) {
                // Show the loading spinner animation
                show( id("qloading") );
```

```
// Make sure that no user is currently selected
curPos = null;

// Get the UL that holds all the results
var results = id("results").lastChild;

// And empty it out
results.innerHTML = "";

// Do a request for new data
ajax({
    // Do a simple GET request to the CGI script which
    // returns an HTML block of LI elements
    type: "GET",
    url: "auto.cgi?q=" + w,

    // Watch for when the HTML comes back
    onSuccess: function(html){
        // Insert it in to the results UL
        results.innerHTML = html;

        // And hide the loading animation
        hide( id("qloading") );

        // Re-initalize the list of users that we've pulled in
        loadDone();

        // Go through each of the returned users
        var li = results.getElementsByTagName( "li" );
        for ( var i = 0; i < li.length; i++ ) {

            // If we're already added the user, remove the LI for it
            if ( doneUsers [ li[i].id ] )
                results.removeChild( li[i--] );

            // Otherwise, bind some events to the user li
            else {

                // Whenever the user mouses over the li,
                // set it to be the currently hilighted user
                li[i].onmouseover = function(){
                    updatePos( this );
                };
```

```
                                // When the user is clicked
                                li[i].onclick = function(){
                                    // Add the user to the input
                                    addUser( this );

                                    // And focus back on the input again
                                    id("q").focus();
                                };
                            }
                        }

                        // Go through the list of user li
                        li = results.getElementsByTagName( "li" );

                        // If there are no users left (we've added them all)
                        if ( li.length == 0 )
                            // Then hide the results
                            hide( id("results") );

                        else {

                            // Add 'odd' classes to each of the remaining users
                            // to give them a striping
                            for ( var i = 1; i < li.length; i += 2 )
                                addClass( li[i], "odd" );

                            // Set the currently selected user to the first one
                            updatePos( li[0] );

                            // And then show the results
                            show( id("results") );
                        }
                    }
                });
            }
        },

        // When the popup needs to be closed
        close: function(){
            // Hide the result set
            hide( id("results") );
        }
    });

    function trim(s) {
        return s.replace(/^\s+/,"").replace(/\s+$/, "");
    }
```

```
// Change the highlight of the user that's currently selected
function updatePos( elem ) {
    // Update the position to the currently selected element
    curPos = elem;

    // Get all the user li elements
    var li = id("results").getElementsByTagName("li");

    // Remove the 'cur' class from the currently selected one
    for ( var i = 0; i < li.length; i++ )
        removeClass( li[i], "cur" );

    // And add the highlight to the current user item
    addClass( curPos, "cur" );

    return false;
}

// Re-initialize the list of users that have already been
// entered into the text input by the user
function loadDone() {
    doneUsers = {};

    // Go through the list of users (separated by commas)
    var users = id("q").value.split(',');
    for ( var i = 0; i < users.length; i++ ) {

        // Save the username (as the key) in an object hash
        doneUsers[ trim( users[i].toLowerCase() ) ] = true;
    }
}

// Add a user to the input text field
function addUser( elem ) {
    // The text value of the text input
    var v = id("to").value;

    // Add the user's name at the end of the end of the input
    // Making sure that it's separated with the correct comma
    id("to").value =
        ( v.indexOf(',') >= 0 ? v.substr(0, v.lastIndexOf(',') + 2 ) : '' )
        + elem.id + ", ";

    // Add the username to the master list (avoids having
    // to completely re-load the list)
    doneUsers[ elem.id ] = true;
```

```
        // Remove the user li element
        elem.parentNode.removeChild( elem );

        // And hide the results list
        hide( id("results") );
    }
});
```

Figure 12-6 shows what the final result looks like.

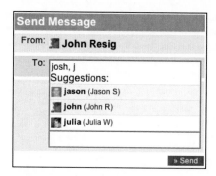

Figure 12-6. *A screenshot of the autocomplete search in action, completing a second username*

The final result is quite impressive and highly useful. The basic concepts of an auto-complete search aren't too complex or hard to implement, but when tied together it creates a nicely interactive result.

Summary

An autocomplete search makes for a nice addition to virtually any application. In almost every text-entry interaction, there is opportunity to help users type in their entries.

In this chapter I covered all the aspects of building an autocomplete search for entering usernames into a simple form. Specifically, you saw how to capture text entry from a user, send a request to a server-side script and pull relevant data back, and allow the user to navigate the results. Taking the concepts presented in this chapter and adapting them to your particular use case will be highly beneficial to your users.

A working demo of this example is available at this book's web site at http:// www.jspro.org/, along with detailed instructions on how to set up the server-side stuff. The source code, as always, is available in the Source Code/Download section of the Apress web site at http://www.apress.com.

■ ■ ■

## CHAPTER 13

An Ajax Wiki

With different server-side MVC frameworks flying to the forefront of web application development (such as Ruby on Rails and Django), I figure now is a good time to look at some of the alternative programming languages used for web application development. The example I explore in this chapter is a simple in-browser wiki.

What Is a Wiki?

According to Wikipedia.org (by far the most popular wiki-based web site), a wiki is a type of web site that allows anyone visiting it to add, remove, or otherwise edit all content very quickly and easily, sometimes without the need for registration. This ease of interaction and operation makes a wiki an effective tool for collaborative writing.

Additionally, a bunch of formatting is provided so that you can customize your wiki entries. Figure 13-1 shows the main page of a wiki after it's been through a number of revisions by different users.

What makes this case study so unique is that the wiki engine logic is written entirely in JavaScript, with the JavaScript code sending database queries directly to the server. This case study demonstrates a number of fundamental concepts necessary for developing a modern web application, even though none of the traditional application logic is taking place on the server.

The application itself is broken down into three portions: client, server, and database (as is the case with most Ajax applications), all of which I will cover extensively. The client is responsible for interacting with the user and manipulating the interface. The server is responsible for managing the communication between the client and the data source.

To understand what exactly this application is, what it's capable of, and how it works, I'm going to walk you through each of the application's features and explain how this application's code can be reused in your own.

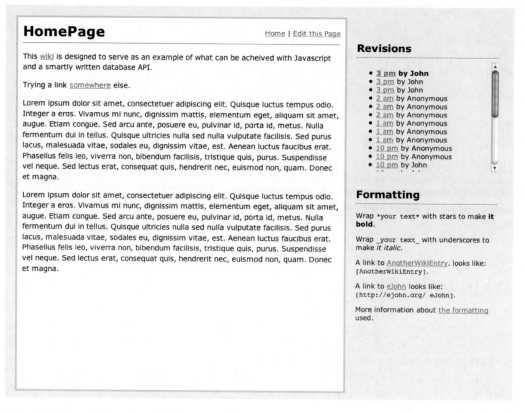

Figure 13-1. *Screenshot of a wiki in action*

Talking With the Database

Each page of a wiki can be created and edited by anyone. This means that you need to store all of this user-contributed content somewhere so that you can access it later. Perhaps the sanest solution is to create a simple database that you can store all of your data in. To be able to make your JavaScript-coded client talk to your database, you need to have a piece of server-side code sit in between it and the wiki database. The flow of each database query looks like what's shown in Figure 13-2. This process is the same for all forms of statements executed (e.g., SELECT, INSERT, etc.).

There are two times that you need to communicate with the database from your client. The first is to query the database, retrieving all the revisions for a particular page. The second is when you insert the data for a new revision into the database. The flow for both of these queries is virtually identical, making it easy to build a common, simple communication layer that you can use for this and other JavaScript applications. Another nice aspect of having this common communication layer is that you can easily step through the full communication flow (shown in Figure 13-2) and look at how the JavaScript is able to communicate with the database.

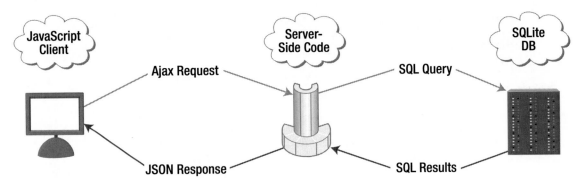

Figure 13-2. *The flow of the application when performing a query from the client*

■Caution It's important to realize that you shouldn't send plain SQL queries from a client to a server; doing so can leave the server and database open to malicious attacks. It is because of this that in your application all SQL queries are mapped to keywords that are transformed to the actual queries on the server side. This allows you to be flexible on the client side while still protecting the database from attacks.

To understand how this flow works, you're going to step through the process of executing a query against the server and database from the JavaScript client.

The Ajax Request

An Ajax request occurs whenever there's a need to communicate with the database (and thus the server). For example, an Ajax request occurs whenever you need to save a revision that you've made to the wiki. A revision consists of four pieces of information:

The title of the wiki page: A common convention for naming wiki pages is using a scheme called CamelCase, which consists of pushing together capitalized words. For example, the main page of your wiki has the name HomePage.

The name of the revision author: Users making the revisions have the option to provide their name. However, they can remain anonymous if they wish (which is a very popular feature of most wikis).

The actual text of the revision: This is a potentially large text entry that the user enters. The contents are formatted with Textile, a popular text-formatting scheme.

The exact time of the revision: This is generated by the client and (hopefully) used as a unique identifier. Since the time is precise to the exact millisecond, this should serve well enough for this application.

Using all of these pieces of data, you can now build a query that you can send to your database. A simplified version of the code needed to save a revision is shown in Listing 13-1.

Listing 13-1. *Code Required to Save Data From the Client to the Server-Side Database*

```
// Insert the revision into the database
sqlExec(
    // A query statement, the actual code of which is stored on the server
    "insert",
    [
        document.title, // The title of the entry
        $("#author").val(), // The author value that the user provided
        $("#text").val(), // The text of the revision
        (new Date()).getTime() // The exact time of the revision
    ],
    // Reload the revision list, once the query is complete
    reload
);
```

Behind the sqlExec function, you prepare the SQL query (which is then converted into a CGI query string), build the request URL, and make an Ajax request. To pull this together, you use jQuery's Ajax functionality, which is capable of handling HTTP POST requests (the POST request is needed to send the long revision text). You'll see the final Ajax request in the "Handling the JSON Response" section of this chapter.

Now that you've made a request to the server, you need to see how the server-side code handles the database query.

The Server-Side Code

The server-side portion of this application has a very simple and reproducible flow. The overall goal is to get a SQL query from the client, execute it against a SQL database, and return the results formatted as a JSON string. To put this application into practice, I decided to refine the application flow and produce duplicate working versions of it in all the popular scripting languages: Perl, PHP, Python, and Ruby. I assume that you have at least tinkered with one of these languages; if not, this is a great time to learn by example.

Handling a Request

The client has just initiated a connection with the server-side portion of the application, requesting that a specific SQL query be executed against the database. You can access this query and the name of the database to execute it against by accessing the CGI parameters passed to the application. In the previous section, you saw that two of the parameters passed to the server-side script are the name of the database and the SQL query text. To understand how the parameters are retrieved, Listing 13-2 shows how it's done in the Ruby version of the server-side code.

Listing 13-2. *Retrieving the CGI Parameters Passed to the Server-Side Portion of the Application Written in Ruby*

```ruby
# Import the CGI library
require 'cgi'

# Create a new CGI object, which will parse
# the incoming CGI parameters
cgi = CGI.new

# Capture the query parameter
sql = cgi['sql']

# Get the database name from the user and make
# sure that no malicious characters were used
d = cgi['db'].gsub(/[^a-zA-Z0-9_-]/, "")
```

Using the retrieved database name and query, you now need to connect to the database, which begs the question, What type of database should you use? I've already decided to use a SQL-based database (since it's such a ubiquitous standard in web application development). For this application, I decided to go with the SQL database called SQLite.

SQLite is an up-and-coming SQL database implementation that is incredibly lightweight and fast. It sacrifices such things as users, roles, and permissions in favor of simplicity and speed. For this particular application, this fits your needs very nicely. SQLite works by running off of a single file on your system, so you can have as many databases as you have files. In addition to being really fast, SQLite serves as a really quick and simple way of setting up a database for simple applications or testing. Rather than require a large database install (such as MySQL, PostgreSQL, or Oracle), SQLite will serve your needs just fine.

Every language that I explored (Perl, PHP, Python, and Ruby) has support for SQLite in one way or another:

- Perl has the DBD::SQLite module. This module is particularly notable because the developers decided to completely implement the SQLite specification inside of the module itself, meaning that no additional downloads are required to get a database up and running.

- PHP 5 has built-in SQLite support. Unfortunately, the language only has support for SQLite 2 (which is fine for some applications), but in order to have complete compatibility between the different code bases, you need to install a PHP SQLite 3 library instead.

- Python and Ruby both have SQLite libraries that hook in directly with the official SQLite installation. Python 2.5 has support for SQLite built straight into the language (which I choose not to use, as it's still relatively new).

I highly recommend that you explore using SQLite in some of your smaller projects. It's a great way to get up and running when you don't need the overhead of a large database installation.

How to connect to the SQLite database is virtually identical in every language. They all require two steps: The first is to include a SQLite library (to provide generic connection functions), and the second is to connect to the database and remember the connection for later. Listing 13-3 shows how this is done in Ruby.

Listing 13-3. *Importing the External SQLite Library and Connecting to the Database in the Ruby Version of the Server-Side Code*

```ruby
# Import the external SQLite library
require 'rubygems'
require_gem 'sqlite3-ruby'

# Later on in the program…

# 'd' needs to be cleaned, to make sure that no
# malicious database file name was provided
d = cgi['db'].gsub(/[^a-zA-Z0-9_-]/, "")

# Connect to the SQLite database, which is just a file
# 'd' contains the name of our database, which is 'wiki'
db = SQLite3::Database.new('../../data/' + d + '.db')
```

With an open connection to the SQLite database, you can now execute the client-sent query and get the results.

Executing and Formatting SQL

With a connection open to the database, you should now be able to execute the SQL query. The ultimate goal is to be able to put the results of a query into a form that can be easily converted to a JSON string and returned to the client. The easiest digestible form for the SQL results is an array of hashes, looking something like the code in Listing 13-4. Each hash represents a row matched in the database. Each key/value pair in the hash represents a column name and a column value within the row.

Listing 13-4. *A Sample JSON Structure Returned From the Server*

```
[
    {
        title: "HomePage",
        author: "John",
        content: "Welcome to my wonderful wiki!",
        date: "20060324122514"
    },
```

```
{
    title: "Test",
    author: "Anonymous",
    content: "Lorem ipsum dolem…",
    date: "20060321101345"
},
. . .
]
```

Depending on the language that you choose to use, the difficulty of putting the SQL results into the desired data structure varies. The most common case, however, is one where the SQL library returns two things: an array of the column names, and an array of arrays containing all the row data, as shown in Listing 13-5.

Listing 13-5. *In Ruby, the Data Structures Returned by Executing an SQL Query Looking for Wiki Revision Information*

```
rows.columns = ["title","author","content","date"]


rows = [
    ["HomePage","John","Welcome to my wonderful wiki!","20060324122514"],
    ["Test","Anonymous","Lorem ipsum dolem…","20060321101345"],
    . . .
]
```

The process of converting the SQL results presented in Listing 13-5 to be more like the data structure shown in Listing 13-4 can be tricky. Essentially, you need to iterate through each matched row, create a temporary hash, populate it with all the column data, and then add the new hash onto the global array. How this is done in Ruby is presented in Listing 13-6.

Listing 13-6. *How an SQL Statement Is Executed in Ruby and Pushed Into the Final Data Structure (Called r)*

```
# If the sql has some returned rows  (e.g. it was a SELECT)
db.query( sql ) do |rows|
    # Go through every returned row
    rows.each do |row|
        # Create a temporary hash
        tmp = {}

        # Force the array columns into Hash Key/Value pairs
        for i in 0 .. rows.columns.length-1
            tmp[rows.columns[i]] = row[i]
        end

        # Add the row hash to the array of found rows
        r.push tmp
    end
end
```

Now that you have a suitable final data structure, you can go about converting it to a JSON string. At its core, JSON is a way of representing values (strings and numbers), arrays of values, and hashes (key/value pairs) using JavaScript-compatible object notation. Since you've taken care and made sure that there is a data structure consisting of nothing but arrays, hashes, and strings, you can easily convert it to a JSON-formatted string.

All the scripting languages that you're using for this application have an implementation of JSON serialization (taking a native data structure and converting it to a JSON string), which is exactly what you need. Additionally, since the output is very lightweight, as is the case with most JSON-formatted data, it becomes very easy to output to the browser. Incidentally, each language's implementation ends up being very similar to the others, simplifying the transition process from one language to another:

- Each implementation is available in the form of a library or a module.

- Each implementation is able to translate native language objects (e.g., strings, arrays, and hashes).

- Each implementation makes it easy to get at a string of the JSON-formatted object.

However, the one language that implements JSON serialization particularly elegantly is Ruby. This is an example of how you would convert an object to a JSON string (after loading in the JSON library) and print it back out to the client:

```
# Convert the object (r) to a JSON string, and print it
print r.to_json
```

I highly recommend that you look over the code for the server implementation in your favorite language and see how it handles SQL querying and JSON serialization. I think you'll be pleasantly surprised at how simple it is.

Handling the JSON Response

You've now received a response from the server that contains the formatted JSON string. Going back to Listing 13-2 you can now write the code necessary to handle and evaluate this JSON code. If there's one thing that JSON is good at, it's simplicity in evaluation and navigation. You don't need a full-blown parser (as you would with XML); instead, all you need is the eval() function (which evaluates JavaScript code, which is exactly what a JSON string is). Using the jQuery library, it is completely taken care of, as you can see in Listing 13-7. All you have to do is specify a data type (named dataType) of "json" and you instantly receive JSON data from the server.

Listing 13-7. *Getting Results From the Server and Sending the JavaScript Data Structure to the Callback Function*

```
// Submit the query to the server
$.ajax({
    // POST to the API URL
    type: "POST",
    url: apiURL,
```

```
    // Serialize the array of data
    data: $.param(p),

    // We're expecting JSON data coming back
    dataType: "json",

    // Wait for the request to finish successfully
    // If a callback was specified by the user, send the data back
    success: callback
});
```

If you'll notice in Listing 13-7, the last action that's performed is the execution of the function named callback (which points to whichever callback function is provided to the sqlExec function). The single argument that's passed to this function is the full data structure that you meticulously built on the server and displayed to the client. To understand how this full sqlExec-Ajax-response flow works, take a look at a simplified version of what actually happens in the wiki, shown in Listing 13-8. The logic is that if revisions for the page exist, the most recent one must be displayed. Otherwise, if none exists, a form should be displayed so that the user can create a new revision.

Listing 13-8. *A Simplified Version of the Code Used in the Client Code to Retreive Revisions From the Server and Display Them on the Site*

```
// Request all the revisions for the current wiki page
// Once loaded, return the data to the 'loaded' function.
sqlExec("select", [$s], loaded);

// Handle the SQL results coming back from the server
function loaded(sql) {
    // If revisions exist for this wiki
    if ( sql.length > 0 ) {
        // Show the wiki page
        showContent();

        // Render the revision, using textile
        $("#content").html(textile(sql[0].content));

        // Make the revision contents editable
        $("textarea").val( sql[0].content );

    // Otherwise, if no revisions exist, show a 'create me' form
    } else {
        // Show the default editing form instead
        showForm();
    }
}
```

The important part of the code shown in Listing 13-8 is the quick snippet `textile` `(sql[0].content)`, which grabs the wiki revision text from the data structure and runs a Textile formatter on it. Much in the way that HTML is a way of marking up content, so is Textile. Textile is significantly simpler, providing basic, understandable formatting for anyone to use. A sample of Textile formatting is shown in Figure 13-3.

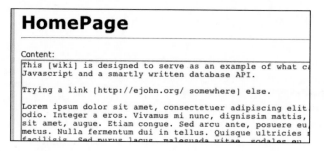

Figure 13-3. *A wiki revision using Textile formatting*

One nice aspect about Textile, however, is that someone has already done all the hard work and created a Textile JavaScript library that's capable of converting Textile-formatted text into final, presentable HTML. More information about Textile can be found on the following web sites:

- Textile overview: `http://www.textism.com/tools/textile/`

- JavaScript Textile implementation (used in this project): `http://jrm.cc/extras/live-textile-preview.php`

Now that the data is coming back from the server formatted and inserted into the document, you have the makings of a full wiki. From this point, I recommend that you set up your own copy of the wiki code and play around. It's all highly commented, so it should be fairly stress-free to maneuver around.

An Extra Case Study: A JavaScript Blog

If you're interested in seeing what else can be done with this client-server-SQLite setup, I've created another demo that you can feel free to explore. This application is a simple, private in-browser blog. It's very easy to use, too; whenever you visit the page you're given your own private blog that you can view and post to. Additionally, there are live previews of your posts and a little SQL console that can be fun to play with. The code and a demo of the blog application are on the book's web site (`http://jspro.org/`). A screenshot of it in action is shown in Figure 13-4.

Figure 13-4. *A screenshot of the in-browser blog and SQL console*

Application Code

The case study presented in this chapter is much more complicated than the case studies previously demonstrated. This section details the primary code needed to make this application run (and directly relates to what is discussed in this chapter).

What follows is a list of all the files needed to power this wiki application. It's a mix of the client-side and server-side code discussed in the chapter, in addition to all the different libraries and style files not directly mentioned in this chapter:

- *index.html*: The main application page, pulling all the client code together.

- *install.html*: The main installation file, to be run before first using the application.

- *css/style.css*: All the CSS styling for the client side of the application.

- *js/wiki.js (shown in Listing 13-9)*: The main JavaScript code, responsible for binding events and running SQL queries.

- *js/sql.js (shown in Listing 13-10)*: The code responsible for communicating with the server, retrieving the JSON data from the SQL queries.

- *js/textile.js*: A copy of the JavaScript Textile library (for converting text to HTML): http://jrm.cc/extras/live-textile-preview.php.

- *js/jquery.js*: A copy of the current release of jQuery: http://jquery.com/.

- *api/*: The main server code responsible for translating SQL query results to JSON and returning them to the client. This directory contains each code version in Perl, PHP, Python, and Ruby. I've included a copy of the Ruby version of the code in Listing 13-11.

- *data/wiki.db*: The SQLite database that stores the wiki.

The full code of the files in this chapter is in the following listings.

Core JavaScript Code

Listing 13-9 shows wiki.js, the main JavaScript code responsible for binding events and interacting with the user.

Listing 13-9. *js/wiki.js*

```
// Get the name of the current page
var $s = window.location.search;
$s = $s.substr(1,$s.length);

// Determine if a revision number
// was provided - if so, remember it's ID
var $r = false;

// Revisions are provided in the format
// ?Title&RevisionID
var tmp = $s.split("&");
if ( tmp.length > 1 ) {
  $s = tmp[0];
  $r = tmp[1];
}

// Go to the homepage, if no page is provided
if (!$s) window.location = "?HomePage";

// Set the name of the database
var db = "wiki";

// We need to wait for the DOM to finish loading
$(document).ready(function(){
```

```
  // Set the title of the page
  document.title = $s;
  $("h1").html($s);

  // Load in all the wiki revisions
  reload();

  // If the 'edit page' link is clicked
  $("#edit").click(showForm);

  // When the user submits a new revision
  $("#post form").submit(function(){
    // Get the author name
    var author = $("#author").val();

    // Get the text
    var text = $("#text").val();

    // Render the contents
    $("#content").html(textile(text));

    // Make the current revision the time
    // (this helps with highlighting)
    $r = (new Date()).getTime();

    // Insert the revision into the database
    sqlExec("insert", [$s,author,text,$r], reload);

    return false;
  });

  // If the user clicked the 'cancel' link
  // inside the editing area
  $("#cancel").click(showContent);
});

// Show the current revision
function showContent() {
  // Show the edit link
  $("#edit,#cancel").css("display","inline");

  // Hide the editing area
  $("#post").hide();

  // Show the content
  $("#content").show();
```

```javascript
    return false;
}

// Show the form to edit the current revision
function showForm() {
  // Hide the edit link
  $("#edit").hide();

  // Show the editing area
  $("#post").show();

  // Hide the content
  $("#content").hide();

  return false;
}

// Load all of the revisions from the database
function reload(t) {
  // Request all the revisions
  sqlExec("select", [$s], function(sql) {
    // If revisions exist for this wiki
    if ( sql.length > 0 ) {
      if ( !$r ) $r = sql[0].date;

      // Show the wiki page
      showContent();

      // Show all the revisions
      $("#side ul").html('');

      // Go through each of the revisions
      for ( var i = 0; i < sql.length; i++ ) {

        // If this revision is the one currently being displayed
        if ( sql[i].date == $r ) {

          // Render the revision
          $("#content").html(textile(sql[i].content));

          // Make the revision contents editable
          $("textarea").val( sql[i].content );

        }

        // Get a workable date object
        var d = new Date( parseInt(sql[i].date) );
```

```
        // Figure out if the revision was made within the last day, or not
        if ( d.getTime() > (new Date()).getTime() - (3600 * 24000) )

          // If it was, make a nice am/pm time
          d = d.getHours() >= 12 ?
            (d.getHours() != 12 ? d.getHours() - 12 : 12 ) + " pm" :
            d.getHours() + " am";

        // Otherwise, display the month and day of the revision
        else {
          var a = d.toUTCString().split(" ");
          d = a[2] + " " + d.getDate();
        }

        // Add the revision to the revision list
        $("#side ul").append("<li class='" + ( $r == sql[i].date ? "cur" : "" )
          + "'><a href='?" + $s + ( i > 0 ? "&" + sql[i].date : "" )
          + "'>" + d + "</a> by " + sql[i].author + "</li>");
      }

    // Otherwise, this page has never been revised
    } else {
      // Say so in the revision panel
      $("#rev").html("<li>No Revisions.</li>");

      // Hide the editing controls
      $("#edit,#cancel").hide();

      // Show the default editing form
      showForm();
    }
  });
}
```

JavaScript SQL Library

Listing 13-10 shows sql.js, the code responsible for communicating with the server and retrieving the JSON data from the SQL queries.

Listing 13-10. *js/sql.js*

```
// UPDATE THIS VARIABLE
// The URL where your Server-Side script is
var apiURL = "api/ruby/";

// Some default global variables
var sqlLoaded = function(){}
```

```
// Handle a long SQL Submission
// This function is capable of sending large amounts of
// data (e.g. a large INSERT), but is only able to send
// to locations on the same server as the client
function sqlExec(q, p, callback) {

  // Load all the arguments into a structured array
  for ( var i = 0; i < p.length; i++ ) {
    p[i] = { name: "arg", value: p[i] };
  }

  // Include the name of the database
  p.push({ name: "db", value: db });

  // And the name of the SQL query to execute
  p.push({ name: "sql", value: q });

  // Submit the query to the server
  $.ajax({
    // POST to the API URL
    type: "POST",
    url: apiURL,

    // Serialize the array of data
    data: $.param(p),

    // We're expecting JSON data coming back
    dataType: "json",

    // Wait for the request to finish successfully
    // If a callback was specified by the user, send the data back
    success: callback
  });

}
```

Ruby Server-Side Code

The following code, in Listing 13-11, represents the server-side portion of the Ajax wiki application. All of this code is written in the Ruby programming language. For examples of the same code, but written in PHP, Perl, or Python, you can visit this book's web site at http://jspro.org/.

Listing 13-11. *The Server-Side Portion of the Wiki Application Written in Ruby*

```ruby
#!/usr/bin/env ruby

# Import all the external libraries
require 'cgi'
require 'rubygems'
require_gem 'sqlite3-ruby'
require 'json/objects'

# Display the Javascript header
print "Content-type: text/javascript\n\n"

# Initalize the application variables
err = ""
r = []
cgi = CGI.new

# Capture parameters passed in by the user
call = cgi['callback']
sql = cgi['sql']

# Get a database from the user and make
# sure that no malicious characters were used
d = cgi['db'].gsub(/[^a-zA-Z0-9_-]/, "")

# If no database was provided, then use 'test'
if d == '' then
  d = "test"
end

# Get the list of arguments that we're
# putting in the SQL query
args = cgi.params['arg']

# We only accept two different SQL queries

# Insert a new wiki revision into the database
if sql == "insert" then
  sql = "INSERT INTO wiki VALUES(?,?,?,?);"

# Get all the revisions for a wiki entry
elsif sql == "select" then
  sql = "SELECT * FROM wiki WHERE title=? ORDER BY date DESC;"
```

```
# Otherwise, fail on the query
else
  sql = ""
end

# If a SQL query was provided
if sql != '' then

  # Go through each of the arguments provided
  for i in 0 .. args.length-1
    # Replace all single quotes with '' (that's the equivalent
    # of escaping them in SQLite), and escape all ?
    args[i] = args[i].gsub(/'/, "''").gsub(/\?/, "\\?")

    # Then go through the SQL query and replace the first matched
    # question mark with the argument data
    sql = sql.sub(/([^\\])\?/, "\\1'" + args[i] + "'")
  end

  # After we're done, un-escape the question marks that we escaped
  sql = sql.gsub(/\\\?/, "?")

  # Make sure that we capture all thrown DB errors
  begin
    # Connect to the SQLite database, which is just a file
    db = SQLite3::Database.new('../../data/' + d + '.db')

    # If the sql has some returned rows
    # (e.g. it was a SELECT)
    db.query( sql ) do |rows|
      # Go through every returned row
      rows.each do |row|
        # Create a temporary hash
        tmp = {}

        # Force the array columns into
        # Hash Key/Value pairs
        for i in 0 .. rows.columns.length-1
          tmp[rows.columns[i]] = row[i]
        end

        # Add the row hash to the array of found rows
        r.push tmp
      end
    end
```

```
  rescue Exception => e
    # If an error occurred, remember the message for later
    err = e
  end
else
  # If no SQL query was provided, display an error
  err = "No query provided."
end

# If an error occurred, return a hash containing
# an error key and a value containing the error message
if err != '' then
  r = { "error" => err }
end

# Convert the return object to a JSON string
jout = r.to_json

# If a callback was provided
if call != '' then
  # Wrap the returned object in the callback string
  print call + "(" + jout + ")"
else
  # Otherwise just print the JSON string
  print jout
end
```

Summary

There are a couple concepts that I hope you'll be able to learn when walking through this particular application. First, JSON is a powerful and viable alternative to using XML in web applications. Second, by keeping your server-side code as simple as possible, you can give the front end more control over what to do with the user data (which should be done in moderation, keeping the most important business logic hidden). Finally, all modern server-side scripting languages can behave very similarly (in that they have many of the same features) and are rather easy to swap in and out (which is why I wrote identical versions of the server-side code in the four most popular scripting languages).

All of the main application code can be found in the "Application Code" section of this chapter. A complete installable version of the application can be found on this book's web site, http://jspro.org/, or at http://www.apress.com/, complete with detailed installation instructions. A live demo can be found here: http://jspro.org/demo/wiki/.

The web site includes full instructions on how to use the code. Additionally, a full forum is provided to discuss any problems that you might encounter when attempting your own installation.

■ ■ ■

## PART 5

The Future of JavaScript

CHAPTER 14

■ ■ ■

Where Is JavaScript Going?

In the past couple years there's been a tremendous amount of development on the JavaScript language—and from many directions. The Mozilla Foundation has been making progress on improving the quality of the JavaScript language, aligning it with ECMAScript 4 (the language that JavaScript is based upon). On another front, the WHAT-WG, a collaboration of web browser manufacturers who want to develop new technologies that allow writing and deploying applications over the Web, has created the specification for the next generation of browser-based applications. Finally, library authors and corporations have been working to solidify the techniques of streaming browser-based applications into the technique called *Comet*. All of this represents the future of the JavaScript language and browser-based development.

In this chapter we're going to look at the advances that have been made in JavaScript 1.6 and 1.7, leading up to the full JavaScript 2.0 release. Next, you'll see one of the advances made with the Web Applications 1.0 specification: the ability to draw using JavaScript. Finally, we'll take a quick look at the premise behind Comet and streaming web applications.

JavaScript 1.6 and 1.7

Since early this decade, the JavaScript language has been slowly marching forward, adding functional improvements. While most modern browsers support JavaScript 1.5 (or an equivalent), they've been quite lax about moving the language forward.

Brendan Eich, and others at the Mozilla Foundation, has been diligently working to bring the language forward, in conjunction with ECMAScript 4. More information about Mozilla's work can be found here:

- *Mozilla's work with JavaScript*: http://www.mozilla.org/js/language/

- *Mozilla's JavaScript 2.0 proposal*: http://www.mozilla.org/js/language/js20/

- *Mozilla's ECMAScript 4 proposal*: http://www.mozilla.org/js/language/es4/

While JavaScript 2.0 has yet to be finalized, Mozilla has already begun making inroads, releasing JavaScript versions 1.6 and 1.7, which include a number of the features that are going to make up the final, revised language. A number of the features that have been added are rather significant, and I'll cover them briefly in this section.

JavaScript 1.6

The first release of the updated JavaScript language came in the form of JavaScript 1.6. It was released in conjunction with the Firefox 1.5 browser, created by the Mozilla Foundation. A short synopsis of the changes made in JavaScript 1.6 can be found at the Mozilla web site: `http://developer.mozilla.org/en/docs/New_in_JavaScript_1.6`.

The two important features in this release are E4X (ECMAScript for XML) and a set of additional functions for arrays. Neither of these features is implemented in any other browser at this time, but it's very likely that Opera and Safari will be the next ones to jump on board. I'll show you the benefits that each of these features has.

ECMAScript for XML (E4X)

E4X adds a set of new syntax to the JavaScript language, giving you the ability to write XML inline, right inside of JavaScript code. The result is rather interesting and, albeit, quite complex. More information about E4X can be found in its specification and on the Mozilla web site:

- *The ECMAScript for XML specification*: `http://www.ecma-international.org/publications/standards/Ecma-357.htm`

- *A quick overview of E4X*: `http://developer.mozilla.org/presentations/xtech2005/e4x/`

In general, the specification allows you to write JavaScript-like syntax that has XML DOM results. For example, writing var img = <img/> + <hr/> will append a horizontal rule after an image element and store the resulting DOM elements in a variable for later use. A more complex example is shown in Listing 14-1. The resulting XML document is shown in Listing 14-2.

Listing 14-1. *Building an HTML Document Using E4X, From a Presentation Given by Brendan Eich*

```
<script type="text/javascript;e4x=1">
    // Create an HTML element and store it in a variable
    var html = <html/>;

    // Set the contents of the title element to a string of text
    // E4X automatically creates all missing elements and takes care
    // of text nodes appropriately
    html.head.title = "My Page Title";

    // Set the background color property of the body element
    // The body element is created automatically
    html.body.@bgcolor = "#e4e4e4";
```

```
        // Add some properties to a form element inside the body
        html.body.form.@name = "myform";
        html.body.form.@action = "someurl.cgi";
        html.body.form.@method = "post";
        html.body.form.@onclick = "return somejs();";

        // Create an empty input element with a specified name
        html.body.form.input[0] = "";
        html.body.form.input[0].@name = "test";
</script>
```

Listing 14-2. *The HTML Document Generated by Calling the E4X Code From Listing 14-1*

```
<html>
    <head>
        <title>My Page Title</title>
    </head>
    <body bgcolor="#e4e4e4">
        <form name="myform" action="someurl.jss"
                method="post" onclick="return somejs();">
            <input name="test"></input>
        </form>
    </body>
</html>
```

While the syntax for E4X is quite a deviation from the normal JavaScript style—and that may be enough to scare off most new users—the result could be quite useful, allowing you to cut down on a number of repetitive DOM operations.

Array Extras

The primary new features added to JavaScript 1.6 are those relating to arrays. In 1.6, arrays now have a number of additional methods that can be used for common operations:

- Two of the operations, indexOf() and lastIndexOf(), are similar to the methods of the same name that exist for string objects. The two methods allow you to find the position of an object within an array, returning the matched index, or -1 if the object does not exist in the array.

- Three new methods, forEach(), some(), and many(), will help simplify common iteration needs, allowing you to execute a function within the context of an array over every one of its contained objects.

- New filter() and map() functions allow you to perform inline array transformations, similar to the map and grep operations that exist in other languages (such as Perl).

Examples of all the new JavaScript 1.6 array functions are shown in Listing 14-3.

Listing 14-3. *Examples of New Array Methods in JavaScript 1.6*

```
// A simple array of numbers
var tmp = [ 1, 2, 3, 4, 5, 3 ];

// indexOf( Object )
// Find the index of an object within an array of objects
tmp.indexOf( 3 ) == 2
tmp.indexOf( 8 ) == -1

// lastIndexOf( Object )
// Find the last of an object within an array of objects
tmp.lastIndexOf( 3 ) == 5

// forEach( Function )
// Call a function on every single object within an array
// The function is passed three arguments: The object, its index,
// and a reference to the array
tmp.forEach( alert );

// every( Function )
// Call the function on every object in the array, if it returns true
// for every object, return true
tmp.every(function(num){
    return num < 6;
}) // true

// some( Function )
// Call the function on every object in the array, if it returns true
// for any object, return true
tmp.some(function(num){
    return num > 6;
}) // false

// filter( Function )
// Trim the array by only keeping objects that match a specified
// criteria. An object is kept if the function returns 'true'.
tmp.filter(function(num){
    return num > 3;
}) // [ 4, 5 ]

// map( Function )
// Convert an array of objects to another set of objects. The result of
// the specified function converts an object to its new value
tmp.map(function(num) {
    return num + 2;
}) // [ 3, 4, 5, 6, 7, 5 ]
```

These simple examples aside, these new methods provide a great amount of much-needed speed and functionality for arrays and JavaScript. I certainly look forward to the day these methods receive greater cross-browser adoption.

JavaScript 1.7

This new release of the JavaScript language adds a great deal of functionality, adding a number of features that bring it closer to other full-featured languages. Additionally, the new JavaScript 1.7 release is even more advanced than what was offered by the previous JavaScript 1.6 update, adding some new features that change the way the language is able to work. This web site details some of the new features available in JavaScript 1.7: `http://developer.mozilla.org/en/docs/New_in_JavaScript_1.7`.

This update to the JavaScript language was released in conjunction with the 2.0 version of Mozilla's Firefox 2.0 browser. This browser includes a full implementation of everything outlined in this section and is still the only browser that has significant, modern updates to the JavaScript language.

Array Comprehension

One nice, new addition allows you to write nifty one-liners that relate to array generation. In order to populate an array with a list of items, previously you would have to iterate through a set and push them onto the final array. Now you can instead use array comprehension to do this in a single, simple step. It's best explained by an example, shown in Listing 14-4.

Listing 14-4. *Array Comprehension in JavaScript 1.7*

```
<script type="application/javascript;version=1.7">
    // Old way of putting a series of numbers into an array
    var array = [];
    for ( var i = 0; i < 10; i++ ) {
        array.push( i );
    }

    // New way
    var array = [ i for ( i = 0; i < 10; i++ ) ];

    // Old way of putting object keys into an array
    var array = []
    for ( var key in obj ) {
        array.push( key );
    }

    // New Way
    var array = [ key for ( key in obj ) ];
</script>
```

This particular language feature is one that's been in other languages (such as Python) for some time, and it's nice to see it making its way to JavaScript.

Let Scoping

Let Scoping is a fantastic new feature and probably one that'll be among the most widely used and adopted. Up until this point, JavaScript hasn't had any block-level scoping (as discussed in Chapter 2). With the addition of the new let statement, expression, and definition, it's now possible to define variable scope on a number of different levels. Listing 14-5 shows a few examples of what's possible with let scoping.

Listing 14-5. *Examples of JavaScript 1.7's Let Scoping*

```
<script type="application/javascript;version=1.7">
    // let Statement
    var test = 10;
    let( test = 20 ) {
        alert( test ); // alerts out 20
    }
    alert( test ); // alerts 10

    // let Expression
    var test = 10;
    alert( let( test = 20 ) test ); // alerts out 20
    alert( test ); // alerts 10

    // let Definition
    var test = 10;
    if ( test == 10 ) {
        let newTest = 20;
        test += newTest;
    }
    alert( test ); // alerts 30
    alert( newTest ); // fails, newText is undefined outside of the if statement

    // Using let in a for block
    for ( let i = 0; i < 10; i++ ) {
        alert( i );
    }
    alert( i ); // fails, i is undefined outside of the for statement
</script>
```

With this simple addition, you'll be able to make your code cleaner, work more efficiently, and avoid a number of common namespace collisions (much of this is working up to the introduction of classes and namespaces in JavaScript 2.0).

Destructuring

The final big concept introduced in JavaScript 1.7 is that of destructuring. This is a concept taken from functional programming languages (such as Lisp) that allows you to have complex data structures on the left-hand side of an operand populated with specified values.

A little more information on destructuring in ECMAScript 4 is on Mozilla's web site: http://developer.mozilla.org/es4/proposals/destructuring_assignment.html.

While the concept of destructuring is not simple, it should definitely warrant some of your time, as it's an excellent concept to understand. A couple examples of how destructuring works in JavaScript 1.7 are shown in Listing 14-6.

Listing 14-6. *Examples of Destructuring in JavaScript 1.7*

```
<script type="application/javascript;version=1.7">
    // An example of using destructuring to swap
    // the values of two variables
    [ b, a ] = [ a, b ]

    // A simple function that returns an array of strings
    function test() {
        return [ "John", "October" ];
    }

    // We can destructure the data that's returned into two
    // new variables - name and month
    var [ name, month ] = test();

    // An example of destructuring using an object
    var { name: myName } = { name: "John" };
    // Now myName == "John"

    // A simple data structure
    var users = [
        { name: "John", month: "October" },
        { name: "Bob", month: "December" },
        { name: "Jane", month: "May" }
    ];

    // Destructuring within a loop
    for ( let { name: name, month: month } in users ) {
        // Prints out alerts for John, Bob, and Jane
        alert( name + " was born in " + month );
    }
</script>
```

All together, the JavaScript language is moving in some very positive directions, generally adopting useful features from other languages (such as Python and Lisp). Much of its usefulness, however, relies upon the implementation effort that different browser vendors put into the language. While the Mozilla Foundation has been very diligent about implementing new features, other browsers have been rather lax. While it'll be a while before you can start using JavaScript 1.6 or 1.7 in cross-browser web applications, you'll be able to begin using it now, developing Mozilla-specific browser extensions (at least until there is a more common implementation of the language).

Web Applications 1.0

The second specification that is pushing forward JavaScript development is that of the WHAT-WG (Web Hypertext Application Technology Working Group) in creating the new Web Applications 1.0 specification. This specification goes in a number of different directions, adding numerous additions to HTML, the DOM, and JavaScript as a whole. Many consider the work going into this specification is what will become HTML 5. Thankfully, unlike new versions of JavaScript, implementations of (portions of) this specification are much easier to come by.

While this entire specification is quite large, I highly recommend that you read through it and look at the new technology that will be available very soon. In this section I'll only be focusing on one particular feature of this new specification: the <canvas> element. This new element allows you to programmatically draw 2D images using JavaScript. Adoption of this technique has been very high, making it an easy topic to learn and test. More information about Web Applications 1.0 and the <canvas> element can be found here:

- *The entire Web Applications 1.0 specification*: http://whatwg.org/specs/web-apps/current-work/

- *The subsection of the specification dealing specifically with the new <canvas> element*: http://whatwg.org/specs/web-apps/current-work/#the-2d

- *A series of examples that utilize the new <canvas> element*: http://developer.mozilla.org/en/docs/Canvas_tutorial:Basic_animations

The <canvas> element fills the needs of many web application developers, allowing them to rotate images, draw lines, and create shapes. This single addition can add on whole new levels of interactivity to web applications.

The usefulness of being able to draw arbitrary shapes has encouraged browser maintainers to rapidly include the Canvas API in their latest browser releases. Currently, every modern browser supports the Canvas API, with the exception of Internet Explorer, and Google has stepped up and implemented the entire Canvas API in IE, using its native VML support. More information about ExplorerCanvas, Google's Internet Explorer Canvas implementation, is at http://code.google.com/p/explorercanvas/.

Next, we're going to take an in-depth look at two of the examples presented in Mozilla's basic <canvas> tutorial.

Building a Clock

The first example is the building of a simple clock. You're going to use the Canvas 2D API to draw every aspect of the clock; no images or extraneous HTML elements will be used in this process. Figure 14-1 shows an example of the clock that you're going to draw.

Figure 14-1. *The animated clock drawn with the Canvas API*

The <canvas> element works something like a real painting canvas. You can draw a single static frame of the animated clock; but in order to draw a new frame, you must completely clear your canvas and draw it anew. If you have experience with the OpenGL API, you'll feel right at home with the Canvas API.

With the Canvas API, you frequently need to rotate the image canvas—but this can cause a lot of confusion, as you may not know what angle you're currently pointing at or where your "brush" is currently located. It's for that reason that the Canvas API works a lot like a stack: you first save the old position and rotation of the canvas, make some changes to how the current image looks, then revert back to the original canvas and continue drawing.

Listing 14-7 contains the code needed to make your animated clock using Canvas; note that code makes extensive use of the stack system in Canvas to make drawing easier.

Listing 14-7. *Drawing an Animated Clock Using the Canvas API*

```
<html>
<head>
  <title>Canvas Clock Demo</title>
<script>
// Wait for the browser to load
window.onload = function() {
  // Draw the clock
  clock();

  // and re-draw the clock every second thereafter
  setInterval(clock, 1000);
};

function clock() {
  // Get the current date and time
  var now = new Date();
  var sec = now.getSeconds();
  var min = now.getMinutes();
  var hr  = now.getHours();
  hr = hr >= 12 ? hr - 12 : hr;

  // Get the drawing context of the <canvas> element
  var ctx = document.getElementById('canvas').getContext('2d');

  ctx.save();
    // Initalize the drawing Canvas
    ctx.clearRect(0,0,150,150);

    // When we draw at 0,0 we're actually drawing at 75,75
    ctx.translate(75,75);

    // Drawing a 100px line actually draws a 40px line
    ctx.scale(0.4,0.4);
```

```javascript
// Start the cursor rotated at 12:00
ctx.rotate(-Math.PI/2);

// Initalize the drawing properties
ctx.strokeStyle = "black";
ctx.fillStyle = "black";
ctx.lineWidth = 8;
ctx.lineCap = "round";

// Hour marks
ctx.save();
  ctx.beginPath();
    // For each hour
    for ( var i = 0; i < 12; i++ ) {
      // Rotate the Canvas 1/12th of the way
      // (remember: A circle = 2 * PI)
      ctx.rotate(Math.PI/6);

      // Move the cursor to near the outside of the Canvas
      ctx.moveTo(100,0);

      // and draw a short (20px) tick
      ctx.lineTo(120,0);
    }
  ctx.stroke();
ctx.restore();

// Minute marks
ctx.save();
  // These ticks will be lighter than the hours
  ctx.lineWidth = 5;

  ctx.beginPath();
    // For each minute
    for ( var i = 0; i < 60; i++ ) {
      // except for the minutes that are 'on the hour'
      if ( i % 5 != 0 ) {
        // Move the cursor farther out
        ctx.moveTo(117,0);

        // And draw a short (3px) line
        ctx.lineTo(120,0);
      }
```

```
          // Rotate the Canvas 1/60th of the way around
          ctx.rotate(Math.PI/30);
        }
    ctx.stroke();
ctx.restore();

// Draw Hour Hand
ctx.save();
   // Rotate the Canvas to the correct position
   ctx.rotate( (Math.PI/6) * hr + (Math.PI/360) * min + (Math.PI/21600) * sec )

   // This line is going to be wide
   ctx.lineWidth = 14;

   ctx.beginPath();
      // Start drawing from just off-center (making it look like a clock hand)
      ctx.moveTo(-20,0);

      // And draw to near the hour ticks
      ctx.lineTo(80,0);
   ctx.stroke();
ctx.restore();

// Draw Minute Hand
ctx.save();
   // Rotate the Canvas to the current minute position
   ctx.rotate( (Math.PI/30) * min + (Math.PI/1800) * sec )

   // This line will be thinner than the hour hand
   ctx.lineWidth = 10;

   ctx.beginPath();
      // But it's also longer, so set it farther back
      ctx.moveTo(-28,0);

      // And draw it farther out
      ctx.lineTo(112,0);
   ctx.stroke();
ctx.restore();

// Draw Second Hand
ctx.save();
   // Rotate the Canvas to the current second position
   ctx.rotate(sec * Math.PI/30);
```

```
            // This line will be redish
            ctx.strokeStyle = "#D40000";
            ctx.fillStyle = "#D40000";

            // and thinner than the other hands
            ctx.lineWidth = 6;

            ctx.beginPath();
              // But also set farther back
              ctx.moveTo(-30,0);

              // But stubbier
              ctx.lineTo(83,0);
            ctx.stroke();
          ctx.restore();

          // Outside Blue Circle
          ctx.save();
            // The border will be wide
            ctx.lineWidth = 14;

            // and blue-ish
            ctx.strokeStyle = '#325FA2';

            ctx.beginPath();
              // Draw a complete circle, 142px out
              ctx.arc(0,0,142,0,Math.PI*2,true);
            ctx.stroke();
          ctx.restore();

      ctx.restore();
    }
    </script>
    </head>
    <body>
      <canvas id="canvas" height="150" width="150"></canvas>
    </body>
    </html>
```

Once you work through all the details and math (which varies, depending on the complexity of what you're attempting to draw), the Canvas 2D API proves to be immensely useful.

Simple Planet Simulation

In this second example you're going to look at the rotation of images, as opposed to the native drawing of shapes. You're going to start with three base images: one of the sun, one of the earth, and one of the moon. You're then going to create a simple simulation (in that it looks nice, but is hardly accurate) showing the rotation of the earth around the sun and the rotation of the moon around the earth. Additionally, you'll roughly show which side of the earth is dark, while rotated away from the sun. Figure 14-2 shows an example of what the final result looks like in motion.

Figure 14-2. *The earth rotating around the sun and the moon rotating around the earth in a simple Canvas planet simulation*

You'll most likely notice a lot of concepts in this code similar to the previous example (saving and restoring Canvas positions, namely), but it's important to note how you handle the drawing and rotation of the individual images. Listing 14-8 shows the full code for the Canvas planet simulation.

Listing 14-8. *A Simulation of the Earth Rotating Around the Sun Using the Canvas 2D API*

```
<html>
<head>
<title>Canvas Sun Demo</title>
<script>
// Initalize the list of images that will be used
var imgs = { sun: null, moon: null, earth: null };

// Wait for the window to completely load
window.onload = function() {
  // Load all the images from the document
  for ( var i in imgs )
    imgs[i] = document.getElementById(i);

  // Start drawing 10 times  per second
  setInterval( draw, 100 );
};
```

```javascript
function draw() {
  // Get the time intervals that we need
  var time = new Date();
  var s = ( (2 * Math.PI) / 6) * time.getSeconds();
  var m = ( (2 * Math.PI) / 6000 ) * time.getMilliseconds();

  // Get the drawing context of the Canvas
  var ctx = document.getElementById('canvas').getContext('2d');

  // Empty the Canvas
  ctx.clearRect(0,0,300,300);

  // New items are always drawn under old items (used for the shadow)
  // More info: http://developer.mozilla.org/en/docs/Canvas_tutorial:Compositing
  ctx.globalCompositeOperation = 'destination-over';

ctx.save();
  // Drawing at 0,0 = drawing at 150,150
  ctx.translate(150,150);

  // Rotate the Canvas to earth's position
  ctx.rotate( (s + m) / 10 );

  // Move 105 pixels out
  ctx.translate(105,0);

  // The fill for the shadow (which will be
  // faded, so that we can see through it)
  ctx.fillStyle = 'rgba(0,0,0,0.4)';
  ctx.strokeStyle = 'rgba(0,153,255,0.4)';

  // Draw the shadow rectangle (its not perfect, but close)
  ctx.fillRect(0,-12,50,24);

  // Draw the earth
  ctx.drawImage(imgs.earth,-12,-12);

  ctx.save();
    // Rotate the Canvas, relative to the rotation of the earth
    ctx.rotate( s + m );

    // Position the moon 'in orbit'
    ctx.translate(0,28.5);

    // Draw the moon image
    ctx.drawImage(imgs.moon,-3.5,-3.5);
  ctx.restore();
```

```
  ctx.restore();

  // Draw the earth's orbit
  ctx.beginPath();
    ctx.arc(150,150,105,0,Math.PI*2,false);
  ctx.stroke();

  // Draw the static sun
  ctx.drawImage(imgs.sun,0,0);
}
</script>
</head>
<body style="background:#000;">
  <canvas id="canvas" height="300" width="300"></canvas>

  <!-- Preload all our source images -->
  <div style="display:none;">
    <img src="sun.png" id="sun"/>
    <img src="moon.png" id="moon"/>
    <img src="earth.png" id="earth"/>
  </div>
</body>
</html>
```

The <canvas> element and the associated API have seen a great amount of traction lately; they're used in both Apple's Dashboard and Opera's Widget area. This is one piece of "future" JavaScript that is, in all practicality, here right now, and you should seriously consider using it in your applications.

Comet

The final new concept that you're going to look at is one that's been recently refined and is in the process of becoming an emerging standard. While the concept of Ajax is fairly straightforward (having a single asynchronous connection), Ajax does not encapsulate any sort of streaming content. The concept of being able to have a stream of new updates coming into your web application is now frequently called *Comet* (as coined by Alex Russell of Dojo). Having the ability to stream updates into a web application gives you a whole new level of freedom, allowing you to build ultraresponsive applications (such as chat applications).

Much as Ajax does not contain new technology, fundamentally, neither does Comet. However, many developers have taken to refining the general streaming concepts posed by web applications into a final standard called *Cometd*. More information about the upcoming Cometd standard and the concept of Comet itself, can be found here:

- *The original post, by Alex Russell, detailing the concepts behind Comet:* http://alex.dojotoolkit.org/?p=545

- *Defining a specification for Comet:* http://cometd.com/

Comet improves current Ajax applications by having a long-lived connection that continually streams new information from a central server. It is this central server's job to distribute communication evenly and to the appropriate channels. Figure 14-3 shows an example of how Comet behaves in comparison to a traditional Ajax application.

The Dojo Foundation is responsible for much of the work that's gone into standardizing Comet and making it readily usable by average web developers. Listing 14-9 shows an example of using the Dojo library to initiate a Comet connection to a server-side resource (which is run using a Cometd server).

Listing 14-9. *Using Dojo and Its Cometd Library to Connect to a Streaming Server and Listen to Different Broadcast Channels*

```
<!DOCTYPE HTML PUBLIC "-//W3C//DTD HTML 4.01//EN"
    "http://www.w3.org/TR/html4/strict.dtd">
<html>
    <head>
    <title>Cometd Client/Server Test Page</title>
    <script type="text/javascript">
        // We're going to be logging all interactions to a debug panel
        djConfig = { isDebug: true };
    </script>
    <script type="text/javascript" src="../dojo/dojo.js"></script>
    <script type="text/javascript">
        dojo.require("dojo.io.cometd");
        dojo.addOnLoad(function(){
            // Set the base URL for all cometd interaction
            cometd.init({}, "/cometd");

            // Subscribe to a  single point of broadcast
            // This will watch for all streaming output coming
            // from this particular service and log it to the debug panel
            cometd.subscribe("/foo/bar/baz", false, dojo, "debugShallow");

            // Broadcast two messages to two different services
            cometd.publish("/foo/bar/baz", { thud: "thonk!"});
            cometd.publish("/foo/bar/baz/xyzzy", { foo: "A simple message" });
        });
    </script>
    </head>
    <body></body>
</html>
```

While the number of applications that use Comet (or Comet-like technology) is still rather small, that number is bound to increase as more people realize just how useful this particular piece of technology is for making high-performance web applications.

Ajax web application model (asynchronous)

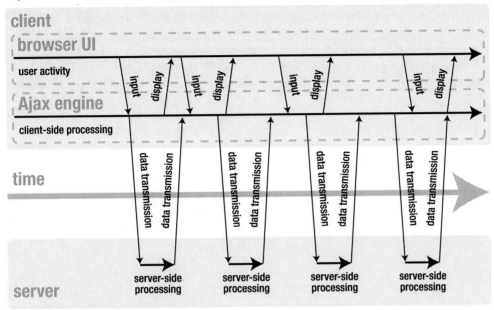

Comet web application model

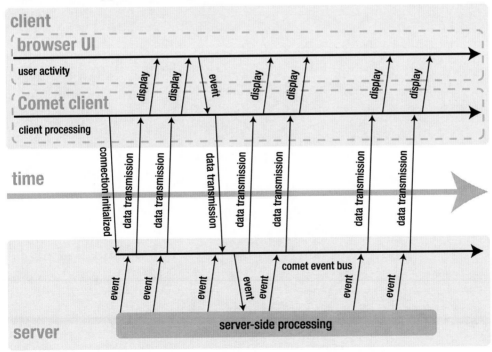

Figure 14-3. *A comparison between the traditional Ajax model and the new Comet-style web application model*

Summary

The technology presented in this chapter comes in a wide range—everything from the complicated and far-off (such as destructuring in JavaScript 1.7) to the current and highly usable (such as the <canvas> element). I hope that I've been able to give you a good feel for the direction in which browser-based web development is heading in the near future.

## PART 6

Appendixes

■ ■ ■

DOM Reference

This appendix serves as a reference for the functionality provided by the Document Object Model discussed in Chapter 5.

Resources

DOM functionality has come in a variety of flavors, starting with the original prespecification DOM Level 0 on up to the well-defined DOM Levels 1 and 2. Since all modern browsers support the W3C's DOM Levels 1 and 2 nearly completely, the W3C's web sites serve as an excellent reference for learning how the DOM should work:

- *DOM Level 1*: http://www.w3.org/TR/REC-DOM-Level-1/level-one-core.html

- *HTML DOM Level 1*: http://www.w3.org/TR/REC-DOM-Level-1/level-one-html.html

- *DOM Level 2*: http://www.w3.org/TR/DOM-Level-2-Core/

- *HTML DOM Level 2*: http://www.w3.org/TR/DOM-Level-2-HTML/

Additionally, there exists a number of excellent references for learning how DOM functionality works, but none is better than the resources that exist at Quirksmode.org, a site run by Peter-Paul Koch. He has comprehensively looked at every available DOM method and compared its results in all modern browsers (plus some). It's an invaluable resource for figuring out what is, or is not, possible in the browsers that you're developing for:

- *W3C DOM Core Levels 1 and 2 reference*: http://www.quirksmode.org/dom/w3c_core. html

- *W3C DOM HTML Levels 1 and 2 reference*: http://www.quirksmode.org/dom/w3c_html. html

Terminology

In Chapter 5 on the Document Object Model and in this appendix, I use common XML and DOM terminology to describe the different aspects of a DOM representation of an XML document. The following words and phrases are terminology that relate to the Document Object Model and XML documents in general. All of the terminology examples will relate to the sample HTML document shown in Listing A-1.

Listing A-1. *A Reference Point for Discussing DOM and XML Terminology*

```
<!DOCTYPE HTML PUBLIC "-//W3C//DTD HTML 4.01//EN"
"http://www.w3.org/TR/html4/strict.dtd">
<html>
<head>
    <title>Introduction to the DOM</title>
</head>
<body>
    <h1>Introduction to the DOM</h1>
    <p class="test">There are a number of reasons why the DOM is awesome,
        here are some:</p>
    <ul>
        <li id="everywhere">It can be found everywhere.</li>
        <li class="test">It's easy to use.</li>
        <li class="test">It can help you to find what you want, really quickly.</li>
    </ul>
</body>
</html>
```

Ancestor

Very similar to the genealogical term, *ancestor* refers to the parent of the current element, and that parent's parent, and that parent's parent, and so on. In Listing A-1 the ancestor elements of the <ul> element are the <body> element and the <html> element.

Attribute

Attributes are properties of elements that contain additional information about them. In Listing A-1 the <p> element has the attribute *class* that contains the value *test*.

Child

Any element can contain any number of nodes (each of which are considered to be *children* of the parent element). In Listing A-1 the <ul> contains seven child nodes; three of the child nodes are the <li> elements, the other four are the endlines that exist in between each element (contained within text nodes).

Document

An XML *document* consists of one element (called the *root node* or *document element*) that contains all other aspects of the document. In Listing A-1 the <html> is the document element containing the rest of the document.

Descendant

An element's *descendants* include its child nodes, its children's children, and their children, and so on. In Listing A-1 the <body> element's descendants include <h1>, <p>, <ul>, all the <li> elements, and all the text nodes contained inside all of them.

Element

An *element* is a container that holds attributes and other nodes. The primary, and most noticeable, component of any HTML document is its elements. In Listing A-1 there are a ton of elements; the <html>, <head>, <title>, <body>, <h1>, <p>, <ul>, and <li> tags all represent elements.

Node

A *node* is the common unit within a DOM representation. Elements, attributes, comments, documents, and text nodes are all nodes and therefore have typical node properties (for example, nodeType, nodeName, and nodeValue exist in every node).

Parent

Parent is the term used to refer to the element that contains the current node. All nodes have a parent, except for the root node. In Listing A-1 the parent of the <p> element is the <body> element.

Sibling

A *sibling* node is a child of the same parent node. Generally this term is used in the context of previousSibling and nextSibling, two attributes found on all DOM nodes. In Listing A-1 the siblings of the <p> element are the <h1> and <ul> elements (along with a couple white space–filled text nodes).

Text Node

A *text node* is a special node that contains only text; this includes visible text and all forms of white space. So when you're seeing text inside of an element (for example, <b>hello world!</b>), there is actually a separate text node inside of the <b> element that contains the "hello world!" text. In Listing A-1, the text "It's easy to use" inside of the second <li> element is contained within a text node.

Global Variables

Global variables exist within the global scope of your code, but they exist to help you work with common DOM operations.

document

This variable contains the active HTML DOM document, which is viewed in the browser. However, just because this variable exists and has a value, doesn't mean that its contents have been fully loaded and parsed. See Chapter 5 for more information on waiting for the DOM to load. Listing A-2 shows some examples of using the document variable that holds a representation of the HTML DOM to access document elements.

Listing A-2. *Using the Document Variable to Access Document Elements*

```
// Locate the element with the ID of 'body'
document.getElementById("body")

// Locate all the elements with the tag name of  <div>.
document.getElementsByTagName("div")
```

HTMLElement

This variable is the superclass object for all HTML DOM elements. Extending the prototype of this element extends all HTML DOM elements. This superclass is available by default in Mozilla-based browsers and Opera. It's possible to add it to Internet Explorer and Safari using the methods described in Chapter 5. Listing A-3 shows an example of binding new functions to a global HTML element superclass. Attaching a hasClass function provides the ability to see whether an element has a specific class.

Listing A-3. *Binding New Functions to a Global HTML Element SuperClass*

```
// Add a new method to all HTML DOM Elements
// that can be used to see if an Element has a specific class, or not.
HTMLElement.prototype.hasClass = function( class ) {
    return new RegExp("(^|\\s)" + class + "(\\s|$)").test( this.className );
};
```

DOM Navigation

The following properties are a part of all DOM elements and can be used to traverse DOM documents.

body

This property of the global HTML DOM document (the document variable) points directly to the HTML <body> element (of which there should only be the one). This particular property is one that has been carried over from the days of DOM 0 JavaScript. Listing A-4 shows some examples of accessing the <body> element from the HTML DOM document.

Listing A-4. *Accessing the <body> Element Inside of an HTML DOM Document*

```
// Change the margins of the <body>
document.body.style.margin = "0px";

// document.body is equivalent to:
document.getElementsByTagName("body")[0]
```

childNodes

This is a property of all DOM elements, containing an array of all child nodes (this includes elements, text nodes, comments, etc.). This property is read-only. Listing A-5 shows how you would use the childNodes property to add a style to all child elements of a parent element.

Listing A-5. *Adding a Red Border Around Child Elements of the <body> Element Using the childNodes Property*

```
// Add a border to all child elements of <body>
var c = document.body.childNodes;
for ( var i = 0; i < c.length; i++ ) {
    // Make sure that the Node is an Element
    if ( c[i].nodeType == 1 )
        c[i].style.border = "1px solid red";
}
```

documentElement

This is a property of all DOM nodes acting as a reference to the root element of the document (in the case of HTML documents, this will always point to the <html> element). Listing A-6 shows an example of using the documentElement to find a DOM element.

Listing A-6. *Example of Locating the Root Document Element From Any DOM Node*

```
// Find the documentElement, to find an Element by ID
someRandomNode.documentElement.getElementById("body")
```

firstChild

This is a property of all DOM elements, pointing to the first child node of that element. If the element has no child nodes, firstChild will be equal to null. Listing A-7 shows an example of using the firstChild property to remove all child nodes from an element.

Listing A-7. *Removing All Child Nodes From an Element*

```
// Remove all child nodes from an element
var e = document.getElementById("body");
while ( e.firstChild )
    e.removeChild( e.firstChild );
```

getElementById(elemID)

This is a powerful function that locates the one element in the document that has the specified ID. The function is only available on the document element. Additionally, the function may not work as intended in non-HTML DOM documents; generally with XML DOM documents you have to explicitly specify the ID attribute in a DTD (Document Type Definition) or schema.

This function takes a single argument: the name of the ID that you're searching for, as demonstrated in Listing A-8.

Listing A-8. *Two Examples of Locating HTML Elements by Their ID Attributes*

```
// Find the Element with an ID of body
document.getElementById("body")


// Hide the Element with an ID of notice
document.getElementById("notice").style.display = 'none';
```

getElementsByTagName(tagName)

This property finds all descendant elements—beginning at the current element—that have the specified tag name. This function works identically in XML DOM and HTML DOM documents.

In all modern browsers, you can specify * as the tag name and find all descendant elements, which is much faster than using a pure-JavaScript recursive function.

This function takes a single argument: the tag name of the elements that you're searching for. Listing A-9 shows examples of getElementsByTagName. The first block adds a highlight class to all <div> elements in the document. The second block finds all the elements inside of the element with an ID of *body*, and hides any that have a class of *highlight*.

Listing A-9. *Two Code Blocks That Demonstrate How getElementsByTagName Is Used*

```
// Find all <div> Elements in the current HTML document
// and set their class to 'highlight'
var d = document.getElementsByTagName("div");
for ( var i = 0; i < d.length; i++ ) {
    d[i].className = 'hilite';
}


// Go through all descendant elements of the element with
// an ID of body. Then find all elements that have one class
// equal to 'hilite'. Then hide all those elements that match.
var all = document.getElementById("body").getElementsByTagName("*");
for ( var i = 0; i < all.length; i++ ) {
    if ( all[i].className == 'hilite' )
        all[i].style.display = 'none';
}
```

lastChild

This is a reference available on all DOM elements, pointing to the last child node of that element. If no child nodes exist, lastChild will be null. Listing A-10 shows an example of using the lastChild property to insert an element into a document.

Listing A-10. *Creating a New <div> Element and Inserting It Before the Last Element in the <body>*

```
// Insert a new Element just before the last element in the <body>
var n = document.createElement("div");
n.innerHTML = "Thanks for visiting!";

document.body.insertBefore( n, document.body.lastChild );
```

nextSibling

This is a reference available on all DOM nodes, pointing to the next sibling node. If the node is the last sibling, nextSibling will be `null`. It's important to remember that nextSibling may point to a DOM element, a comment, or even a text node; it does not serve as an exclusive way to navigate DOM elements. Listing A-11 is an example of using the nextSibling property to create an interactive definition list.

Listing A-11. *Making All <dt> Elements Expand Their Sibling <dd> Elements Once Clicked*

```
// Find all <dt> (Defintion Term) elements
var dt = document.getElementsByTagName("dt");
for ( var i = 0; i < dt.length; i++ ) {
    // Watch for when the term is clicked
    dt[i].onclick = function() {
        // Since each Term has an adjacent <dd> (Definition) element
        // We can display it when it's clicked

        // NOTE: Only works when there's no whitespace between <dd> elements
        this.nextSibling.style.display = 'block';
    };
}
```

parentNode

This is a property of all DOM nodes. Every DOM node's parentNode points to the element that contains it, except for the document element, which points to `null` (since nothing contains the root element). Listing A-12 is an example of using the parentNode property to create a custom interaction. Clicking the Cancel button hides the parent element.

Listing A-12. *Using the parentNode Property to Create a Custom Interaction*

```
// Watch for when a link is clicked (e.g. a Cancel link)
// and hide the parent element
document.getElementById("cancel").onclick = function(){
    this.parentNode.style.display = 'none';
};
```

previousSibling

This is a reference available on all DOM nodes, pointing to the previous sibling node. If the node is the first sibling, the previousSibling will be `null`. It's important to remember that previousSibling may point to a DOM element, a comment, or even a text node; it does not serve as an exclusive way to navigate DOM elements. Listing A-13 shows an example of using the previousSibling property to hide elements.

Listing A-13. *Hiding All Elements Before the Current Element*

```
// Find all elements before this one and hide them
var cur = this.previousSibling;
while ( cur != null ) {
    cur.style.display = 'none';
    cur = this.previousSibling;
}
```

Node Information

These properties exist on most DOM elements in order to give you easy access to common element information.

innerText

This is a property of all DOM elements (which only exists in non-Mozilla-based browsers, as it's not part of a W3C standard). This property returns a string containing all the text inside of the current element. Since this property is not supported in Mozilla-based browsers, you can utilize a workaround similar to the one described in Chapter 5 (where you use a function to collect the values of descendant text nodes). Listing A-14 shows an example of using the innerText property and the text() function from Chapter 5.

Listing A-14. *Using the innerText Property to Extract Text Information From an Element*

```
// Let's assume that we have an <li> element like this, stored in the variable 'li':
// <li>Please visit <a href="http://mysite.com/">my web site</a>.</li>

// Using the innerText property
li.innerText

// or the text() function described in Chapter 5
text( li )

// The result of either the property or the function is:
"Please visit my web site."
```

nodeName

This is a property available on all DOM elements that contains an uppercase version of the element name. For example, if you have an <li> element and you access its nodeName property, it will return LI. Listing A-15 shows an example of using the nodeName property to modify the class names of parent elements.

Listing A-15. *Locating All Parent <li> Elements and Setting Their Class to current*

```
// Find all the parents of this node, that are an <li> element
var cur = this.parentNode;
while ( cur != null ) {
    // Once the element is found, and the name verified, add a class
    if ( cur.nodeName == 'LI' )
        cur.className += " current";
    cur = this.parentNode;
}
```

nodeType

This is a common property of all DOM nodes, containing a number corresponding to the type of node that it is. The three most popular node types used in HTML documents are the following:

- Element node (a value of 1 or document.ELEMENT_NODE)

- Text node (a value of 3 or document.TEXT_NODE)

- Document node (a value of 9 or document.DOCUMENT_NODE)

Using the nodeType property is a reliable way of making sure that the node that you're trying to access has all the properties that you think it does (e.g., a nodeName property is only useful on a DOM element; so you could use nodeType to make sure that it's equal to 1 before accessing it). Listing A-16 shows an example of using the nodeType property to add a class to a number of elements.

Listing A-16. *Locating the First Element in the HTML <body> and Applying a header Class to It*

```
// Find the first element in the <body>
var cur = document.body.firstChild;
while ( cur != null ) {
    // If an element was found, add the header class to it
    if ( cur.nodeType == 1 ) {
        cur.className += " header";
        cur = null;
```

```
        // Otherwise, continue navigating through the child nodes
        } else {
            cur = cur.nextSibling;
        }
    }
}
```

nodeValue

This is a useful property of text nodes that can be used to access and manipulate the text that they contain. The best example of this in use is the text function presented in Chapter 5, which is used to retrieve all the text contents of an element. Listing A-17 shows an example of using the nodeValue property to build a simple text value function.

Listing A-17. *A Function That Accepts an Element and Returns the Text Contents of It and All Its Descendant Elements*

```
function text(e) {
    var t = "";

    // If an element was passed, get its children,
    // otherwise assume it's an array
    e = e.childNodes || e;

    // Look through all child nodes
    for ( var j = 0; j < e.length; j++ ) {
        // If it's not an element, append its text value
        // Otherwise, recurse through all the element's children
        t += e[j].nodeType != 1 ?
            e[j].nodeValue : text(e[j].childNodes);
    }

    // Return the matched text
    return t;
}
```

Attributes

Most attributes are available as properties of their containing element. For example, the attribute ID can be accessed using the simple element.id. This feature is residual from the DOM 0 days, but it's very likely that it's not going anywhere, due to its simplicity and popularity.

className

This property allows you to add and remove classes from a DOM element. This property exists on all DOM elements. The reason I'm mentioning this specifically is that its name, className, is very different from the expected name of *class*. The strange naming is due to the fact that the word *class* is a reserved word in most object-oriented programming languages; so its use is avoided to limit difficulties in programming a web browser. Listing A-18 shows an example of using the className property to hide a number of elements.

Listing A-18. *Finding All <div> Elements That Have a Class of special and Hiding Them*

```
// Find all the <div> elements in the document
var div = document.getElementsByTagName("div");
for ( var i = 0; i < div.length; i++ ) {
    // Find all the <div> elements that have a single class of 'special'
    if ( div[i].className == "special" ) {
        // And hide them
        div[i].style.display = 'none';
    }
}
```

getAttribute(attrName)

This is a function that serves as the proper way of accessing an attribute value contained within a DOM element. Attributes are initialized with the values that the user has provided in the straight HTML document.

The function takes a single argument: the name of the attribute that you want to retrieve. Listing A-19 shows an example of using the getAttribute() function to find input elements of a specific type.

Listing A-19. *Finding the <input> Element Named text and Copying Its Value Into an Element With an ID of preview*

```
// Find all the form input elements
var input = document.getElementsByTagName("input");
for ( var i = 0; i < input.length; i++ ) {

    // Find the element that has a name of "text"
    if ( input[i].getAttribute("name") == "text" ) {

        // Copy the value into another element
        document.getElementById("preview").innerHTML =
            input[i].getAttribute("value");

    }

}
```

removeAttribute(attrName)

This is a function that can be used to completely remove an attribute from an element. Typically, the result of using this function is comparable to doing a setAttribute with a value of " " (an empty string) or null; in practice, however, you should be sure to always clean up extra attributes in order to avoid any unexpected consequences.

This function takes a single argument: the name of the attribute that you wish to remove. Listing A-20 shows an example of unchecking some check boxes in a form.

Listing A-20. *Finding All Check Boxes in a Document and Unchecking Them*

```
// Find all the form input elements
var input = document.getElementsByTagName("input");
for ( var i = 0; i < input.length; i++ ) {

    // Find all the checkboxes
    if ( input[i].getAttribute("type") == "checkbox" ) {

        // Uncheck the checkbox
        input[i].removeAttribute("checked");

    }

}
```

setAttribute(attrName, attrValue)

This is a function that serves as a way of setting the value of an attribute contained within a DOM element. Additionally, it's possible to add in custom attributes that can be accessed again later while leaving the appearance of the DOM elements unaffected. setAttribute tends to behave rather strangely in Internet Explorer, keeping you from setting particular attributes (such as class or maxlength). This is explained more in Chapter 5.

The function takes two arguments. The first is the name of the attribute. The second is the value to set the attribute to. Listing A-21 shows an example of setting the value of an attribute on a DOM element.

Listing A-21. *Using the setAttribute Function to Create an <a> Link to Google*

```
// Create a new <a> element
var a = document.createElement("a").

// Set the URL to visit to Google's web site
a.setAttribute("href","http://google.com/");

// Add the inner text, giving the user something to click
a.appendChild( document.createTextNode( "Visit Google!" ) );

// Add the link at the end of the document
document.body.appendChild( a );
```

DOM Modification

The following are all the properties and functions that are available to manipulate the DOM.

appendChild(nodeToAppend)

This is a function that can be used to add a child node to a containing element. If the node that's being appended already exists in the document, it is moved from its current location and appended to the current element. The appendChild function must be called on the element that you wish to append into.

The function takes one argument: a reference to a DOM node (this could be one that you just created or a reference to a node that exists elsewhere in the document). Listing A-22 shows an example of creating a new <ul> element and moving all <li> elements into it from their original location in the DOM, then appending the new <ul> to the document body.

Listing A-22. *Appending a Series of <li> Elements to a Single <ul>*

```
// Create a new <ul> element
var ul = document.createElement("ul");

// Find all the first <li> elements
var li = document.getElementsByTagName("li");
for ( var i = 0; i < li.length; i++ ) {

    // append each matched <li> into  our new <ul> element
    ul.appendChild( li[i] );

}

// Append our new <ul> element at the end of the body
document.body.appendChild( ul );
```

cloneNode(true|false)

This function is a way for developers to simplify their code by duplicating existing nodes, which can then be inserted into the DOM. Since doing a normal insertBefore or appendChild call will physically move a DOM node in the document, the cloneNode function can be used to duplicate it instead.

The function takes one true or false argument. If the argument is true, the node and everything inside of it is cloned; if false, only the node itself is cloned. Listing A-23 shows an example of using this function to clone an element and append it to itself.

Listing A-23. *Finding the First <ul> Element in a Document, Making a Complete Copy of It, and Appending It to Itself*

```
// Find the first <ul> element
var ul = document.getElementsByTagName("ul")[0];

// Clone the node and append it after the old one
ul.parentNode.appendChild( ul.cloneNode( true ) );
```

createElement(tagName)

This is the primary function used for creating new elements within a DOM structure. The function exists as a property of the document within which you wish to create the element.

Note If you're using XHTML served with a content-type of application/xhtml+xml instead of regular HTML served with a content-type of text/html, you should use the createElementNS function instead of the createElement function.

This function takes one argument: the tag name of the element to create. Listing A-24 shows an example of using this function to create an element and wrap it around some other elements.

Listing A-24. *Wrapping the Contents of a <p> Element in a <strong> Element*

```
// Create a new <strong> element
var s = document.createElement("strong");

// Find the first paragraph
var p = document.getElementsByTagName("p")[0];

// Wrap the contents of the <p> in the <strong> element
while ( p.firstChild ) {
    s.appendChild( p.firstChild );
}

// Put the <strong> element (containing the old <p> contents)
// back into the <p> element
p.appendChild( s );
```

createElementNS(namespace, tagName)

This function is very similar to the createElement function, in that it creates a new element; however, it also provides the ability to specify a namespace for the element (for example, if you're adding an item to an XML or XHTML document).

This function takes two arguments: the namespace of the element that you're adding, and the tag name of the element. Listing A-25 shows an example of using this function to create a DOM element in a valid XHTML document.

Listing A-25. *Creating a New XHTML <p> Element, Filling It With Some Text, and Appending It to the Document Body*

```
// Create a new XHTML-compliant <p>
var p = document.createElementNS("http://www.w3.org/1999/xhtml", "p");

// Add some text into the <p> element
p.appendChild( document.createTextNode( "Welcome to my site." ) );

// Add the <p> element into the document
document.body.insertBefore( p, document.body.firstChild );
```

createTextNode(textString)

This is the proper way to create a new text string to be inserted into a DOM document. Since text nodes are just DOM-only wrappers for text, it is important to remember that they cannot be styled or appended to. The function only exists as a property of a DOM document.

The function takes one argument: the string that will become the contents of the text node. Listing A-26 shows an example of using this function to create a new text node and appending it to the body of an HTML page.

Listing A-26. *Creating an <h1> Element and Appending a New Text Node*

```
// Create a new <h1> element
var h = document.createElement("h1");

// Create the header text and add it to the <h1> element
h.appendChild( document.createTextNode("Main Page") );

// Add the header to the start of the <body>
document.body.insertBefore( h, document.body.firstChild );
```

innerHTML

This is an HTML DOM–specific property for accessing and manipulating a string version of the HTML contents of a DOM element. If you're only working with an HTML document (and not an XML one), this method can be incredibly useful, as the code it takes to generate a new DOM element can be cut down drastically (not to mention it is a faster alternative to traditional DOM methods). While this property is not part of any particular W3C standard, it still exists in every modern browser. Listing A-27 shows an example of using the innerHTML property to change the contents of an element whenever the contents of a <textarea> are changed.

Listing A-27. *Watching a <textarea> for Changes and Updating a Live Preview With Its Value*

```
// Get the textarea to watch for updates
var t = document.getElementsByTagName("textarea")[0];

// Grab the current value of a <textarea> and update a live preview,
// everytime that it's changed
t.onkeypress = function() {
    document.getElementById("preview").innerHTML = this.value;
};
```

insertBefore(nodeToInsert, nodeToInsertBefore)

This function is used to insert a DOM node anywhere into a document. The function must be called on the parent element of the node that you wish to insert it before. This is done so that you can specify null for nodeToInsertBefore and have your node inserted as the last child node.

The function takes two arguments. The first argument is the node that you wish to insert into the DOM; the second is the DOM node that you're inserting before. This should be a reference to a valid node. Listing A-28 shows an example of using this function to insert the *favicon* (the icon that you see next to a URL in the address bar of a browser) of a site next to a set of URLs on a page.

Listing A-28. *Going Through All <a> Elements and Adding an Icon Consisting of the Site's Favicon*

```
// Find all the <a> links within the document
var a = document.getElementsByTagName("a");
for ( var i = 0; i < a.length; i++ ) {

    // Create an image of the linked-to site's favicon
    var img = document.createElement("img");
    img.src = a[i].href.split('/').splice(0,3).join('/') + '/favicon.ico';

    // Insert the image before the link
    a[i].parentNode.insertBefore( img, a[i] );

}
```

removeChild(nodeToRemove)

This function is used to remove a node from a DOM document. The removeChild function must be called on the parent element of the node that you wish to remove.

The function takes one argument: a reference to the DOM node to remove from the document. Listing A-29 shows an example of running through all the <div> elements in the document, removing any that have a single class of *warning*.

Listing A-29. *Removing All Elements That Have a Particular Class Name*

```
// Find all <div> elements
var div = document.getElementsByTagName("div");
for ( var i = 0; i < div.length; i++ ) {
    // If  the <div> has one class of 'warning'
    if ( div[i].className == "warning" ) {

        // Remove the <div> from the document
        div[i].parentNode.removeChild( div[i] );

    }
}
```

replaceChild(nodeToInsert, nodeToReplace)

This function serves as an alternative to the process of removing a node and inserting another node in its place. This function must be called by the parent element of the node that you are replacing.

This function takes two arguments: the node that you wish to insert into the DOM, and the node that you are going to replace. Listing A-30 shows an example of replacing all <a> elements with a <strong> element containing the URL originally being linked to.

Listing A-30. *Converting a Set of Links Into Plain URLs*

```
// Convert all links to visible URLs (good for printing
// Find all <a> links in the document
var a = document.getElementsByTagName("a");
while ( a.length ) {

    // Create a <strong> element
    var s = document.createElement("strong");

    // Make the contents equal to the <a> link URL
    s.appendChild( document.createTextNode( a[i].href ) );

    // Replace the original <a> with the new <strong> element
    a[i].replaceChild( s, a[i] );

}
```

APPENDIX B

■ ■ ■

Events Reference

This appendix serves as a reference for Chapter 6 on events. It provides comprehensive coverage of all possible DOM events, to complement the general theory presented in Chapter 6. Here you will find resources for more information, definitions of common event-related terminology, and explanations of all common event objects and interactions.

Resources

If there is one resource you should access to find more information about events, it is Quirksmode.org. This site provides a side-by-side comparison for every event in all the modern browsers. I highly recommend that you visit it to get a feel for the events each browser supports (`http://www.quirksmode.org/js/events_compinfo.html`).

Additionally, the two most popular specifications currently used are the W3C's DOM events and Internet Explorer's HTML events. Each site has a comprehensive listing of all the possible events and each aspect of how they behave:

- *W3C DOM Level 2 events*: `http://www.w3.org/TR/DOM-Level-2-Events/events.html`

- *Internet Explorer HTML events*: `http://msdn.microsoft.com/workshop/author/dhtml/reference/events.asp`

Terminology

This section defines a number of new terms introduced in the topic of JavaScript event handling that may be unfamiliar to those who have not dealt with JavaScript events or asynchronous event handling.

Asynchronous

Asynchronous events have a general callback structure, in contrast to a threaded application structure. This means that a single piece of code (a *callback*) is registered with an event handler. When that event occurs, the callback is executed.

Attach / Bind / Register a Callback

Attaching (sometimes called *binding*), a callback to an event handler is how code is registered in an asynchronous event model. Once an event occurs, the event handler is called, which contains a reference to the registered callback. A *callback* is a piece of code in the form of a function reference that is called once an event is completed.

Bubbling

The *bubbling* phase of an event occurs after the capturing phase of an event. The bubbling phase begins at the source of the event (such as the link that a user clicks) and traverses up the DOM tree to the root of the document.

Capturing

The *capturing* phase of an event (which occurs only in the W3C event model) is the first event phase to occur and consists of an event moving down the DOM tree to the location of the element that instantiated the event.

Default Action

The *default* action is a browser-based action that occurs regardless of whether a user has an event handler bound or not. An example of a default action provided by the browser is when a user clicks a link and is taken to another web page.

Event

An *event* is an action that is fired (initiated) within a web page. Generally, events are initiated by the user (such as moving a mouse, pressing a key, etc.), but can also occur without interaction (such as the page loading, or an error occurring).

Event Handler

An *event handler* (such as a function reference) is the code that is called whenever an event is fired. If a callback hasn't been registered with the event handler, nothing will occur (beyond the default action).

Threaded

In a *threaded* application, there typically exists a number of disparate process flows that are performing a continual task (such as checking to see if a resource is available). JavaScript does not handle threads in any respect and exists only as an asynchronous language.

Event Object

The event object is an object that's provided, or is available, inside of every event handler function. How it's handled in Internet Explorer and other browsers varies.

W3C-compatible browsers provide a single argument to the event handler function, which contains a reference to the event object. Internet Explorer's event object is always available at the window.event property, which should only be accessed while within an event handler.

General Properties

A number of properties exist on the event object for every type of event being captured. All of these event object properties relate directly to the event itself and nothing is event-type specific. What follows is a list of all the event object properties with explanations and example code.

type

This property contains the name of the event currently being fired (such as click, mouseover, etc.). This can be used to provide a generic event handler function, which then deterministically executes related functions (such as the addEvent/removeEvent functions discussed in Chapter 6). Listing B-1 shows an example of using this property to make a handler have a different effect, based upon its event type.

Listing B-1. *Using the type Property to Provide Hoverlike Functionality for an Element*

```
// Locate the <div> that we want to hover over
var div = document.getElementsByTagName('div')[0];

// Bind a single function to both the mouseover and mouseout events
div.onmouseover = div.onmouseout = function(e){
    // Normalize the Event object
    e = e || window.event;

    // Toggle the background color of the <div>, depending on the
    // type of mouse event that occurred
    this.style.background = (e.type == 'mouseover') ? '#EEE' : '#FFF';
};
```

target / srcElement

This property contains a reference to the element that fired to the event. For example, binding a click handler to an <a> element would have a target property equal to the <a> element itself. The srcElement property is equivalent to target, but works in Internet Explorer. Listing B-2 shows an example of using this property to handle a global event handler.

Listing B-2. *Double-Clicking Any Node in the HTML DOM and Having It Removed*

```
// Bind a Double-Click listener to the document
document.ondblclick = function(e) {
    // Neutralize the Event object
    e = e || window.event;

    // Find thet correct target node
    var t = e.target || e.srcElement;
```

```
        // remove the node from the DOM
        t.parentNode.removeChild( t );
};
```

stopPropagation() / cancelBubble

The stopPropagation() method stops the event bubbling (or capturing) process, making the current element the last one to receive the particular event. The event phases are explained fully in Chapter 6. The cancelBubble property is available in Internet Explorer; setting it to true is equivalent to calling the stopPropagation() method in a W3C-compatible browser. Listing B-3 shows an example of using this technique to stop the propagation of an event.

Listing B-3. *Dynamic Highlighting of All the <li> Elements Within a Document*

```
// Find all the <li> elements in the document
var li = document.getElementsByTagName('li');
for ( var i = 0; i < li.length; i++ ) {

    // Watch for the user to move his mouse over an <li>
    li[i].onmouseover = function(e){
        // If this is a W3C-compatible browser
        if ( e )
            // Use stopPropogation to stop the event bubbling
            e.stopPropagation();

        // Otherwise, it's Internet Explorer
        else
            // So set cancelBubble to true to stop the event bubbling
            e.cancelBubble = true;

        // finally, highlight the background of the <li>
        this.style.background = '#EEE';
    };

    // When the mouse if moved back out of the <li>
    li[i].onmouseout = function(){
        // Reset the backgound color back to white
        this.style.background = '#FFF';
    };

}
```

preventDefault() / returnValue = false

Calling the preventDefault() method stops the browser's default action from occurring in all modern W3C-compliant browsers. Internet Explorer requires that you set the returnValue property of the event object to false in order to stop the default browser action.

An explanation of the default action process can be found in Chapter 6. The code in
Listing B-4 makes it so that anytime a link is clicked on a page, instead of visiting the page
(like it normally would), it sets the title of the document to be the URL of the link.

Listing B-4. *Preventing the Default Browser Action*

```
// Locate all <a> elements on the page
var a = document.getElementsByTagName('a');
for ( var i = 0; i < a.length; i++ ) {

    // Bind a click handler to the <a>
    a[i].onclick = function(e) {
        // Set the title of the page to the URL of this link, instead of visiting it
        document.title = this.href;

        // Prevent the browser from ever visiting the web site pointed to from
        // the <a> (which is the default action)
        if ( e ) {
            e.preventDefault();

        // Prevent the default action in IE
        } else {
            window.event.returnValue = false;
        }
    };

}
```

Mouse Properties

Mouse properties only exist within the event object when a mouse-related event is initiated
(such as click, mousedown, mouseup, mouseover, mousemove, and mouseout). At any other
time, you can assume that the values being returned do not exist, or are not reliably present.
This section lists all the properties that exist on the event object during a mouse event.

clientX / clientY

These properties contain the *x* and *y* coordinates of the mouse cursor relative to the browser
window. For an example of these properties, see the code shown in Listing B-5.

Listing B-5. *Finding the Current Position of the Mouse Cursor Within the Web Page*

```
// Find the horizontal position of the cursor
function getX(e) {
    // Check for the non-IE position, then the IE position, and finally return 0
    return e.pageX || (e.clientX +
        (document.documentElement.scrollLeft || document.body.scrollLeft));
}
```

```
// Find the vertical position of the cursor
function getY(e) {
    // Check for the non-IE position, then the IE position, and finally return 0
    return e.pageY || (e.clientY +
        (document.documentElement.scrollTop || document.body.scrollTop));
```

pageX / pageY

These properties contain the *x* and *y* coordinates of the mouse cursor relative to the rendered document (for example, if you've scrolled a ways down a document, the number would no longer match what is contained within the clientX/clientY properties). They do not work in Internet Explorer. To get the position of the cursor in IE, you should use the clientX/clientY properties and add the current scroll offset to them.

layerX / layerY and offsetX / offsetY

These properties contain the *x* and *y* coordinates of the mouse cursor relative to the event's target element. The layerX/layerY properties are only available in Mozilla-based browsers and Safari, while offsetX/offsetY are available in Opera and Internet Explorer. (You can see an example of them in use in Listing B-17.)

button

This property is a number representing the mouse button that's currently being clicked (only available on the click, mousedown, and mouseup events). Unfortunately, there is also some confusion over what number to use to represent which mouse button is pressed. Fortunately, 2 is used to represent a right-click in all browsers; so you can feel safe testing for that, at the very least. Table B-1 shows all the possible values of the button property in both Internet Explorer and W3C-compatible browsers.

Table B-1. *Possible Values for the button Property of the event Object*

Click	Internet Explorer	W3C
Left	1	0
Right	2	2
Middle	4	1

Listing B-6 shows a code snippet that prevents the user from right-clicking (and bringing up a menu) anywhere on a web page.

Listing B-6. *Using the button Property of the event Object*

```
// Bind a click handler to the entire document
document.onclick = function(e) {
    // Normalize the Event objct
    e = e || window.event;
```

```
        // If a right-click was performed
        if ( e.button == 2 ) {
            // Prevent the default action from occurring
            e.preventDefault();
            return false;
        }
};
```

relatedTarget

This event property contains a reference to the element that the mouse has just left. More often than not, this is used in situations where you need to use mouseover/mouseout, but you need to know where the mouse just was, or is going to. Listing B-7 shows a variation on a tree menu (<ol> elements containing other <ol> elements) in which the subtrees only display the first time the user moves the mouse over the <li> subelement.

Listing B-7. *Using the relatedTarget Property to Create a Navigable Tree*

```
// Find all the <li> elements in the document
var li = document.getElementsByTagName('li');
for ( var i = 0; i < li.length; i++ ) {

    // and attach mouseover handlers to them
    li[i].onmouseover = function(e){

        // If the mouse is entering for the first time (from the parent)
        if ( e.relatedTarget == this.parentNode ) {
            // display the last child element (which happens to be another <ol>)
            this.lastChild.style.display = 'block';
        }

    };

}

// Sample HTML:
<ol>
    <li>Hello <ol>
        <li>Another</li>
        <li>Item</li>
    </ol></li>
    <li>Test <ol>
        <li>More</li>
        <li>Items</li>
    </ol></li>
</ol>
```

Keyboard Properties

Keyboard properties generally only exist within the event object when a keyboard-related event is initiated (such as keydown, keyup, and keypress). The exception to this rule is for the ctrlKey and shiftKey properties, which are available during mouse events (allowing you to Ctrl+Click an element). At any other time, you can assume that the values contained within a property do not exist, or are not reliably present.

ctrlKey

This property returns a Boolean value representing whether the keyboard Ctrl key is being held down. This property is available for both keyboard and mouse events. The code in Listing B-8 watches for a user clicking a mouse button and holding down the control key; when this occurs, the clicked item is removed from the document.

Listing B-8. *Using the ctrlKey Property to Create a Type of Mouse-Click Interaction*

```
// Bind a click handler onto the entire document
document.onclick = function(e){
    // Neutralize the Event object
    e = e || window.event;
    var t = e.target || e.srcElement;

    // If the control key was held down while the click was made
    if ( e.ctrlKey )
        // Remove the clicked node
        t.parentNode.removeChild( t );
};
```

keyCode

This property contains a number corresponding to the different keys on a keyboard. The availability of certain keys (such as Page Up and Home) can fluctuate, but generally speaking, all other keys work reliably. Table B-2 is a reference for all of the commonly used keyboard keys and their associated key codes.

Table B-2. *Commonly Used Key Codes*

Key	Key Code
Backspace	8
Tab	9
Enter	13
Space	32
Left arrow	37
Up arrow	38

Key	Key Code
Right arrow	39
Down arrow	40
0–9	48–57
A–Z	65–90

Listing B-9 shows the code necessary to run a simple slideshow. This code assumes that there are a number of <li> elements inside of a single <ol> or <ul> element. Each <li> can contain anything (such as an image). When the left and right arrow keys are pressed, the previous or next <li> is revealed to the user.

Listing B-9. *Using the keyCode Property to Create a Simple Slideshow*

```
// Locate the first <li> element on the page
var cur = document.getElementsByTagName('li')[0];

// and make sure that it's visible
cur.style.display = 'block';

// Watch for any keypresses on the page
document.onkeyup = function(e){
    // Normalize the Event object
    e = e || window.event;

    // If the left or right arrow keys were pressed
    if ( e.keyCode == 37 || e.keyCode == 39 ) {

        // hide the currently displayed <li> element
        cur.style.display = 'none';

        // If the left arrow was pressed, find the previous <li> element
        // (or loop back around and go to the last one)
        if ( e.keyCode == 37 )
            cur = cur.previousSibling || cur.parentNode.lastChild;

        // If the right arrow key was pressed, find the next <li> element
        // or if we're at the end, go back to the first <li> element
        else if ( e.keyCode == 39 )
            cur = cur.nextSibling || cur.parentNode.firstChild;

        // show the next <li> in the sequence
        cur.style.display = 'block';
    }

};
```

shiftKey

This property returns a Boolean value representing whether the keyboard Shift key is being held down. This property is available for both keyboard and mouse events. Listing B-10 shows code that watches for a user clicking a mouse button and holding down the Shift key; when this occurs, a contextual menu is displayed.

Listing B-10. *Using the shiftKey Property to Display a Special Menu*

```
// Bind a click handler onto the entire document
document.onclick = function(e){
    // Neutralize the Event object
    e = e || window.event;

    // If the shift key was held down while the click was made
    if ( e.shiftKey )
        // Display the menu
        document.getElementById('menu').style.display = 'block';
};
```

Page Events

All page events deal specifically with the function and status of the entire page. The majority of the event types handle the loading and unloading of a page (whenever a user visits the page and then leaves again).

load

The load event is fired once the page has completely finished loading; this event includes all images, external JavaScript files, and external CSS files. This can be used as a way to launch your DOM-related code; however, if you need a faster response time, you should look into the domReady() function explained in Chapter 6.

Listing B-11 shows code that waits for the page to load, upon which it binds a click handler to the element with an ID of cancel. Once the click handler is fired, it will hide the element that has the ID of main.

Listing B-11. *Using the load Event to Wait for the Entire Page to Finish Loading*

```
// Wait for the page to finish loading
window.onload = function(){

    // Locate the element with an ID of 'cancel' and bind a click handler
    document.getElementById('cancel').onclick = function(){
```

```
    // That when clicked, hides the 'main' element
    document.getElementById('main').style.display = 'none';

  };

};
```

beforeunload

This event is something of an oddity, as it's completely nonstandard but widely supported. It behaves very similarly to the unload event, with an important difference. Within your event handler for the beforeunload event, if you return a string, that string will be shown in a confirmation message asking users if they wish to leave the current page. If they decline, the user will be able to stay on the current page. Dynamic web applications, such as Gmail, use this to prevent users from potentially losing any unsaved data.

Listing B-12 attaches a simple event handler (that only returns a string) explaining why the user should not leave the current page that he or she is on. The browser will display a confirmation box with a full explanation, including your custom message.

Listing B-12. *Using the beforeunload Event to Stop People from Leaving a Page*

```
// Attach to the beforeunload handler
window.onbeforeunload = function(){

    // Return an explanation for why the user should not leave the page.
    return 'Your data will not be saved.';

};
```

error

The error event is fired every time an error occurs within your JavaScript code. This can serve as a way to capture error messages and display or handle them gracefully. This event handler behaves differently than others, in that instead of passing in an event object, it includes a message explaining the specific error that occurred.

Listing B-13 shows a custom way for handling and displaying error messages in a bulleted list, as opposed to the traditional error console.

Listing B-13. *Using the error Event to Keep a Viewable Error Log*

```
// Attach an error event handler
window.onerror = function( message ){

    // Create an <li> element to store our error message
    var li = document.createElement('li');
    li.innerHTML = message;
```

```
        // Find our error list (which has an ID of 'errors')
        var errors = document.getElementById('errors');

        // and add our error message to the top of the list
        errors.insertBefore( li, errors.firstChild );

};
```

resize

The resize event occurs every time the user resizes the browser window. When the user adjusts the size of the browser window, the resize event will only fire once the resize is complete, not at every step of the way.

Listing B-14 shows code that watches for instances where the user resizes the browser window too small, applying an alternate class to the document element (to provide better document styling for the smaller window).

Listing B-14. *Using the resize Event to Dynamically Resize an Element*

```
// Watch for the user resizing the browser window
window.onresize = function() {
    // Locate the document element (to be used to find the window width)
    var de = document.documentElement;

    // Figure out the width of the browser
    // (unfortunately, every browser likes to do this differently)
    var w = window.innerWidth || (de && de.clientWidth)
        || document.body.clientWidth;

    // If the window is too small, add a class to document element
    de.className = w < 990 ? 'small' : '';
};
```

scroll

The scroll event occurs when the user moves the position of the document within the browser window. This can occur from keyboard presses (such as using the arrow keys, Page Up/Down, or the spacebar) or by using the scrollbar.

unload

This event fires whenever the user leaves the current page (this could be the user clicking a link, hitting the Back button, or even closing the browser window). Preventing the default action does not work for this event (the next best thing is the beforeunload event).

Listing B-15 shows code that binds an event handler to the unload event, displaying a message to the user when he leaves the current page.

Listing B-15. *The unload Event*

```
// Watch for the user leaving the web site
window.onunload = function(){

    // Display a message to the user, thanking them for visiting
    alert( 'Thanks for visiting!' );

};
```

UI Events

User interface events deal with how the user is interacting with the browser or page elements themselves. The UI events can help you determine what elements on the page the user is currently interacting with and provide them with more context (such as highlighting or help menus).

focus

The focus event is a way of determining where the page cursor is currently located. By default, it is within the entire document; however, whenever a link or a form input element is clicked or tabbed into using the keyboard, the focus moves to that instead. (An example of this event is shown in Listing B-18.)

blur

The blur event occurs when the user shifts his focus from one element to another (within the context of links, input elements, or the page itself). (An example of this event is shown in Listing B-18.)

Mouse Events

Mouse events occur either when the user moves the mouse pointer or when the user clicks one of the mouse buttons.

click

A click event occurs when a user presses the left mouse button down on an element (see the mousedown event) and releases the mouse button (see the mouseup event) on the same element. Listing B-16 shows an example of using the click event to prevent the user from visiting links that link to the current page.

Listing B-16. *Disabling All Click Attempts on Links That Point to the Current Page*

```
// Find all <a> elements within the document
var a = document.getElementsByTagName('a');
for ( var i = 0; i < a.length; i++ ) {

    // If the link points to the same  page that we're currently on
    if ( a[i].href == window.location.href ) {

        // Make it such that the link no longer 'works' when clicked
        a[i].onclick = function(e){
            return false;
        };

    }

}
```

dblclick

The dblclick event occurs after the user has completed two click events in rapid succession. The rate of the double click depends upon the settings of the operating system.

mousedown

The mousedown event occurs when the user presses down a mouse button. Unlike the keydown event, this event will only fire once while the mouse is down. For an example of this event, see the code shown in Listing B-17.

mouseup

The mouseup event occurs when the user releases the pressed mouse button. If the button is released on the same element that the button is pressed on, a click event also occurs. For an example of this event, see the code shown in Listing B-17.

mousemove

A mousemove event occurs whenever the user moves the mouse pointer at least one pixel on the page. How many mousemove events are fired (for a full movement of the mouse) depends on how fast the user is moving the mouse and how fast the browser is at keeping up with the updates. Listing B-17 shows an example of a simple drag-and-drop implementation.

Listing B-17. *Elements with a Class Name of draggable Will Be Able to Be Dragged By the User*

```
// Initialize all the variables that we're going to use
var curDrag, origX, origY;
```

```
// Watch for any time that the user clicks down on an element
document.onmousedown = function(e){
    // Normalize the Event object
    e = fixEvent( e );

    // Only drag elements that have a class of 'draggable'
    if ( e.target.className == 'draggable' ) {
        // The element that we're currently dragging
        curDrag = e.target;

        // Remember where the cursor position started, and where the
        // element was located
        origX = getX( e ) + (parseInt( curDrag.style.left ) || 0);
        origY = getY( e ) + (parseInt( curDrag.style.top ) || 0);

        // Watch for the mouse to move, or lift
        document.onmousemove = dragMove;
        document.onmouseup = dragStop;
    }

};

// Watch for the mouse to move
function dragMove(e) {
    // Normalize the Event object
    e = fixEvent( e );

    // Make sure that we're watching the right element
    if ( !curDrag || e.target == curDrag ) return;

    // Set the new cursor position
    curDrag.style.left = (getX(e)) + 'px';
    curDrag.style.top = (getY(e)) + 'px';
}

// Look for the drag to end
function dragStop(e) {
    // Normalize the Event object
    e = fixEvent( e );

    // Reset all of our watcher methods
    curDrag = document.mousemove = document.mouseup = null;
}
```

```
// Adjust the event object, to make it sane
function fixEvent(e) {
    // Make all the IE-centric parameters be W3C-like
    if (!e) {
        e = window.event;
        e.target = e.srcElement;
        e.layerX = e.offsetX;
        e.layerY = e.offsetY;
    }
    return e;
}
```

mouseover

The mouseover event occurs whenever the user moves the mouse into an element from another. If you wish to know which element the user has come from, use the relatedTarget property. For an example of this event, see the code shown in Listing B-18.

mouseout

The mouseout event occurs whenever the user moves the mouse outside of an element. This includes moving the mouse from a parent element to a child element (which may seem unintuitive at first). If you wish to know which element the user is going to, use the relatedTarget property.

Listing B-18 shows an example of attaching pairs of events to elements to allow for keyboard-accessible (and mouse-accessible) web page use. Whenever the user moves his mouse over a link, or whenever he uses the keyboard to navigate to it, the link will receive some additional color highlighting.

Listing B-18. *Creating a Hover Effect by Using the mouseover and mouseout Events*

```
// Find all the <a> elements, to attach the event handlers to them
var a = document.getElementsByTagName('a');
for ( var i = 0; i < a.length; i++ ) {

    // Attach a mouseover and focus event handler to the <a> element,
    // which changes the <a>s background to blue when the user either
    // mouses over the link, or focuses on it (using the keyboard)
    a[i].onmouseover = a[i].onfocus = function() {
        this.style.backgroundColor = 'blue';
    };
```

```
// Attach a mouseout and blur event handler to the <a> element
// which changes the <li>s background back to its default white
// when the user moves away from the link
a[i].onmouseout = a[i].onblur = function() {
    this.style.backgroundColor = 'white';
};
```

}

Keyboard Events

Keyboard events handle all instances of a user pressing keys on the keyboard, whether it is inside or outside of a text input area.

keydown / keypress

The keydown event is the first keyboard event to occur when a key is pressed. If the user continues to hold down the key, the keydown event will continue to fire. The keypress event is a common synonym for the keydown event; they behave virtually identically, with one exception: if you wish to prevent the default action of a key being pressed, you must do it on the keypress event. Listing B-19 shows an example of using the keypress handler to prevent particular keys from being pressed within an <input> element.

Listing B-19. *Stopping the Enter Key From Inadvertantly Submitting a Form From an* <input> *Element*

```
// Find all <input> elements in the document
var input = document.getElementsByTagName('input');
for ( var i = 0; i < input.length; i++ ) {

    // Bind a keypress handler to the <input> element
    input[i].onkeypress = function(e) {
        // Prevent the default action, if the user presses the enter key
        return e.keyCode != 13;
    };

}
```

keyup

The keyup event is the last keyboard event to occur (after the keydown event). Unlike with the keydown event, this event will only fire once when released (since you can't release a key for a long period of time).

Form Events

Form events deal primarily with <form>, <input>, <select>, <button>, and <textarea> elements, the staples of HTML forms.

select

The select event fires every time a user selects a different block of text within an input area, using the mouse. With this event, you can redefine how a user interacts with a form. Listing B-20 shows an example of using the select event to prevent text selection within a form field.

Listing B-20. *Preventing a User From Selecting Text Within a <textarea>*

```
// Locate the first <textarea> on the page
var textarea = document.getElementsByTagName('textarea')[0];

// Bind a select event listener
textarea.onselect = function(){
    // When a new selection is made, prevent the action
    return false;
};
```

change

The change event occurs when the value of an input element (this includes <select> and <textarea> elements) is modified by a user. The event only fires after the user has already left the element, letting it lose focus.

The code shown in Listing B-21 is capable of watching an element with an ID of entryArea (which should be a <textarea>) for changes and updating an associated live preview with its contents.

Listing B-21. *Watching the change Event to Update an Associated Element*

```
// Watch the 'entryArea' (which is a <textarea>) for any changes
document.getElementById('entryArea').onchange = function(){

    // When the area has been changed, update the live preview
    document.getElementById('preview').innerHTML = this.value;

};
```

submit

The submit event occurs only in forms and only when a user clicks a Submit button (located within the form) or hits Enter/Return within one of the input elements. By binding a submit handler to the form, and not a click handler to the Submit button, you'll be sure to capture all attempts to submit the form by the user.

Listing B-22 shows the code that watches for the first form on a page, intercepts the submission, and displays a message to the user, instead of sending the results to a server.

Listing B-22. *Using submit to Perform an Alternative Action*

```
// Bind a submit handler the the first form in the document
document.getElementsByTagName('form')[0].onsubmit = function(e) {

    // Get the name that the user entered
    var name = document.getElementById('name').value;

    // Set the <h1> element to contain Hello Name! (where name is the name
    // that the user entered into the form)
    document.getElementsByTagName('h1')[0].innerHTML =
        'Hello ' + name + '!';

    // Make sure that the form is not submitted to the server
    return false;

};
```

reset

The reset event only occurs when a user clicks a Reset button inside of a form (as opposed to the Submit button, which can be duplicated by hitting the Enter key). Listing B-23 shows an example of watching a form's reset event to provide an alternative action.

Listing B-23. *A Quick and Dirty Way to Handle Resetting a Form*

```
// Find the first form on the page
var form = document.getElementsByTagName('form')[0];

// Watch for when the reset button is hit
form.onreset = function(){

    // Find all the <input> elements inside of the form
    var input = form.getElementsByTagName('input');

    // and reset their values to an empty string
    for ( var i = 0; i < input.length; i++ )
        input[i].value = '';

};
```

APPENDIX C

∎∎∎

The Browsers

JavaScript programming has always been driven by development of web browsers. Since the use of JavaScript in nonbrowser settings (e.g., server-side JavaScript) is still rather experimental, the feature set of JavaScript is still very browser-centric. Thus, the features available in JavaScript are very closely tied to how browsers evolve and which features they (or their users) deem as the most important.

Modern Browsers

Of all the possible browsers available on the Internet, there are only a few that keep up to date with the latest technologies, and even fewer that push the boundaries of what's possible with a browser. In the end, the browsers you choose to support will most likely depend on who your audience is and how much time you're willing to put into making your applications work right for everyone.

With that said, it is now much easier than it used to be to develop successful JavaScript applications. With the standardization of many practices (DOM, XMLHttpRequest, etc.), it is only a matter of time before there will be no additional effort required to support all modern browsers. However, that day is not today. So for now, here are the most popular modern browsers and what they support.

Internet Explorer

Created by Microsoft and packaged with its operating system (beginning with Windows 95), Internet Explorer is by far the most popular web browser. Development on the browser has slowed over the years, as Microsoft has enjoyed its dominant position in the browser market. Recently, the browser team has started work again, because of the release of Windows Vista, the new Microsoft operating system (which features Internet Explorer 7).

Versions 5.5 and 6.0

Version 5.5 is the updated version of IE in Windows 98, and version 6.0 is the default browser for Windows XP. While both have some level of bugs and inconsistencies in their CSS and DOM implementations, they are very functional browsers that should be supported by any web application.

Version 7

The latest version of the Internet Explorer browser is available for Windows XP and for Windows Vista. While adoption rates are still limited, expect it to really take off when Vista adoption picks up.

While very little has changed within the JavaScript engine, the rendering engine has had a ton of CSS-related bugs fixed. One JavaScript item to note is that instead of having to use the ActiveXObject for XMLHttpRequests, you can now just use XMLHttpRequest directly (which is provided by default).

Mozilla

Born from the remnants of Netscape, Mozilla represents the open source effort to develop a popular browser; and with the recent release of Firefox and its rise to popularity, Mozilla has taken a front seat in modern browser development.

Firefox 1.0, Netscape 8, and Mozilla 1.7

These three browsers are all based upon the 1.7 version of the Gecko rendering engine. This engine has full compliance with all modern scripting techniques. These are all solid, stable, usable browsers.

Firefox 1.5 and 2.0

The latest version of the Gecko rendering engine (1.8), which is used in the latest Firefox browsers, supports a number of new advantages that will play a larger part in upcoming years, including partial SVG 1.1 support, <canvas> element support, and support for JavaScript 1.6. I discuss these different features in Chapter 14.

Safari

Safari is Apple's foray into making a better browser for OS X (when compared to the unsightly Internet Explorer 5). When it began (at 1.0), its rendering engine was rather rough, making developers wary of fully supporting it. However, as new releases have come out, the engine has steadily improved.

The most common versions of Safari (1.3 for OS X 10.3, 2.0 for OS X 10.4) contain a substantial number of bug fixes and new features. It is not uncommon to find that your applications will work quite well when loaded in Safari.

Additionally, these browsers introduced support for the new <canvas> element, which allows developers to physically draw on a web page, an important feature for highly dynamic applications.

Opera

A veteran of the browser wars with Netscape and Microsoft, Opera's popularity soared after the Norwegian browser became completely free (previously it was ad-supported or licensable). Along with Mozilla, Opera has been highly active in developing and planning the new HTML 5 specification and implementing portions of the spec into its browser.

Version 8.5

Version 8.5 was the first completely free version of the Opera browser, therefore its use is much more widespread than other versions. It has solid support for all modern features, although developers will occasionally find its CSS implementation differing from other browsers; its JavaScript implementation is more than sufficient.

Version 9.0

The most recent update of the Opera browser includes a number of bug fixes to its JavaScript engine, along with support for the new <canvas> element.

Index

You Need the Companion eBook

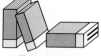